CW01430969

FRENCH AND FRANCOPHONE STUDIES

Haunting Presences

Series Editors

Hanna Diamond (University of Bath)
Claire Gorrara (Cardiff University)

Editorial Board

Ronan le Coadic (Université Rennes 2)
Nicola Cooper (Swansea University)
Colin Davis (Royal Holloway, University of London)
Didier Francfort (Université Nancy 2)
Sharif Gemie (University of Glamorgan)
H. R. Kedward (Sussex University)
Margaret Majumdar (Goldsmiths College, University of London)
Nicholas Parsons (Cardiff University)

Haunting Presences

Ghosts in French Literature and Culture

Edited by
Kate Griffiths and David Evans

UNIVERSITY OF WALES PRESS
CARDIFF
2009

© The Contributors, 2009

All rights reserved. No part of this book may be reproduced in any
material form (including photocopying or storing it in any medium by
electronic means and whether or not transiently or incidentally to some
other use of this publication) without the written permission of the
copyright owner except in accordance with the provisions of the
Copyright, Designs and Patents Act 1988 or under the terms of a licence
issued by the Copyright Licensing Agency Ltd, Saffron House, 6–10 Kirby
Street, London, EC1N 8TS. Applications for the copyright owner's
written permission to reproduce any part of this publication should be
addressed to the University of Wales Press, 10 Columbus Walk,
Brigantine Place, Cardiff, CF10 4UP.
www.uwp.co.uk

British Library Cataloguing-in-Publication Data
A catalogue record for this book is available from the British Library.

ISBN 978-0-7083-2181-2

The rights of the Contributors to be identified separately as authors
of their contributions has been asserted by them in accordance with sections 77 and 78 of the Copyright, Designs and Patents Act 1988.

Typeset by Mark Heslington Ltd, Scarborough, North Yorkshire
Printed in Great Britain by CPI Antony Rowe, Wiltshire

Contents

Acknowledgements

This book brings together essays developed from some of the best papers presented at 'Haunting Presences: Ghosts in French and Francophone Literature, Art and Film', a conference held at the Institute of Germanic and Romance Studies (IGRS) in January 2006. Heartfelt thanks go to Cathy Wardle, the co-organizer of that conference. Her insight, organizational skills and unfailing good humour were central to the conference's success. We would like to thank the bodies who generously provided the funding which enabled the conference to go ahead, namely the Society for French Studies and the French Department at Royal Holloway. Thanks are also extended to the speakers and delegates at the conference for their stimulating insights and to Rosemary Lloyd at the IGRS for ensuring the conference ran so smoothly.

In the process of editing this collection, we have been helped by a host of friends and colleagues at Swansea University, St Andrews and elsewhere. We are especially grateful to Katie Halsey for her insight at various stages of the project and to Susan Harrow for her support. The help of Sarah Lewis from University of Wales Press has also been invaluable. A special thank you is offered to each of the contributors to this volume. We have enjoyed reading their essays and have appreciated their engagement with the editing process.

Notes on Contributors

ANDREW ASIBONG is Lecturer in French at Birkbeck, University of London. His publications include: *François Ozon* (Manchester/New York: Manchester University Press, 2007); '*Moja sestra*: horrific kinship in the works of Marie NDiaye', in I. McNeill and B. Stephens (eds), *Transmission: Essays in French Literature, Thought and Culture* (Oxford: Peter Lang, 2007); 'Meat, murder, metamorphosis: the transformational ethics of François Ozon', *French Studies*, 59, 2 (2005) and '*Mulier Sacra*: Marie Chauvet, Marie Darrieussecq, and the sexual metamorphoses of "Bare Life"', *French Cultural Studies*, 14, 2 (2003).

FIONA COX is Lecturer in French at the National University of Ireland, Cork. Her research interests range from nineteenth-century French literature, particularly Hugo, on whom she has published extensively, to the reception of classical literature in modern France. Her book *Aeneas Takes the Metro: Virgil's Presence in Twentieth-Century French Literature* was published by Legenda in 1999.

COLIN DAVIS is Professor of French at Royal Holloway, University of London. His research falls mainly in the area of post-war French fiction and thought. His principal publications are *Michel Tournier: Philosophy and Fiction* (Oxford: Oxford University Press, 1988), *Elie Wiesel's Secretive Texts* (Gainesville: University of Florida, 1994), *Levinas: An Introduction* (Cambridge: Polity Press, 1996), *Ethical Issues in Twentieth-Century French Fiction: Killing the Other* (London: MacMillan, 2000), *French Fiction in the Mitterrand Years: Memory, Narrative, Desire* (co-authored with Elizabeth Fallaize, Oxford: Oxford University Press, 2000), *After Poststructuralism: Reading, Stories and Theory* (London/New York: Routledge, 2004) and *Haunted Subjects: Deconstruction, Psychoanalysis and the Return of the Dead* (Basingstoke: Palgrave Macmillan, 2007).

SUZANNE DOW is Lecturer in French and Francophone Studies at the University of Nottingham. She works on twentieth-century French literature and thought, especially women's writing, feminist theory and Lacanian psychoanalysis. She has published articles on Violette Leduc, Simone de Beauvoir, Marguerite Duras and madness in twentieth-century French women's writing.

DAVID EVANS is Lecturer in French at the University of St Andrews. He works on nineteenth- and twentieth-century poetry, and in particular questions of form, rhythm and musicality. He has published *Rhythm, Illusion and the Poetic Idea: Baudelaire, Rimbaud, Mallarmé* (Amsterdam: Rodopi, 2004) and articles on Théodore de Banville and Michel Houellebecq.

KATE GRIFFITHS is Lecturer in French at Swansea University. Her research relates mainly to nineteenth-century naturalism and the question of cinematic adaptation. She has published a variety of articles in this area, including two specifically on the question of haunting: 'Scribbling ghosts. The textual spectres and spectral texts of Émile Zola', in J. Horn and L. Russell-Watts (eds), *Possessions: Essays in French Literature, Cinema and Theory* (Oxford: Peter Lang, 2003) and 'The ghost of the author: Zola, Renoir and *La Bête humaine*', *Excavatio*, 21 (2006). She recently completed a monograph entitled *Émile Zola and the Artistry of Adaptation*.

JOSEPH HARRIS is Lecturer in French at Royal Holloway, University of London. He is author of *Hidden Agendas: Cross-Dressing in Seventeenth-Century France* (Tübingen: Narr, 2005) and various articles on gender, laughter and identification in early modern drama and prose. He is currently writing a book on subjectivity and spectatorship in French theatre from the Renaissance to the Revolution, and is editing a journal volume of *Nottingham French Studies* entitled 'Identification before Freud: French perspectives'.

HENRIETTE KORTHALS ALTES is currently working as a College Lecturer at Somerville College, Oxford while finishing her D.Phil. thesis on subjectivity and mourning in the works of Jean Echenoz, Pierre Michon and Pascal Quignard. She has presented a wide range of conference papers on related topics and reviewed contemporary French fiction for the *TLS* and the *Guardian.*

JOHN NASSICHUK is Assistant Professor of French and Neo-Latin at the University of Western Ontario, Canada. His publications include articles on Ronsard, Jodelle, Des Masures, Pontano and Flaminio.

FRÉDÉRIC REGARD was educated at the École Normale Supérieure de Saint-Cloud, Paris, and wrote his Doctorat d'État under the supervision of Hélène Cixous. He is currently professor at the Sorbonne. His latest publications in the field of contemporary French literature include 'On Cixous's tongue (beyond scopic desire)', *Angelaki: Journal of the Theoretical Humanities*, 9, 1 (2004), and 'Autobiography as linguistic incompetence: Jacques Derrida's readings of Joyce and Cixous', *Textual Practice*, 19, 2 (2005).

JEAN-XAVIER RIDON is Senior Lecturer at the University of Nottingham. He is the author of books and articles on contemporary French and francophone literature and films. His last book *Le Voyage en son miroir* (Paris: Kimé, 2002) deals with questions of displacement, identity and representation in contemporary travel narratives.

LYNSEY RUSSELL-WATTS is Lecturer in French at the University of Nottingham. She specializes in contemporary French cinema, but also has interests in women's writing and photography and in feminist and psychoanalytic theory. She has published on Breillat and Duras and is currently working on a book on Breillat.

HELEN J. SWIFT is Fellow and Tutor, and university Lecturer, in Medieval French at St Hilda's College, Oxford. The seeds of the present article were sown in an earlier article on 'The ghost(s) of the author(s)', in *Medium Aevum*, 73 (2004); a more fully developed discussion of spectropoetics applied to the *querelle des femmes* appears in her book, *Gender, Writing, and Performance: Men Defending Women in Late Medieval France (1440–1538)* (Oxford: Oxford University Press, 2008).

SARAH TRIBOUT-JOSEPH is Lecturer in French and Comparative Literature at Edinburgh University. Her publications include

Proust and Joyce in Dialogue (Oxford: Legenda, 2008). She has published various articles on both Proust and Joyce. Her interest in Pinget stems from his use of oral narrative.

Introduction
Textual Spectres and Spectral Texts

Kate Griffiths and David Evans

Ghosts have long fascinated the French creative mind. That this fascination appears more pronounced in specific eras and movements is clear. As has been well documented, ghosts are comparatively common currency in much of the nineteenth century, most notably in the rich seam of literature of the fantastic.[1] Ghosts are frequent in the pages and images of Romanticism. Lamartine and Hugo, haunted by the premature deaths of their loved ones, give them a degree of spectral life through verse, just as Ronsard's muse survives in the *Sonnets pour Hélène*, or Jeanne Duval in Baudelaire's 'Je te donne ces vers' (l. 6). Yet in Ronsard, the poet too remains a phantomatic presence, 'fantôme sans os' ('Quand vous serez bien vieille', l. 8) and this shift of focus from the ghost-life of the addressee to that of the poet, and of poetry itself, continues into post-Romantic poetry with Baudelaire's 'Le Revenant' and Mallarmé's series of 'Tombeaux'.[2] However, ghosts also appear where least expected in the nineteenth century. The naturalist novelist Émile Zola rejects Romanticism and the literature of the fantastic, focusing instead on the materiality of reality. Yet, Zola's 1888 novel *Le Rêve* is haunted by generations of wives from the Hautecœur family:

> *Toutes revenaient, Ysabeau, Gudule, Yvonne, Austreberthe, toutes les Mortes heureuses, aimées de la mort qui leur avait épargné la vie, en les enlevant d'un coup d'aile, très jeunes, dans le ravissement de leur premier bonheur. Certaines nuits, leur vol blanc emplissait le château, ainsi qu'un vol de colombes.[3]*

Similarly, the structures of the Second Empire, the regime of which Zola was so critical, are presented in comparably ghost-like terms in

Zola's 1892 novel *La Débâcle*. A regiment of soldiers appear as 'une chevauchée de fantômes'.[4] A captain walks 'd'une légèreté d'apparition'.[5] The emperor himself comes and goes 'comme un spectre'.[6] Reality itself even appears spectral at times: 'on distinguait confusément les fantômes du Palais-Bourbon et de la Madeleine'.[7]

Ghosts, then, cannot be confined to schools. Nor can they be confined to eras. They traverse, as this book will underline, genres and media. Despite the *Encyclopédie*'s subsequent injunction not to believe in ghosts (1751–72), an injunction discussed by Colin Davis in chapter one, Voltaire stages the presence of a literal ghost in his play *Sémiramis* (1748), albeit on one occasion with real difficulty. According to Robert Niklaus, in his introduction to the play,

> On the first night Legrand, playing the ghost of Ninus, was unable to make his entrance because the 'petits-maîtres' seated on the stage blocked the way. An attendant guarding the tomb cried out 'Messieurs, place à l'Ombre'. Laughter ensued, so Voltaire requested that two exempts be posted on the floor of the stage to restrict the number of spectators.[8]

This type of spectre, a literal ghost, may be paralleled with the metaphorical ghosts explored by other authors. Guy de Maupassant, for example, in his short stories 'Fini' and 'Adieu', analyses the ghost of the protagonists' former life. In both stories the resurrection of the protagonists' memories is triggered by the metaphorical return of their former lovers in the form of their strikingly similar daughters.[9] The classification of ghosts is, by its very nature, an elusive task since ghosts in many respects defy categorization, being neither fully living nor fully dead. However, to the literal and metaphorical ghosts already discussed might be added a third category of spectres: the metatextual. Through his 1635 *L'Illusion comique*, Corneille explores the power of theatre to blur the boundaries between the living and the dead. Corneille uses the image of the ghost to evaluate the potency of his own artistic form, assessing the spectral status of art itself. Pridamant watches the ghost of his son inexplicably mingling with the living:

> Je vois Clindor, Rosine, ah! Dieu! quelle surprise!
> Je vois leur assassin, je vois sa femme et Lise!
> Quel charme en un moment étouffe leur discords
> Pour assembler ainsi les vivants et les morts? (ll. 1749–52)

What seems at first to be a return from beyond the grave is subsequently explained and rationalized. Pridamant is still alive, his death was part of a performance on stage in his new profession as an actor. Similarly, in *L'Ombre du cocher* (1722), a play published in Lesage and d'Orneval's *Théâtre de la foire*, spectrality is inextricably entwined with the artistic act as a ghost is conjured by a magician in order to teach a troupe of puppet actors to sing vaudeville.[10] As will become clear in the course of this volume, a variety of authors and artists, in very different eras, use the spectral as a means to evaluate their own artistic act.

Ghosts, whatever their form, be they literal, metaphorical or metatextual, have not been exorcized by modern culture. Indeed, Colin Davis's recent work *Haunted Subjects: Deconstruction, Psychoanalysis and the Return of the Dead* testifies to the prevalence of the dead and the undead in twentieth- and twenty-first-century artistic and theoretical output.[11] According to Davis, the majority of ghosts in the sphere of contemporary popular culture follow the 'unfinished business' model of haunting. They return to right a wrong or reveal a secret and can subsequently be dispatched, the boundary between the living and the dead maintained. The relationships of contemporary theorists with ghosts are, however, more complex. Davis expertly unpicks the ways in which the theories of the deconstructive thinker Jacques Derrida and the psychoanalysts Nicolas Abraham and Maria Torok, in very different ways, demonstrate that the irruption of the spectral tears a hole in the ontology of our lives, a hole neither easily mended, ignored nor explained.

The work of Davis, Derrida, Abraham and Torok threads this current volume as specific chapters engage with various strands of hauntology. *Haunting Presences*, however, turns to historicize the twentieth- and twenty-first centuries' haunting by the image of the ghost, teasing out the way in which a number of hauntology's concerns are, to an extent, shared by and enhanced through the study of pre-twentieth-century works. Colin Davis's opening chapter spans historical eras to draw conclusions about modernity's simultaneous need to believe in and disbelieve the ghost. Chapters two to five then trace the spectre's evolution in successive eras: the medieval, Renaissance, early modern and the nineteenth century. Each focuses on a literary genre key to the era: poetry, drama, the novel. Chapters six to eleven subsequently consider ghosts in media central to the twentieth and twenty-first centuries: film,

photography, theory and literature. Despite its chronological and
genre/media-based approach, this collection does not offer a
universal history of the ghost in French literature and culture.
Rather, it hopes to have created something of a haunting structure
as texts, theories and issues explored in early chapters return, like
the ghosts they discuss, to communicate with works at the heart of
later contributions.

In these cross-century spectral dialogues, no single model of
textual haunting emerges, but rather a cluster of key concerns recur
amidst the plurality of approaches taken by the chapters as a whole.
Perhaps surprisingly, literal ghosts are comparatively few in this
collection. Rather, the volume's chapters focus more predominantly
on metaphorical ghosts in relation to two central issues: subjectivity
and textuality; authorship, be it personal or artistic. Characters are
variously haunted by their own power or lack thereof, by the past, by
memories as well as their absence. Personal memory finds an echo in
the textual memory explored by a number of the chapters in this
collection. Authors and artists self-consciously explore the way in
which they are haunted, in a manner at times creative, at times disem-
powering, by the ghosts of past texts and authors/artists, by the
spectres of future readers and authors. Ghosts within works at times
act as indicators of a broader metatextual evaluation being under-
taken by these works. Put simply, spectres in texts occasionally serve
as a means to allow texts to consider their own spectral textual status.

If many texts have their spectres, traces, however impalpable, of
earlier works and authors, the ghost behind the initial call for
papers for the conference which inspired this volume was that of
Jacques Lacan. Lacan is largely absent from this volume, a volume
whose chapters draw on a wide range of very different theoreticians
and approaches. However, granting him a fleeting presence in its
introduction is perhaps useful, for Lacan's spectral conceptualiza-
tion of identity and textuality resonates with a number of the textual
spectres and spectral texts explored by *Haunting Presences*. That for
Lacan the self is a trace present yet absent in the gaze of the other is
clear. Underlining the other's ability to make the self present, he
writes: 'Ce qui me détermine foncièrement dans le visible, c'est le
regard qui est au-dehors. C'est par le regard que j'entre dans la
lumière.'[12] Yet this subjective presence generated by the mirror or
the gaze of the other is always simultaneously an absence: 'qu'est-ce
que je vais voir dans le miroir? Premièrement, ma propre figure, là

où elle n'est pas.'[13] The present absence of identity in Lacanian thought has useful parallels with the present absence that is the ghost.

Moreover, Lacan parallels the ghostly structures of subjectivity with those of textuality and artistry. Lacan conceives of identity as a text or an art work. It is a photograph ('le regard est l'instrument par où ... je suis photo-graphié'),[14] a painting ('le tableau, certes, est dans mon œil. Mais moi, je suis dans le tableau'),[15] a statue ('c'est ce que j'appelle le corps idéal, statutaire, ou statue')[16] and even a text. Lacan talks of 'la furieuse passion, qui spécifie l'homme d'imprimer dans la réalité son image'.[17] However, perhaps more interestingly in the light of the findings of a number of the chapters in this volume, Lacan goes on to explore the ghost-like status of his own identity, of his own artistic enterprise, underlining the ghosts of past texts which haunt his enterprise and the ghostly trace he will become in texts and the gaze of future readers. Lacan clearly states his conception of love as a means for the self to construct itself. He writes: 'L'amour de celui qui désire être aimé, est essentiellement une tentative de capturer l'autre dans soi-même, dans soi-même comme objet.'[18] Lacan, in his seminar tellingly entitled 'Une lettre d'amour', implicates himself in this loving creative process, claiming to be constructing himself, problematically authoring the text of his identity via the love of his audience: 'Je vous écrivais quoi, en somme? – la seule chose qu'on puisse faire d'un peu sérieux, la lettre d'amour.'[19]

The subjective text Lacan creates for himself is one self-consciously haunted by the ghosts of past works. Throughout his *oeuvre*, Lacan plays with and analyses the constructive role of the textual ghosts who haunt his work largely by means of literary citation. He makes frequent use of literary sources. Initially the relationship between Lacanian psychoanalysis and literature is clear. Lacan invokes literature only to reinforce his points: 'mais j'ai plus de confiance dans la fable de La Fontaine pour nous introduire aux structures de mythe'.[20] Citations are acknowledged and remain distinct as earlier authors are granted a clear presence in Lacan's work: 'Elle [la découverte freudienne] s'exprime assez bien par la fulgurante formule de Rimbaud.'[21] However, Lacan moves to blur the boundary between his theory and the literary sources it uses: 'La vie ne songe qu'à mourir – *Mourir, dormir, rêver* peut-être comme a dit un certain monsieur, au moment précisément où il s'agissait de ça – to be or not to be.'[22] His acknowledgements become teasingly hazy as he signals the presence of earlier authors in his work only to afford them a tantalizingly shadowy absence: 'Comme le remarque fort justement un poète bel esprit, le miroir ferait bien de réfléchir un peu plus avant de nous renvoyer son image.'[23] Ultimately Lacan erodes the citational name plates of literature, rewriting them in his own voice. He ingests and reworks Descartes's cogito: 'Je pense où je ne suis pas, donc je suis où je ne pense pas.'[24] Shakespeare's 'être ou ne pas être, dormir, rêver peut-être' loses even its hinted-at author in its second invocation and Molière's 'tarte à la crème' from *L'École des femmes* passes similarly unattributed.[25] However, far from naturalizing this process, Lacan draws our attention to it. He weaves the words of three of the most canonical writers of all time into his work, specifically playing with their most celebrated lines. Descartes's 'cogito ergo sum', Shakespeare's 'to be or not to be' and Molière's 'tarte à la crème' have become clichés in their own right, fragments of text whose provenance can never fully be erased. He demonstrates that the text upon which you write yourself always retains a trace of the other as author, always partly points to some other ghost, someone earlier, leading you back in time, space and direction. This movement back through the texts of ghosts past is seemingly never ending for the texts which haunt Lacan might themselves have their own ghostly forebears. Lacan states: 'Vous connaissez tous le thème de l'*Anneau de Hans Carvel*, bonne histoire du Moyen Âge, dont La Fontaine a fait un conte et que Balzac a reprise dans ses *Contes drôlatiques*.'[26] Writing, for Lacan, is the recognition of the ghosts of past texts and subjectivities.[27]

Lacan's seminars not only give voice to the ghosts of previous works, they also allow Lacan to contemplate his own textual spectre. As Lacan has self-consciously written himself on those who went before him, so those who read him will appropriate his image, integrating it into their own fictions. He will become the matter of citation, a spectral trace in the voice of others. Lacan is fascinated by a book by Manuel de Dieguez. He claims, 'tout y est, et aussi d'énormes morceaux de ce que je raconte', though the whole book is written without citing him and, indeed, deforms him: 'je ne me croyais pas si transcendental'.[28] He enacts his future textual alienation in his own reading gaze, citing himself in the abstract. He talks of 'le stade du miroir classique de Jacques Lacan',[29] stating elsewhere: 'pour la première fois nous irons à un texte de Jacques

Lacan. Je l'ai relu récemment, et j'ai trouvé qu'il était compréhensible.'[30] If Lacan rereads himself, acts as his own reader, and still finds himself alienated in his own gaze as other, no hope of recuperation or plenitude lies in the vast gaze of the reading public at large.

As Lacan's work plays with the processes and ghosts of textual reworking, so Colin Davis opens this current volume with a chapter focused on a specific ghostly reworking. In 1779 an English aristocrat named Lord Lyttelton was warned by a ghost that he would die at the stroke of midnight in three days' time. He did. In the nineteenth century Jules Janin rewrote and transformed the story of Lord Lyttelton (or Littleton in his spelling), allowing his protagonist to survive the ghostly prediction of his demise. Davis demonstrates the way in which Janin simultaneously demystifies the ghost story, mocking our need to believe in spectres, and remystifies it, using the figure of the ghost to question the fixity of the boundary between the living and the dead. Via the tales of Lord Lyttelton, this chapter discusses what is at stake in the ghost story from the height of the Enlightenment to the present day. It considers why and how, with what structures of narrative and belief, the ghost story survives into a sceptical, post-modern age when we may think we no longer believe in ghosts, but continue to act as if we do.

The ghost of earlier authorship is likewise the focus of chapter two. Helen Swift considers the ghostly relationship set up by certain fifteenth-century poets writing literary defences of women. These poets address the misogynistic authors with whom their pro-feminine texts take issue. Their works conjure up the ghosts both of the person of the earlier author and the spectral trace of their texts. Via the work of Harold Bloom on inheritance and the concept of 'spectropoetics' drawn from the 'spectropolitics' Derrida enunciates in *Spectres de Marx*, Swift identifies two possible outcomes for this conjuring. Either, in the words of Bloom, 'the strong dead return to darken the living', as subsequent authors reproduce and perpetuate the texts which they oppose, or, as Swift points out, it is possible to lay the ghost of the earlier author through an act of radical rewriting.[31]

If ghosts are a source of potential disorder in Swift's chapter, as medieval poets struggle with their spectral forebears, in chapter three John Nassichuk underlines the power of the ghost prologue in two Renaissance plays to restore order, be it at the level of plot or at the level of interpretation. Nassichuk offers a comparison of two important ghost characters, Marc Antoine in Étienne Jodelle's *Cléopâtre captive* (1552) and Égée in Robert Garnier's *Hippolyte* (1573). Jodelle's Marc Antoine, the first French Renaissance tragic ghost, serves as a messenger whose authority is absolute. He appears to Cléopâtre, ordering her to commit suicide. He thus determines the outcome of the plot, an outcome he justifies by invoking the ethical principle of 'Holy Equity'. In contrast, Garnier's Égée does not intervene in the action. Rather, he simply foretells, observes and philosophizes about the dramatic action. Égée occupies something of a median position, at once human and yet not of the living, existing somewhere between the characters of the action and the gods who distribute justice. His position is, Nassichuk suggests, similar to that of the audience, as the ghost of the spectator finds itself incorporated into the fabric of the play.

If ghosts open plays in chapter three, they close them in chapter four as Joseph Harris evaluates the spectral denouement of Racine's *Andromaque*. The Greek ambassador Oreste, traumatized at having caused, if only indirectly, the deaths of his beloved Hermione and the King Pyrrhus, descends into madness on stage and is haunted by the internal visions of the dead and other supernatural beings. Unlike the Renaissance spectres just examined, Racine's ghosts neither cause the action nor externally comment upon it. Instead they are the internalized consequences of that action. The ghostly reappearance of Pyrrhus and Hermione functions as a visual short-hand for Oreste's own dramatic impotence throughout the play as well as internalizing a motif that overshadows a play whose charac-ters are all incessantly haunted by the past. Moreover, working from writing from Corneille to Dubos, Harris extends his chapter beyond the ghosts in Racine's text, to suggest that ghosts also provide a potent metaphor for the play of presences, absence and belief that underlines theatrical performance as a whole. Spectres in the text can be paralleled with the spectral status of drama.

The psychological spectres identified by Harris in Racine find parallels in the metaphorical novelistic ghosts unearthed by Fiona Cox in chapter five. Cox presents Victor Hugo's *Les Misérables* as a text peopled by ghosts at the level of characterization. Hugo refers to Valjean as a 'passant' or a 'fantôme' whose name is effaced even from his gravestone. Hugo's insistence on the insubstantiality of his characters is, Cox suggests, intimately linked not only to his existential concerns, but also to his attempt to write the supreme epic, an epic that will surpass those of Homer, Virgil and Dante. *Les Misérables* is haunted not only by its protagonists, but also by the memories of texts such as the *Commedia*, that appear to offer fixed and final meanings while Hugo writes, in Malcolm Bowie's terms, 'a self-deflating epic'.[32] Hugo's subversion of his epic ambitions points to the ghosts of texts future, heralding the stylistic innovations and preoccupations of the *nouveau roman* as his novel inhabits the space between the death of the realist, totalizing novel and self-reflexive modernism.

Section II, in a manner comparable with section I, explores the ghosts of identity and textuality, but it does so in relation to the twentieth and twenty-first centuries, exploring many of the media which are key to modernity. Photography is the first medium scrutinized. In chapter six Lynsey Russell-Watts uses theories of the ghostly developed principally from Derrida to explore the personal and artistic ghosts of the work of Annie Ernaux and Marc Marie: *L'Usage de la photo*. In this dual-authored photo-text, texts and images, though linked, are also undeniably separate. The relationship between them is much less one of fusion than of haunting. Text is haunted by text, text by photo, photo by text, photo by absent body, and photo-text by the thematic spectral presences of memory, death, illness and loss. These formal and thematic hauntings are compounded by the feelings, memories and personal ghosts evoked not just by the writers, but also in the mind of the reader. Interrogating the haunted spaces of *L'Usage de la photo*, this chapter lays bare the dialogues it carries out with text-image theory and with notions of authorship and therapy, underlining the usefulness of the spectral as an analytical and critical category.

Chapter seven considers the relationship of the photographic image with its cinematic counterpart as Jean-Xavier Ridon unpicks the layers of haunting at the core of Chris Marker's documentary film *Sans soleil* (1982). The film is haunted by a scene of happiness with which the work starts and ends: the scene of three children on a path in Iceland recorded by Marker in 1963. Marker's film makes clear that, like photography, cinema offers a way to present what is no more and as such has a close association with death. Nevertheless, the picture created is not the memory itself, rather it is a tool that may help the return of the memory. Marker's film thus distinguishes two types of ghost: the cinematic document as a form of objective ghost that preserves a moment in time and the ghost as a form of haunting (a memory) within a subjectivity. Marker creates a new cinematic discourse that attempts to represent the very dynamism of memory and incorporates the phenomenon of oblivion, a discourse structured around the metaphor of the ghost.

Cinema is also the focus of chapter eight as Andrew Asibong turns to consider the spectacular array of ghosts gluing together the eclectic *oeuvre* of French filmmaker François Ozon. Surveying Ozon's career backwards from *Le Temps qui reste* (2005) to his graduating short *Victor* (1993), this chapter maintains that the increasing 'fleshiness' of the spectres the further backwards we move in Ozon's trajectory is of key importance. It is the degree of solidity of a given film's ghosts – and the ghosts' form of cinematic exorcism – that seems to determine the haunted protagonist's capacity to establish viable relations with that film's community of (living and dead) characters. Where Ozon's recent films rehearse (significantly feminized) characters' endless failure to meet the barely perceptible spectre structuring and policing their desire, earlier features explore the possibility of confronting an embodied (and hyper-masculinized) spectre via an experience of unmediated (corporeal) horror. The more grotesquely 'solid' the phantom (that is, the closer Ozon moves towards the representation of actual horror), the greater chance the film has of working as a machine of genuinely unprecedented – and politicized – transformation.

A number of the works explored in this collection are haunted by the ghosts of previous authors; however, perhaps none are more visibly haunted than the text featured in chapter nine: Hélène Cixous's *Portrait de Derrida en jeune singe juif*. Focusing on the textual spectre haunting a number of the chapters of *Haunting Presences*, Frédéric Regard analyses the nine famously provocative pages where Cixous offers her readers a facsimile of her manuscript annotations of Derrida's 'Circonfession' (the autobiographical memoir inserted into Geoffrey Bennington's 1991 *Jacques Derrida*). Cixous's portrait consists in underlining unexpected sections of Derrida's sentences or words, which are retranscribed in the margins of Derrida's own text, as if Cixous's hand had managed to operate the text of its own unconscious ghost-like message. The reader is thus invited to consider Cixous's own writing to be intimately haunted by the presence of Derrida's letter, of Cixous's reading of Derrida to the letter.

Having explored specific twentieth- and twenty-first-century ghosts in photography, film and theory, *Haunting Presences* closes with a literary focus on this era. Whilst previous chapters have analysed works haunted by memory, in chapter ten Sarah Tribout-Joseph explores the haunting lack of memory in Robert Pinget's *Passacaille*. The text is haunted by persistent apparitions of a dead and mutilated body, apparitions which signal that something is amiss, without clarifying what it is. Tribout-Joseph suggests that the body is the central character's memory come back to haunt him, that the writer in *Passacaille* is haunted by himself and that the work may thus be read as a spectral staging of conscience.

Perhaps appropriately for a volume which seeks to open cross-century spectral dialogues, *Haunting Presences* closes, in chapter eleven, with Henriette Korthals Altes's exploration of the way in which canonical texts from Plato to Stendhal are at once transmuted and subverted by Pascal Quignard's *Vie secrète* (1998). The book opens with autobiographical fragments relating the affair the narrator has had with his now deceased violin teacher. Affect and emotion (the narrative of lost love) are transformed into theory (aphorisms on love, knowledge, reading and music), whilst canonical texts are transformed into a new work. The book therefore rests on several layers of transformation as both individuals and texts are haunted. In *Vie secrète*, to allow oneself to be haunted by figures of the past is a form of self-effacement. However, it does not correspond to a feeling of dispossession or a melancholic stance. Korthals Altes shows that, on the contrary, for Quignard such self-effacement and capacity to find resonance with the voices of the past is a moment of plenitude. It defines the process of loving and stands at the origin of any creative act.

The layers of haunting explored by this volume are thus numerous. Characters are haunted by memory, by its lack, by their own potency. Authors and artists are haunted by illness, death, the past, by the textual or artistic process, by the gaze of the reader or spectator. Works are haunted by the voices of earlier works, by the spectre of future transformation, by the boundaries of their own art form. The vocabulary of haunting is conventionally associated with anxiety, horror and paralysis. However, this volume hopes to underline the productivity of the ghost for creative spirits, its core importance to considerations of the structures of identity and artistry, by dipping into the huge range of French works which make use of the spectre in all manner of forms. From ghosts, literal or metaphorical, subjective or artistic, texts, films, photographs and theories spring.

Notes

1 See, *inter alia*, Amy J. Ransom, *The Feminine as Fantastic in the Conte fantastique* (New York: Peter Lang, 1995), and Tobin Siebers, *The Romantic Fantastic* (Ithaca/London: Cornell University Press, 1984).

2 For a study of this poetics of death and rebirth, see David Evans, 'Le Tombeau de la Poésie: strategies of textual resurrection in Mallarmé and Banville', in Lisa Downing, Nigel Harkness, Sonya Stephens and Tim Unwin (eds), *Birth and Death in Nineteenth-Century French Culture* (Amsterdam: Rodopi, 2007), pp. 63–79.

3 Émile Zola, *Le Rêve*, in *Les Rougon-Macquart. Histoire naturelle et sociale d'une famille sous le Second Empire*, ed. Henri Mitterand, 5 vols (Paris: Gallimard, Bibliothèque de la Pléiade, 1960–7), IV (1966), pp. 813–994 (p. 866). For further details of the metaphor of the ghost in Zola's fiction, see Kate Griffiths, 'Scribbling ghosts: the textual spectres and spectral texts of Émile Zola', in J. Horn and L. Russell-Watts (eds), *Possessions: Essays in French Literature, Cinema and Theory* (Oxford: Peter Lang, 2003), pp. 51–65.

4 Émile Zola, *La Débâcle*, in *Les Rougon-Macquart. Histoire naturelle et sociale d'une famille sous le Second Empire*, ed. Henri Mitterand, 5 vols (Paris: Gallimard, Bibliothèque de la Pléiade, 1960–7), V (1966), pp. 399–912 (p. 592).

5 Ibid., p. 610.

6 Ibid., p. 580.

7 Ibid., p. 895.

8 Voltaire, *Œuvres de 1746–1748 (I)* (Oxford: Voltaire Foundation, 2003), p. 43.

9 Guy de Maupassant, *Contes et nouvelles*, ed. Louis Forestier, 2 vols (Paris: Gallimard, Bibliothèque de la Pléiade, 1974–9), II (1979), pp. 513–18, and I (1974), pp. 1246–50.

10 The author of this play cannot be fully identified. Authors of works, if they are identified at all in this collection, are designated only by their initials. However, in many later volumes there is simply a note stating that all the plays are by Lesage, d'Orneval and Fuzelier.

11 Colin Davis, *Haunted Subjects: Deconstruction, Psychoanalysis and the Return of the Dead* (Basingstoke: Palgrave Macmillan, 2007).

12 Jacques Lacan, *Le Séminaire de Jacques Lacan. Livre XI* (Paris: Seuil, 1973), p. 98.

13 Jacques Lacan, *Le Séminaire de Jacques Lacan. Livre I* (Paris: Seuil, 1975), p. 144.

14 Lacan, *Livre XI*, p. 98.

15 Ibid., p. 89.

16 Lacan, *Livre I*, p. 171.

17 Jacques Lacan, *Écrits* (Paris: Seuil, 1966), p. 116.
18 Lacan, *Livre I*, p. 304.
19 Jacques Lacan, *Le Séminaire de Jacques Lacan. Livre XX* (Paris: Seuil, 1975), p. 78.
20 Lacan, *Écrits*, p. 448.
21 Jacques Lacan, *Le Séminaire de Jacques Lacan. Livre II* (Paris: Seuil, 1978), p. 16.
22 Ibid., p. 272.
23 Lacan, *Écrits*, p. 428.
24 Ibid., p. 517.
25 Ibid., pp. 627, 252, 525.
26 Jacques Lacan, *Le Séminaire de Jacques Lacan. Livre III* (Paris: Seuil, 1981), p. 356.
27 For more details on Lacan and the question of citation, see Kate Griffiths, 'Descartes and Lacan: print and the subject of citation', *New Zealand Journal of French Studies*, 27, 2 (2006), 16–28. We are grateful to *NZJFS* for allowing the reproduction of one aspect of this article here.
28 Jacques Lacan, *Le Séminaire de Jacques Lacan. Livre XVII* (Paris: Seuil, 1991), p. 169.
29 Lacan, *Livre I*, p. 169.
30 Ibid., p. 195.
31 Harold Bloom, *The Anxiety of Influence: A Theory of Poetry*, 2nd edn (New York/Oxford: Oxford University Press, 1997), p. 139.
32 Malcolm Bowie, *Proust Among the Stars* (New York: Columbia University Press, 1998), p. 105.

Chapter One
Ghosts, Hearsay and Lies: the Strange Case(s) of Lord Lyttelton

Colin Davis

In 1674 a Dutch lawyer named Hugo Boxel engaged the philosopher Spinoza in a correspondence about ghosts. Boxel gave a number of (in his view) telling reasons for believing in their existence: the universe would be less perfect without them; it is plausible that God would create creatures more like himself than corporeal beings; since there are bodies without souls, there must be souls without bodies; and finally, space cannot be empty, so it must be full of spirits. Boxel concludes that there must be spirits of all kinds, except, he suspects, those of the female sex. One can almost hear Spinoza's laughter as he patiently refutes Boxel's reasoning. In comparison with Spinoza's intelligent scepticism, Boxel appears to be a credulous fool. His arguments do not bear scrutiny. It is surely time for rational beings to stop believing in ghosts.

Boxel, though, offers a crucial counter-argument: we should believe in ghosts because there are numerous ancient and modern stories about them. He even tells one himself:

> *Un bourgmestre, homme savant et sage, et qui vit encore, m'a raconté un jour qu'il avait entendu dire que dans la brasserie de sa mère, il se faisait autant de travail de nuit que de jour quand on brassait la bière. Il attestait que cela s'était produit maintes fois. Ce récit m'a été fait à diverses reprises de sorte que, à cause de ces expériences et pour les raisons que j'ai dites plus haut, je suis obligé de croire aux spectres.*[1]

The story is extremely vague. No specific claim is made about what might have been going on in the brewery at night, though its ghostly significance is assumed. The story's plausibility is enhanced by the fact that it was recounted by someone known to Boxel, even though the burgermeister did not witness the supernatural events himself. In the end, what makes the story utterly compelling is its repetition. Boxel finds himself *obliged* to believe in ghosts because he has heard tell of them so often ('Ce récit m'a été fait à diverses reprises de sorte que ... je suis obligé de croire aux spectres'). Boxel appears to be gullible to such an extreme extent that, from a modern perspective, we might begin to suspect that his whole argument is a parody. And yet, Spinoza's rational calm is impotent in the face of Boxel's insistent will to believe. We know ghosts exist because we have heard ghost stories; and if we do not believe stories told by men who seem plausible, then we are lost. Boxel proffers no argument worth considering, yet the urgency of his case is strangely compelling. Spinoza dispenses with Boxel's silly belief in ghosts, but the ghosts do not quite go away.

One conclusion to draw from this is that, despite Spinoza's efforts, our business with the dead is still unfinished; or in other words, the dead are not yet fully dead. Slavoj Žižek suggests that the return of the living dead deserves to be called 'the fundamental fantasy of contemporary mass culture'.[2] In Žižek's account the dead return because our symbolic debt to them remains unpaid. Our business with them and their business with us is unfinished; and, I shall argue, stories of ghosts persist because they continue to convey something that is of value to us, even if many of us do not strictly believe in them any longer. Modern ghost stories exploit the clash between belief and disbelief, making our scepticism and its apparent rebuttal one of their central concerns. To examine the status of the modern ghost story, I shall consider the case of the second Lord Lyttelton, who died in mysterious circumstances at the age of thirty-five in 1779.[3] Lord Lyttelton had apparently led a wicked and debauched life. Like many wicked and debauched people he had been a member of Parliament until he was unseated for bribery. When he inherited his title on the death of his father in 1773 he was abroad with a barmaid, and he subsequently took his father's seat in the House of Lords. His life was unremarkable except for its excesses; what ensured his notoriety through the late eighteenth and nineteenth centuries was the manner of his death, which made of it what Dr Johnson called 'the most extraordinary thing which has happened in my day'.[4] It seems that Lord Lyttelton was informed by a ghost that he would die at midnight in three days' time. Three days later, at midnight, he was indeed dead. Like the ghost story recounted by Boxel, Dr Johnson heard of Lord Lyttelton's death from someone he was inclined to trust, his uncle Lord Westcote; and he was willing to believe it because he was, as he put it, 'so glad to have every evidence to the spiritual world'. In other words, he accepted it as true because it could be taken to confirm what he already believed.

It is highly significant that this incident occurred, and quickly became well known, in the late eighteenth century, at the height of the Age of Reason. Spinoza tried and failed to convince Hugo Boxel that ghosts did not exist. The thinkers of the Enlightenment wanted to achieve what Spinoza could not by putting an end to superstition once and for all. The entry on *superstition* in the *Encyclopédie* (1751–72) of Diderot and D'Alembert lists 'les spectres, les songes et les visions' as the tools of fear and imagination. The entry on *fantôme* is more forceful still in its insistence that ghosts do not exist; they are the product of bad education, and it is the role of philosophy to root out foolish beliefs. The mission of the Enlightenment, then, was to get rid of ghosts definitively. And yet, stories of the supernatural persisted. The Age of Reason also witnessed the huge popularity in France of Dom Augustin Calmet's collection of vampire stories, the rise of gothic literature, and what Terry Castle calls 'the invention of the uncanny'.[5] Indeed, Castle suggests that the aggressive rationalism of the eighteenth century 'also produced, like a kind of toxic side effect, a new human experience of strangeness, anxiety, bafflement, and intellectual impasse'.[6] In Castle's account, Enlightenment thinking aimed to put an end to superstition, and in the process to make spirits and ghosts obsolete; but rather than abolishing ghosts, it gave them a new hold on the human mind:

> *The rationalists did not so much negate the traditional spirit world as displace it into the realm of psychology. Ghosts were not exorcized – only internalized and reinterpreted as hallucinatory thoughts. Yet this internalization of apparitions introduced a latent irrationalism into the realm of mental experience. If ghosts were thoughts, then thoughts themselves took on – at least notionally – the haunting reality of ghosts. The mind became subject to spectral presences. The epistemologically unstable, potentially fantastic metaphor of the phantasmagoria simply condensed the historical paradox: by relocating*

the world of ghosts in the closed space of the imagination, one ended up super-naturalizing the mind itself.[7]

This is, according to Castle, 'a momentous event in the history of Western consciousness'.[8] The ghosts are now inside our heads rather than roaming the outside world, and human subjectivity has been infiltrated by alien, irrational, spectral forces. This relocation of ghosts into the mind sets the stage for Freudian psychoanalysis, which aims to free us from irrational anxieties whilst introducing the demonic into the very core of subjectivity. Rather than exorcizing the supernatural, psychoanalysis identifies the darkest powers as originating within ourselves rather than in the outside world; so, far from clearing away diabolic forces, it turns them into an integral part of what it means to be human. Paralleling the ambiguous achievement of psychoanalysis, part of what is at stake in the modern ghost story is whether it repeats our crazy fears in order to rid us of them or to chain us to them more effectively.

Lord Lyttelton's encounter with a ghost comes at a historical conjuncture when such things should no longer occur, as if it were produced precisely as a response to the denial of its possibility. The ghost appears not only to the doomed lord but also, by becoming the subject of hearsay and storytelling, to the whole of the Enlightened world, to tell us that there is more in the universe than the rationalists might want us to believe. After Lyttelton's death the suspicion quickly arose that he might have committed suicide, telling the story of the apparition as a final joke on the world. But this suspicion is disproved by a detail in the story of his death. Because those around him were worried by his increasing anxiety as midnight on the fatal day approached, all clocks and watches were put forward by half an hour so that they registered midnight when it was in fact 11.30. Lord Lyttelton thought he had survived the ghost's prediction, only to die half an hour later when it was really the appointed time. If he had intended to kill himself at midnight – so the argument goes – he would have followed the clocks and unwittingly done the deed half an hour early; the spirit world, though, cannot be deceived as to the time by the paltry expedient of changing the clocks.

So the demise of Lord Lyttelton is a kind of proof that ghosts exist, reinforcing beliefs that the thinkers of the Enlightenment had tried to stigmatize as superstition. In fact, the visitation three days

before his death is neither the beginning nor the end of the return
of the dead in Lord Lyttelton's story. His father, the first Lord
Lyttelton, was a minor political and literary figure in the eighteenth
century, the author of, amongst other things, a collection of
Dialogues of the Dead following the lead of Lucian, Fénelon and
Fontenelle. The second Lord Lyttelton's prehistory, then, already
involved voices of the deceased returning to inform the living. And,
not content to *witness* a ghost, Lord Lyttelton himself *became* a ghost
to haunt others, as his story would continue to haunt nineteenth-
century Europe. One night, Lord Lyttelton appeared to a friend of
his, a certain Miles Peter Andrews. The following account of the visitation draws on a text published in 1828, but it was already
circulating within days of Lyttelton's death:

> One night after Mr Andrews had left Pitt Place and gone to Dartford, where
> he owned powder-mills, his bed-curtains were pulled open and Lord Lyttelton
> appeared before him in his robe de chambre and nightcap. Mr Andrews
> reproached him for coming to Dartford Mills in such a guise, at such a time of
> night, and, turning to the other side of the bed, rang the bell, when Lord
> Lyttelton had disappeared. The house and garden were searched in vain; and
> about four in the afternoon a friend arrived at Dartford with tidings of his
> lordship's death.[9]

So the interference of the dead in the world of the living is everywhere in Lord Lyttelton's story, as it doggedly obstructs attempts at
rationalization. But what did he actually see on the night of his
fateful visitation? Here, the accounts of those close to him, some
written many years after the event, are full of contradiction. He may
have died in Epsom or Berkeley Square; he may have reported that
the ghost appeared in a dream or while he was awake; he saw a
young woman and a robin redbreast, or he saw a bird, which may
have been a robin or a dove, which became a woman; the woman
may have been a deserted lover, or the mother of sisters he had
seduced, or someone unknown; the apparition may or may not have
been accompanied by a preternatural light or a fluttering sound.
For some, such as Dr Johnson, the event may have provided
evidence of the spirit world, but quite what the event was which
provided this evidence remains clouded in mystery. The story gets
told and retold, acquiring greater credence as it goes, but with each
teller, as Frost puts it, 'varying the circumstances, and omitting some
of the details or adding others'.[10]

The story of Lord Lyttelton's death arose and was widely reported in the late eighteenth century, I suggest, precisely because it contradicted the rationalist assumptions of Enlightenment thought. It can be understood as part of what Castle calls the 'toxic side effect' of rationalism, reasserting the inscrutability of the world we inhabit at a time when some thinkers believed they were close to solving its mysteries. Moreover, the mysteries which the story affirms derive from a very conventional morality: a notorious miscreant is warned of the fate awaiting him; he will be punished for his wicked actions, and those of us who hear of his tale are reminded of the spiritual order which watches over us. However, a nineteenth-century reworking of the story of Lord Lyttelton by the French author Jules Janin marks an important shift. No longer representing merely one side in the stand-off between reason and faith, the ghost story embraces its modern condition by incorporating a self-doubting element within itself. Janin's 'Une histoire de revenant', dating from 1834, refers unmistakably to Lyttelton's death.[11] The text begins and ends with a short framing narrative, to which I shall return. Its main body tells the story of a certain Lord Littleton who, despite a change of spelling and some deviations from source versions, is clearly modelled on the English aristocrat. In Janin's version, Littleton's abandoned lover drowns herself in the Thames and returns to him as a ghost to tell him that he will die in a week's time at the stroke of midnight. Littleton is unable to sleep and becomes increasingly anxious through the week. On the appointed day his worried friends advance the clocks by half an hour so that he believes he is still alive at midnight. We might anticipate that he will die half an hour later like the real Lord Lyttelton, but the story in fact ends in anticlimax as the narrator tells his audience that Littleton has survived: 'il se porte aussi bien que vous et moi, Messieurs; l'heure a passé sans emporter Sa Seigneurie: à l'heure qu'il est, il mange, il boit, il dort, il monte à cheval, il est heureux à tous les jeux, il n'a pas une seule maîtresse, et je vous conseille d'en faire autant'.

The title of 'Une histoire de revenant' indicates that the story is about something that returns, that is, something that survives in some (albeit spectral) form even after it should have died. The *revenant* of the title is of course Littleton's mistress, but it is also in a sense Littleton himself, who survives in the story even though he seems doomed, and whose story itself has survived and returns in

Janin's version fifty-five years after the death of the historical Lyttelton. The story is also about Janin's survival. Born in 1804, he reached the age of thirty in 1834, the year of the story's publication. This is reflected in the text by the fact that, whereas the historical Lyttelton had been thirty-five at the time of his death, Janin stresses that his character is in his thirtieth year: 'il était arrivé à cette belle trentième année où la passion raisonne, où l'amour hésite, où le cœur ne bat plus qu'à certaines heures dans le jour'. Two further references underscore Littleton's age. In case Janin might have been worrying that his own heart might cease beating at the age of thirty, his story reassures him of the possibility of surviving that fateful age.

If 'Une histoire de revenant' narrates the survival and return of Littleton and of Janin, it also tells of the unlikely survival of the ghost story as a literary form, not killed off by Enlightenment rationalism or the materialism of a secular society in the process of industrialization. The ghost and the ghost story return, after all. Yet if the *revenant* returns, it cannot be as it was in former times. The ghost of Littleton's lover is even more beautiful than she was in life: 'c'était bien sa taille élégante et souple comme le jonc, mais plus svelte encore, grand Dieu!' Her body on the other hand, when it is fished out of the Thames, is 'si défiguré, hélas! et si violet et si contracté par la mort et si horriblement petit, étroit, mort, difforme, que son amant ne l'aurait pas reconnu'. She is both the same as she was and unrecognizable, both more and less than her living self. This discrepancy between the ghost and its physical remains reflects the sense that the ghost story itself, if it is to survive, must also be transformed. The ghost story returns, but here it returns as something to be gently mocked. This explains its most significant deviation from its source: the survival of Lord Littleton. The death of the historical lord and his subsequent reappearance as a ghost confirmed the reality of the supernatural and could be heralded by Dr Johnson as 'the most extraordinary thing which has happened in my day'. The ghost returns to tell of what no human could know; whether it be a dream or an apparition, a woman or a bird, or a woman who turns into a bird, it delivers a message that can come only from a transcendent source. Underlying the ghost's warning that Lord Lyttelton is soon to die is a much more important lesson addressed to those of us who live on to hear the tale: do not believe what the rationalists, the sceptics and the atheists are telling you; there is a plan and a moral order, there is a supervising presence which watches over human affairs, and the wicked will be punished. By contrast, the anticlimax of Littleton's survival in Janin's story mocks the role of the ghost as supernatural messenger. The wicked Lord Lyttelton of history has been replaced by a less dissolute character, described by Janin's narrator as 'un honnête et noble gentilhomme, riche, heureux, sachant commander à ses passions'. His only crime, so far as we know, is to abandon a lover. So the warning of death appears as a spurned lover's vengeance rather than a moral punishment; and in any case the ghost is mistaken or mendacious rather than the messenger of a higher truth. If spirits exist, the story seems to ask, do they really have nothing better to do, no deeper purpose, than to tell us malicious lies? The ghost story survives and returns, but makes a mockery of itself as it does so.

The transition from the historical Lord Lyttelton to Janin's fictional Lord Littleton sketches a process of demystification taking place within the ghost story itself. It withdraws credibility from the belief – that nevertheless underpins the authority of the ghost story – that the spirit world exists and that a higher moral order presides over us and may sometimes communicate with us. To put this in Lacanian terms, the ghost story depends on the fiction of the big Other. The purpose of the psychoanalytic cure is precisely to rid us of this fiction. The cure is complete only when the analysand has learnt to recognize meaningless contingency for what it is, namely meaningless and contingent. We must see through the imposture of the big Other. Here is Žižek's account of the process:

> At the end of the psychoanalytic cure, the analysand has to suspend the urge to symbolize/internalize, to interpret, to search for a 'deeper meaning'; he has to accept that the traumatic encounters which traced out the itinerary of his life were utterly contingent and indifferent, that they bear no 'deeper message' … at the moment of 'exit from transference' which marks the end of the cure, the subject is able to perceive the events around which his life story is crystallized into a meaningful Whole in their senseless contingency.[12]

A century before Lacan, Janin's text enacts the ghost story's self-cure, debunking as a silly fiction the transcendental truth that speaks to us through ghosts. The big Other who dispatches spirits towards us to make us pay for our wickedness is in fact just a deceiver, unable to sustain the moral order. Lord Littleton's survival marks the failure of his life to achieve the meaningful coherence of a destiny and abandons him to its pure senselessness. At the end, he eats, drinks, sleeps and rides without a care, thus coping admirably with an existence of contingent pleasures outside the gaze of the big Other.

So far, my account of 'Une histoire de revenant' depicts it as a sort of self-destruction of the ghost story, as it demystifies the beliefs which sustain its own conditions of possibility. However, this leaves open the question of why the ghost story precisely survives and returns after it should have withered away. I want to suggest that the demystification operated here is shadowed by a gesture of re-mystification which restores some of the ghost story's credibility. This is where the framing narrative, which opens and closes the story, becomes important. The first two paragraphs of 'Une histoire de revenant' present the circumstances in which the story of Lord Littleton is narrated. A group of people including an unnamed first-person narrator (or pre-narrator) are gathered together and begin to talk about ghosts; an Englishman offers to tell a story allegedly well known in London and, on the urging of those present, he proceeds to narrate the main part of the text. Like the ghost story recounted by Boxel to Spinoza, the tale of Lord Littleton is presented as an example of hearsay, gaining authority not because anyone present has first-hand knowledge of it but because of the prestige of the storyteller and the fact that it is claimed to be well known. At the end of the story the frame narrative is briefly reintro-duced and the text concludes with a one-sentence paragraph. This sentence explicitly marks a distance from what has preceded: 'On trouva généralement que cette histoire de lord Littleton n'avait pas de sens commun, et je suis de l'avis général.' The story lacks common sense, so the pre-narrator disowns its implausible implica-tions. This lack of common sense is not, I suggest, because it tells of ghosts, but because it tells of ghosts *who lie*. Who could believe such a thing? We might readily accept that a ghost could appear, but not that it should appear to no good purpose or in accordance with no higher plan. This would make a nonsense of the whole history of supernatural visitations. So the story's conclusion, which ironizes the foundations of the ghost story, is itself debunked. The text enters into a spiral of seriousness and self-mockery, demystification and re-mystification, which offers no prospect of settling into a stable perspective.

The frame narrative adds an element of excess which seems unnecessary to the main story, but at the same time it introduces elements which reflect and inflect the sense or senselessness of what it contains. The impression of disruptive excess is evident from the opening words: 'Nous étions réunis l'autre jour quelques amis français et étrangers qui ne nous étions jamais vus, et qui cependant nous connaissions depuis longtemps: poètes, écrivains, hommes riches, tous gens qui se conviennent au premier abord et qui se comprennent tout de suite à la première poignée de main.' So this is a gathering of friends who have never met, people who have known each other for a long time and understand each other fully on first contact. They speak of everything and nothing ('on ne parla de rien, c'est-à-dire qu'on parla de toutes choses') as if in this company opposites are reunited. The second paragraph introduces the Englishman who will tell the story of Lord Littleton: 'Un des nôtres, un Anglais'. He is a man, we are told, who can drink without getting drunk and who can eat without putting on weight. This reference to eating and drinking reflects a concern in the main narrative. After dismissing his lover, Lord Littleton goes out to dine; he loses his appetite and thirst after his visitation by the ghost but recovers them when he believes it is midnight on the day prescribed for his death.

So eating and drinking appear as key activities for the characters in the frame narrative as they are for the protagonist of the main story. There is, then, a continuity of interests between the narrative and its frame which blurs the division between them. One of the most important of these shared interests is the question of community and belonging. I said earlier that the ghost of Lord Littleton's lover tells him that he is to die. This is not exactly correct; what she in fact says is that he will join her kind: 'vous serez des nôtres'. He will join with her in the community of the dead. This theme of community is also foregrounded in the frame narrative, from its opening words, 'Nous étions réunis', and again in the first words of the second paragraph which introduce the Englishman as 'Un des nôtres'. Since the community of 'our kind' referred to in the main text is that of the dead, it may carry some resonance of this in the frame narrative also. This community of people who know each other without ever having met, who talk of everything and nothing, who drink and eat without effect, has something distinctly eerie about it. Perhaps what is described here is a gathering of the dead.

If this were the case, the ghost story would be about ghosts, and it would be recounted by and to ghosts. Rather than stabilizing the story as a silly anecdote told to pass the time, the frame narrative serves to put back in doubt the demystification effected in the main text. The dividing line between the living and the dead begins to crumble away. The dead are a little less dead because they can return to us, but as a consequence the living are also a little less alive. The anonymous 'Nous' which begins the text and the 'On' which begins its final sentence are faceless, uncanny, barely alive, a band of ghosts recalling to themselves the story of a ghost which offends their common sense: how, if you are a ghost, could you possibly believe that ghosts were so pointless?

'Une histoire de revenant' sets the conditions of possibility of the modern ghost story. It is constructed around a double gesture, represented here by the distinction and then by the interference between the frame narrative and the main text. It does not believe its own tale of spiritual visitation, so it reproduces it with a final twist (Lord Littleton does not die) which mocks gullible readers seeking messages from beyond the grave. But this self-repudiation marks a crisis for the ghost story which, if fully followed through, would signal its demise; so the story, by means of its uncanny frame narrative, restores some of the plausibility of the supernatural which the rest of the text had eroded. The ghost story does not believe in its founding presumption that ghosts are messengers of a higher order; but neither does it believe its lack of belief. Its demystification is re-mystified. This kind of underlying self-contradiction makes possible modern tales of horror and the supernatural, for example, in a film such as *The Ring*. Both the Japanese and American versions of *The Ring* adopt a premise which recalls the ghost's warning to Lord Littleton in 'Une histoire de revenant' that he will die in a week's time. In *The Ring* anyone who watches a certain video tape immediately receives a telephone call by which they are informed that they will die in a week, a prophecy which, unlike the one in Janin's story, turns out to be true. Is the film really trying to warn us that a video tape may be the vehicle of supernatural evil? Surely not. But the fact that we may not believe, or be asked to believe, the film's premise does not make it any less frightening, as if we believed it without believing it. It produces effects of terror which may originate in fears and fantasies which have survived our conscious rejection of them.

The dead will not go away despite our best efforts. Correspondingly, stories of ghosts and the undead are as popular as ever, even though the superstitions and belief systems that sustained them have supposedly been dispelled. Think, for example, of films such as *Ghost, The Sixth Sense, The Others, Truly, Madly, Deeply,* George A. Romero's zombie films beginning with *Night of the Living Dead,* and the seven television series of *Buffy the Vampire Slayer.* We may for the most part no longer believe that the dead return, but we have not entirely given up on them either. Octave Mannoni's formula of fetishism, 'Je sais bien, mais quand même' is pertinent here: I know ghosts do not exist, but I still believe in them; or alternatively, I do not believe in ghosts, but I do not entirely believe my lack of belief.[13] Žižek concurs that this is how we are believers today: 'we make fun of our beliefs, while continuing to practise them, that is, to rely on them as the underlying structure of our daily practices'.[14] Perhaps we want the dead to be with us as much as we need to be rid of them. In any case, on a daily basis the popular media dramatize the return of the dead; and, however ironic, metaphoric or playful this return might be, however much it is presented as mere entertainment not to be taken too seriously, even so it continues to correspond to unsurmounted needs, fears or desires which are as urgent now as they ever were: the need to believe that something of us and of what we love will survive; the fear that we are haunted by the dead, or alternatively that we have been deserted by them; and the desire to know that we are not alone, that we are free to follow our own path but that something nevertheless watches over and accompanies us.

Lord Littleton's survival is described as an affront to common sense because to believe that ghosts lie would mean giving up too much that is still precious to us. Perhaps the dead do not return; we have no debt to them and they have no business with us. And yet, things do go bump in the night. We know there is nothing there, but we fear or hope or believe that there might be. It turns out to be as difficult to do without the dead as it is to live with their recriminating voices.

Notes

1   Quoted from 'Une idée des spectres', at *http://www.vacarme.eu.org/article367.html.* For further discussion of the correspondence between

Spinoza and Boxel and other issues touched upon here, see my *Haunted Subjects: Deconstruction, Psychoanalysis and the Return of the Dead* (Basingstoke: Palgrave MacMillan, 2007). In particular, the discussion of Lord Lyttelton draws on and develops material from chapter four of *Haunted Subjects.*

2   Slavoj Žižek, *Looking Awry: An Introduction to Jacques Lacan Through Popular Culture* (Cambridge, MA/London: The MIT Press, 1991), p. 22.

3   Information about Lord Lyttelton's life and death are taken from Andrew Lang, *The Valet's Tragedy, and Other Stories* (1903), at *http://www.gutenberg.org/dirs/etext00/vlttr10.txt*, and Thomas Frost, *The Wicked Lord Lyttelton* (Stroud: Nonsuch Publishing Ltd, 2006; first published 1876).

4   Quoted, for example, in Frost, *The Wicked Lord Lyttelton*, p. 225.

5   See Terry Castle, *The Female Thermometer: Eighteenth-Century Culture and the Invention of the Uncanny* (New York/Oxford: Oxford University Press, 1995). Dom Augustin Calmet's collection of stories of ghosts and vampires, *Dissertation sur les apparitions des anges, des démons et des esprits, et sur les revenants et vampires de Hongrie, de Bohême, de Moravie et de Silésie*, was first published in 1746. The book quickly sold out, and was subsequently expanded, reprinted and translated into a number of languages.

6   Castle, *The Female Thermometer*, p. 8.

7   Ibid., p. 161. The phantasmagoria to which Castle refers here were ghost-shows from the late eighteenth and early nineteenth centuries in which ghosts were made to appear by the use of magic lanterns.

8   Ibid., p. 171.

9   Quoted from Lang, *The Valet's Tragedy, and Other Stories.*

10 Frost, *The Wicked Lord Lyttelton*, p. 228.

11 Quotations from Janin's 'Une histoire de revenant' are taken from the online version available at *http://www.bmlisieux.com/litterature/janin/histoire.htm.*

12 Slavoj Žižek, *The Indivisible Remainder: An Essay on Schelling and Related Matters* (London/New York: Verso, 1996), pp. 94–5.

13 See Octave Mannoni, 'Je sais bien, mais quand même ...', in *Clefs pour l'imaginaire* (Paris: Seuil, 1968). The fetishist's version of the formula is 'I know that Mother doesn't have a penis but all the same I believe that she has'. For discussion of the formula, see Slavoj Žižek, *For They Know Not What They Do: Enjoyment as a Political Factor* (London/New York: Verso, 1991), pp. 245–53.

14 Slavoj Žižek, *Welcome to the Desert of the Real: Five Essays on September 11 and Related Dates* (London/New York: Verso, 2002), p. 71.

Part I

Ghostly Antecedents

Chapter Two

Haunting Text and Image: Having it Out with Misogynistic Authorities in the Late Medieval *querelle des femmes*

Helen J. Swift

In the introduction to *The Anxiety of Influence*, Harold Bloom 'offers a theory of poetry by way of a description of poetic influence, or the story of intra-poetic relationships'.[1] I wish to argue in the present essay for one particular theory in a specific group of related poems, namely late medieval French literary debates written in defence of women, part of the body of works now referred to under the umbrella term *la querelle des femmes*. I propose that this corpus's 'story of intra-poetic relationships' can most fruitfully be read as a history of ghosts. It is a story of how fifteenth-century writers such as Martin Le Franc, Jacques Milet and Pierre Michault address the misogynistic authorities with which their pro-feminine personae take issue. This manner of address occurs as a literary resurrection of and negotiation with 'the mighty dead',[2] namely the alleged anti-feminine *auctors* Jean de Meun, Matheolus[3] and, often, Boccaccio.[4] It is in particular the looming spectre of Jean de Meun, the late thirteenth-century provocative continuator of Guillaume de Lorris's portion of the *Roman de la Rose*, that will be my focus in this essay. I enlist Bloom's phrase 'intra-poetic relationships' as it enables me to evoke the complex interrelation of inter*text*uality and inter*person*ality that underpins these authors' conception of their misogynist forebears.

My discussion of Jean de Meun's spectral return will tackle the thorny issue of literary authority in the *querelle des femmes* in a way that relates to but differs from Bloom's idea that 'the strong dead

return ... and they do not come back without darkening the living'.[5]
I shall investigate the precise poetic implications of this 'darkening',
namely the equivocal balance of power between ancestor and inheriting poet when the heir in question is obliged to conjure up a
misogynist's ghost in order to refute him or subversively to rewrite
his text. It is in this regard especially that I employ the hermeneutic
apparatus of ghosts provided by Derrida's *Spectres de Marx*.[6] Derrida
describes the complex negotiation with spectres that occurs when a
new generation denounces the communist political inheritance
embodied in the figure and writings of Karl Marx. Derrida's theory
of a 'spectropolitics' may be transposed into what I call a 'spectropoetics', where analogous negotiations occur with regard to the
perceived embodiment of late medieval misogyny, Jean de Meun.
The particular aptness of Derridean spectrality is twofold. First, it
provides an analytical language for describing the ontology of Jean
de Meun's textual ghost that is consonant with the spectral
concerns implied by fifteenth-century writers. Secondly, Derrida
insists upon the struggle for authority that is entailed in the act of
inheritance. In my texts, the inheriting poet who opposes the *Rose*'s
misogyny *is* free to rewrite his predecessor but this act of appropria-
tion occurs, to quote Derrida, '*dans la condition de l'autre*':[7] on terms
imposed by the ultimately ineffaceable face of the dead-though-still-
mighty Jean de Meun.

I choose the word 'face' advisedly since, in miniaturists' illustra-
tive interpretations of my pro-feminine writers' texts, it is their
visualization of the vernacular *auctoritas* as a person, a bodily or
facial presence, that is initially most striking. Much evidence is
provided by manuscripts and early editions of Martin Le Franc's
Champion des dames (*c.* 1442), a judicial debate between the eponymous Champion, Franc Vouloir, and various representatives of his
adversary, Malebouche. The iconographic programmes of two
related manuscripts, *P2* and *Z*, picture Jean de Meun alongside the
debaters as a conjured up presence to accompany the Champion's
criticism of the *Rose* (figure 1).[8] The physicality of the *auctor*'s presence is also manifested in a later incunable through the representation of Jean de Meun looming behind the characters from his text
that the Champion is discussing at this moment, namely La Vieille
and Bel Accueil (figure 2). This visual evidence of the poem's
contemporary reception may prompt a reappraisal of modern critical assumptions about medieval views of authorship and literary

Figure 1 Jean de Meun conjured up between the debaters, Martin Le Franc, *Le Champion des dames*. Paris, BnF MS fr. 841, fol. 98r. Bibliothèque nationale de France.

Figure 2 Jean de Meun looms behind Bel Accueil and La Vieille, Martin Le Franc, *Le Champion des dames*. Paris, BnF, RES YE-27, fol. O3v. Bibliothèque nationale de France.

authority, to which it has generally been assumed that modern ideas of the author as personality are anathema.

It may be helpful to step back momentarily from the *querelle* to set the late medieval scene forming the literary backdrop to my discussions of haunted pro-feminine texts. Much fifteenth- and early sixteenth-century French literature, both poetic and historiographical, seems to have been notably caught up in a proto-Derridean 'chasse au fantôme'.[9] This fascination intersects with the artistic phenomenon of the *danse macabre*, for which the resurrected dead were staged in texts, miniatures, murals, sculptures and dramatic performances.[10] Interest in an 'afterlife' is evidenced by the vogue of the *testament* and *complainte* as literary forms.[11] The idea of specifically literary survival beyond the grave appears in numerous poetic cemeteries, as in Octovien de Saint-Gelais's *Séjour d'honneur* (1494). Saint-Gelais's narrator records epitaphs from the tombstones of deceased literary giants, including Jean de Meun, thereby perpetuating these writers' renown. Similarly, through a poetic dialogue with the late Burgundian celebrity Jean Molinet, Jean Lemaire de Belges underscores the role of historiographers (*indiciaires*) in sustaining life through textual representation: 'Ceulx cy font les gens vivre'.[12] These revived authorities frequently return through the medium of a dream vision, like Guillaume Crétin's *Apparition du Mareschal sans reproche* (1525), where they are perceived as a material presence; the eponymous marshal appears as 'la statue et ymage | d'homme'.[13] One such oneiric encounter with a deceased *auctoritas*, Honoré Bouvet's *Apparicion Maistre Jehan de Meun* (1398), may be used to define my lines of enquiry. Bouvet's narrator-persona recounts how, after dinner one evening,

> ens le jardin de la Tournelle hors de Paris, qui fu jadis maistre Jehan de Meun ... [je] prins telle ymaginacion qu'elle me tint tant longuement que, se m'endormay, soit en bonne heure. Mais vecy venir un grant clerc bien fourré de menu ver, sy me commença a tancer ...[14]

Three issues are raised here: the ontology of the spectre, the locus of the apparition, and the balance of power between the *revenant* and its host. First, appearing to the narrator in 'ymaginacion', Jean de Meun's presence is ambiguous: seeming to appear of his own, autonomous volition ('vecy venir'), he is yet a product of the narrator's dream vision. He may thus be seen to partake of the sort of equivocal ontology that Derrida explains thus: 'Un spectre *paraît* se présenter, lors d'une visitation. On se le représente mais il n'est pas présent, lui-même, en chair et en os.'[15] Secondly, Jean de Meun returns in his own former garden, wherein, we are told, he composed his *chef d'œuvre*: 'fis cy le Rommant de la Rose'.[16] I shall pursue below the important connection between place and inheritance when considering the narrative framework in which *querelle* debates locate their challenges to misogynistic ancestors. Thirdly, the *Apparicion* demonstrates how the struggle for authority is always an issue even when poetic resurrection is intended wholly in homage to the returning spectre. Anxiety strikes as the narrator declares his intellectual deficiency in relation to his illustrious ancestor: 'car je ne sauroye pas estudier comme vous fistes jadis'.[17]

The *Apparicion*'s literary resuscitation of Jean de Meun is essentially a strategy to fuel the inheriting poet Honoré Bouvet's own poetic creativity. Two years later, the *Rose* continuator's spectre fulfils the same function in the *querelle du 'Roman de la Rose'* (*c.*1400–2), the famous literary debate sparked by Christine de Pizan's denunciation of the *Rose* as dissolute, and of its author as a misogynist.[18] 'Ghost-hunting' here becomes the persecution rather than the positive conjuring forth of Jean de Meun, but it is de Meun's polemic which provides the essential impetus and pretext for literary production. This production here assumes the form of epistolary exchange between his detractors, Christine and Jean Gerson, chancellor of Paris University, and his humanist supporters, Jean de Montreuil and the Col brothers. If it reaches no other conclusion, the '*Rose*' *querelle* emphatically asserts the status of Jean de Meun's continuation as a master text, however troubling its authority. Derrida neatly articulates the spectrality of any *chef d'œuvre*'s interpretative translation by its inheritors: 'L'œuvre animée ... *s'ingénie* à habiter sans proprement habiter, soit à hanter, tel un insaisissable spectre, et la mémoire et la traduction. Un chef d'œuvre toujours se meut, par définition, à la manière d'un fantôme'.[19]

A similar concept of inheritance seems to have obtained amongst certain heirs to the *Rose*. Gerson inveighs against its ungovernable 'movement': 'opus illud chaos informe recte nominator, ... et Protheus in omnes se formas mutans'.[20] He thereby attributes a certain autonomy and animation to the poem's legacy, an attribution which troubles the chancellor's desire to put an end to this nefarious work: 'Si soit ung tel livre osté et exterminé'.[21] This desire is expressed by Gerson's anti-*Rose* advocate Eloquance Theologienne before the court of Justice Canonique within the allegorical juridical

fiction of his *Traité contre 'le Roman de la Rose'* (1402). Whilst ostensibly
seeking to suppress the 'masterpiece', Gerson gestures towards the
master's potential spectral resurrection when Eloquance Theologienne voices her wish that Jean de Meun were present in court to
face charges in person: 'Je vouldré bien ... que l'aucteur que on
accuse fust present en sa persone par retournant de mort a vie.'[22] Her
wish may be seen to respond to earlier suggestions in the *querelle* that
any literary challenge to Jean de Meun constitutes a negotiation with
the dead. Jean de Montreuil opposed Christine's prosecution of his
'master' as an illegitimate persecution of the deceased: 'quasi in
pretorio causam ageres, nudiustertius contra mortuum verba
faciens.'[23] However, through his textual treatment in the *querelle*, Jean
de Meun's spirit appears very much alive. The sequels to the *'Rose'*
querelle, those works by Le Franc, Milet and Michault which
contribute to the later *querelle des femmes* by taking issue with the *Rose*'s
alleged misogyny, seem quite specifically to respond to Eloquance
Theologienne's wish to revive the author: they stage his textual
return 'de mort a vie' in the poetic fictions of their trial debates. Such
literary resurrection is pointed up by Michault in his *Procès d'Honneur*
Féminin (*c.*1461), where he envisages his anti-feminine advocate,
Faux Parler, in a courtroom 'acompaignié d'aucuns trespassés, come
Matheole, Juvenal, Maistre Jehan de Meun, acteur de la Rose, et
aucuns vivans'.[24] Michault effectively collapses temporal and ontological boundaries to revive 'l'aucteur en sa persone', 'Maistre Jehan
de Meun', in the company of past misogynists juxtaposed with their
present counterparts alongside the *Procès*'s own diegetic, personified
adversary in one textual moment.[25]

The *'Rose' querelle* writers' varied discussion of Jean de Meun in
terms of his death and resurrection, the desire to see him again face
to face, gestures towards the peculiarly embodied concept of
auctoritas that was demonstrated in the illustrations with which I
opened this essay.[26] What was it, we should now ask, within the texts
of the *querelle des femmes* which inspired such an interpretation of
authorial authority in their miniatures? In Jacques Milet's *Forest de*
tristesse (1459), the convicted misogynists Matheolus and Jean de
Meun await sentencing in the court of Dame Justice, thereby
indicating that the pro-feminine case is as preoccupied with
authors' persons as with their literary products.[27] The *Forest*'s
narrator seems aware of this dual conception of *auctoritas* when he
expresses his opinion regarding the prisoners' fate: 'Je tiens leur *vie*

pour destruicte | Et leurs *livres* ars et deffaiz'.[28] It is in Le Franc's *Champion des dames* that the interpersonality of intra-poetic dialogue is most strikingly presented. The conjuring up of de Meun's spectre is a direct invocation as the eponymous Champion tries to have it out with him in person:

> Ha, Jean de Meun, grandement
> Tu as failly, ce m'est advis,
> Tu as parlé trop baudement.[29]

Like Eloquance Theologienne claiming that 'tout semble estre dit en sa persone',[30] Le Franc's Champion imputes all responsibility to Jean de Meun for the anti-feminine discourse voiced by characters within his *Rose*:

> En quelque guise que l'on sache,
> Il vous ensengne tromperie.
> Amours n'est pas, ains lescherie
> Ce qu'il vous devise en sa Rose.[31]

This concept of personality-oriented *auctoritas*, concerning primarily the ineffaceable author behind the text, not only personalizes literary authority but embodies it in a totemic image of the shadowy 'Maistre Jehan de Meun'. The shadowy figure is implicitly or explicitly revived 'en sa persone' in a more or less face-to-face encounter each time that his text is challenged. Figures 1 and 2 make visually explicit this new understanding of *auctoritas* and it is to illustrate the lines just quoted from the *Champion* that these images were devised.

Having established the peculiar ontology of the misogynistic ghosts that haunt the *querelle des femmes*, we should consider finally how these writers used the resources of poetic fiction to subvert the authority of Jean de Meun's spectre, to overcome their indebtedness to a misogynist inheritance by rewriting his pernicious text. The spectral dilemma of attempting to revolutionize an inheritance is encapsulated succinctly in Derrida's wordplay on the polysemy of the French *conjurer*, with its possible nominalizations as *conjuration* and *conjurement*: he argues that it is impossible to con*jure* a spectre, to overturn its power, without first *con*juring it up.[32] Pierre Col pinpoints one aspect of this problematic paradox for anti-*Rose* protestors when he writes to Christine de Pizan:

> Toy et aultres – qui s'eufforcent comme toy a impugner ce tres noble escripvain Meung – le loués plus en le cuidant blasmer que je ne pouroye le louer pour y user tous mes membres, fussent ilz ores tous convertis en langues.[33]

Col's point is that, by emphasizing how nefarious de Meun's writings are, his detractors inadvertently accord his work additional sensationalizing publicity. In this double bind of promotion-through- denunciation there lies yet another complication: the slippery interrelation of pro-feminine discourse with its ethical antithesis. This inescapable slipperiness is succinctly explained by Michault's anti-feminine advocate: answering an accusation by the pro-feminine advocate, Noble Vouloir, that 'Tous maux entassés, / Tous biens rabaissiez', Faux Parler states with smug irony:

> *On en parle assés*
> *Mais, serez ou tassés,*
> *Fault que vous passés*
> *Par notre langaige.*[34]

The dialectical opposition of *pro* and *contra* is collapsed. The misogynist highlights how an argument in defence can define itself only in relation to, and on the terms proposed by, the case for the prosecution; the former is unavoidably haunted by the latter in a troubling fashion. This doubleness features throughout the *querelle* as a source of anxiety, since the speaker 'passing through' misogynist discourse risks being held culpable for its articulation. Le Franc's Champion expresses this anxiety when he finds his own discourse has become inextricably mired in the language of the *Rose*, exclaiming: 'j'en dis trop, ce parler est ort'.[35]

Querelle des femmes poets can be seen to use the locus of a trial to marry together the promotion-through-denunciation paradox and the double bind of culpability. They do so in order to propose the juridical framework precisely as a means of overcoming these bedevilling dilemmas of responsibility; there is a legal requirement that misogynists' words should be pronounced before the court in order to serve as valid evidence against them.[36] Thus, whilst Milet's Noble Vouloir is cautious about repeating misogynists' defamatory language, he justifies his action by the juridical need to hear recited the author's precise words:

> *Et reciter grant mal me fait*
> *Tes villains motz entre mes ditz*
> *Mais pour racompter ton meffait*
> *Aux dames de quoy tu mesdis*
> *Je parle aussi comme tu dis.*[37]

This intrusion of anti-woman rhetoric into the defence of women is portrayed as a necessary evil. The fictional frame of the trial narrative provides a vehicle for literary reflexive enquiry into the mechanics of pro-feminine discourse; it is a vehicle whose manoeuvres may enlighteningly be explained in spectropoetic terms of the indelible spectre of misogyny haunting successive writers.

The strong dead return and darken the living, but it is equally possible, as these trial fictions suggest, for the inheriting living poet successfully to overturn the power of his ancestor by establishing what Bloom calls a 'revisionary relationship' with the mighty dead: laying the ghost by radical rewriting of it.[38] It is through such a relationship that Le Franc's Champion succeeds in rhetorically recuperating the notorious defloration of the rose-maiden that concludes Jean de Meun's *Rose* continuation. The Champion rewrites the rape as a sacred miracle of consummation modelled on the Annunciation:

> *Vierge, il entra ta chambre close,*
> *Close, reclose et close arriere.*
> *Pas ne pouoit estre desclose,*
> *Je le sçay, devant ne derriere.*
> ...
> *Ainsy nonobstant la barriere*
> *Entra ton clos sans fleur corrumpre.*[39]

The virtuoso handling of interlaced antitheses (close/desclose, devant/derriere) and synonyms (arriere/derriere), and use of *traductio* foreground this act of hermeneutic revision. It lays the ghost of the *Rose* through implicit textual transformation in a manner which complements the Champion's direct trying of Jean de Meun in person.

As Bloom remarks, it is *how* the dead return that is decisive; rather than returning 'intact', the mighty dead must 'return in our colours, and speaking in our voices, at least in part, at least in moments', if 'we', that is living poets, are convincingly to appropriate the potent spectre.[40] Revisionary intra-poetic relationships show how conjuration of the *Rose* is, in Derrida's terms, both 'fragile' and 'powerful'.[41] The *Rose* is a potent and troublesome authority that continually fuels new literary creation and inescapably engages new texts' audiences in the processes of intertextual reading. It is equally just another text, whose rhetorical structures are constantly open to rewriting and metamorphosis. The vital and complex conjunction of these two aspects of intra-poetic relationships – totemic power and textual fragility in the inheritance of Jean de Meun's *Rose* – is what this essay has revealed through the analytical lens of spectropoetics. Inter*personally*, we see the 'corps *fantomal*' of Jean de Meun repeatedly conjured up on the stage of an oneiric juridical court;[42] inter*text*ually, however, his spectre is revolutionized by those heirs who denounce their inheritance of misogynistic discourse.

The sort of intertextual rewriting that I have been exploring may be aligned with Derrida's notion of the active effort of inheritance ('l'héritage … c'est toujours une tâche'),[43] whose work can be accomplished through 'revisionary relationships' of hermeneutic reappropriation. The living poet is no longer confined merely to 'bearing witness to' his inheritance ('en *témoigner*'),[44] but can engage in active negotiation with it. However, the fundamental paradox of indebtedness or double bind remains: 'une radicalisa-tion [such as the Champion's recasting of the *Rose* defloration] est toujours endettée auprès de cela même qu'elle radicalise'.[45] In conclusion, we may turn to the persona of *L'Apparicion Jehan de Meun* to summarize the essence of intra-poetic haunting in his pithy remark: 'uns hom vault tant com tient son dit'.[46] Jean de Meun's *dit* is still 'holding on' (*tient*) over two centuries after his continuation of the *Rose*, in the literary cemetery of Octovien de Saint-Gelais's *Séjour d'honneur*. Saint-Gelais's narrator recounts: 'Si apperceu lors maistre Jehan de Meun, | Tenant encor son Rommant de la Rose.'[47] The possessive adjective is the significant item here: the master is envisaged still holding onto *his* book. It is implied that acts of poetic challenge, judicial trying and hermeneutic revision have not succeeded in wrenching the *Rose* from its author, from whose looming spectre the book is indissociable. If the *Rose* cannot be separated from its author, then the inheritors of this book can no more write independently of its author's influence.

In late medieval French poetry, and the *querelle des femmes* in particular, the *Rose* is perceived as the force to be reckoned with. It must, therefore, if it is to stimulate new creativity in successive generations of inheriting poets, be 'gard[é] près de soi et laiss[é] revenir'[48] in a story of intra-poetic relationships that can most fruit-fully be understood as a history of ghosts.

Notes

1 Harold Bloom, *The Anxiety of Influence: A Theory of Poetry*, 2nd edn (New York/Oxford: Oxford University Press, 1997), p. 5.
2 Ibid., p. 141.
3 For Jean de Meun, see below. Matheolus wrote the deeply misogynist and misogamist *Liber lamentationum Matheoluli* (1295), whose popularity in France was further promoted by a vernacular translation by Jean Le Fèvre (1371–2). Jean de Meun and Matheolus are first cited as the twin targets of pro-feminine argument in Le Fèvre's own rebuttal of his translated *Lamentations*, *Le Livre de leesce* (*c.*1373).
4 Boccaccio's *De mulieribus claris* (1361–2) was regarded somewhat ambivalently as a pro-feminine treatise, presenting as it does both famous and apparently infamous women of the past. Its circulation in France was buoyed by an anonymous vernacular translation, *Des cleres et nobles femmes* (1401). Boccaccio also wrote overtly anti-feminist texts, such as *Il Corbaccio* (1355). It is not surprising, therefore, that Boccaccio received mixed press amongst pro-feminine *querelle* authors: Christine de Pizan and Antoine Dufour explicitly write against him, whereas Pierre Michault cites him amongst the champions of women. See Helen J. Swift, *Gender, Writing and Performance: Men Defending Women in Late Medieval France (1440–1538)* (Oxford: Oxford University Press, 2008), in particular chapter three.
5 Bloom, *Anxiety*, p. 139. I limit myself here to the general terms of Bloom's thesis, as opposed to the detailed 'revisionary ratios' he contrives to classify different types of intra-poetic relationship (p. 14).
6 Jacques Derrida, *Spectres de Marx: l'état de la dette, le travail du deuil, et la nouvelle Internationale* (Paris: Galilée, 1993).
7 Ibid., p. 176. All italics in quotations from *Spectres de Marx* are Derrida's own emphases.
8 The *Champion* is extant in nine manuscripts, one incunable and one early printed edition. The manuscripts designated by the sigla *G*, *P2* and *Z* constitute a family of related witnesses from around 1470: their text is copied from the same exemplar, and their extensive iconographic programmes (*G*, for example, has 182 miniatures) share many visual models. For further details of the poem's publication history, see Swift, *Gender, Writing and Performance*, Appendix 2A.
9 *Spectres*, p. 83. See Christine Martineau-Génieys, *Le Thème de la mort dans la poésie française de 1450 à 1550* (Paris: Champion, 1978). A heightened awareness of, and obsession with, death is generally acknowledged as a key cultural phenomenon that shaped the pan-European late medieval mentality. Various causes are cited, for which see Edelgard DuBruck, 'Death: poetic perception and imagination (Continental Europe)', in Edelgard E. DuBruck and Barbara I. Gusick (eds), *Death and Dying in the Middle Ages* (New York: Peter Lang, 1999), pp. 295–313 (p. 309); Margaret Aston, 'Death', in Rosemary Horrox (ed.), *Fifteenth-Century Attitudes: Perceptions of Society*

in Late Medieval England (Cambridge: Cambridge University Press, 1994), pp. 202–28 (pp. 203, 206); Jane H. M. Taylor, 'Un miroer salutaire', in Jane H. M. Taylor (ed.), *Dies Illa: Death in the Middle Ages,* (Liverpool: Cairns, 1984), pp. 29–43 (p. 40); R. C. Finucane, *Appearances of the Dead: A Cultural History of Ghosts* (London: Junction, 1982), pp. 50–5.

10   For the history of the *danse* and general descriptions of the different frescoes all over France, see J. M. Clark, *The Dance of Death in the Middle Ages and the Renaissance* (Glasgow: Glasgow University Press, 1950), pp. 22–40. For a more recent discussion, contesting some of Clark's conclusions, see Jane H. M. Taylor, 'The dialogues of the Dance of Death and the limits of late-medieval theatre', *Fifteenth-Century Studies*, 16 (1990), 215–32; 'Un miroer salutaire'.

11   See Jacqueline Cerquiglini-Toulet, *L'Écriture testamentaire à la fin du moyen âge: identité, dispersion, trace* (Oxford: EHRC, 1999). A fundamental structural irony operates in many *complaintes* that appear to rail against Death as a disinheriting force, such as the dialogue between Mort and Vertu in Pierre Michault's *Complainte sur la mort d'Ysabeau de Bourbon* (1465): the act of poetic lamentation itself sustains the subject's reputation and secures the literary heritage of the writer. A similar irony is perceived by Cerquiglini-Toulet to underpin the titles of Hélinand de Froidmont's and Robert Le Clerc's poems, *Les Vers de la mort*. The polyvalent figure of the *vers* (both 'worms' and 'lines of verse') encapsulates the dual nature of literary testating: acknowledging inevitable physical decomposition, whilst performing an act of composition through poetic creation which militates against the decay of the testator's name (*L'Écriture testamentaire*, p. 13). See also a dramatic context for the return of the dead in the anonymous *La Farce nouvelle ... de la resurrection de Jenin Landore*. Jenin returns from Paradise and defines his ontological state thus: 'Je suis mort et je suis en vie' (*Ancien théâtre français*, ed. M. Viollet le Duc, 10 vols (Paris, 1854–7), II (1854), pp. 21–34 (p. 23). This is precisely the sort of paradox that seems to have fascinated the late medieval *mentalité*.

12   He highlights also how the memory (*monumentz*) of past poets are to be found in the *bouches* and *escriptz* of their successors: *Épitaphe en maniere de dialogue*, in *Œuvres*, ed. J. Stecher, 4 vols (Geneva: Droz, 1969), IV, pp. 318–38 (vv. 30, 34).

13   Crétin, *Apparition du Mareschal sans reproche*, in *Œuvres poétiques de Guillaume Crétin*, ed. Kathleen Chesney (Paris: Firmin-Didot, 1932), pp. 143–81 (vv. 151–2). Jacques de Chabannes is the eponymous marshal; he returns from his grave shortly after his death at the battle of Pavia in order to counsel the narrator.

14   Honoré Bouvet, *Medieval Muslims, Christians, and Jews in Dialogue: The 'Apparicion Maistre Jehan de Meun' of Honorat Bovet* (Tempe: Arizona Center for Medieval and Renaissance Studies, 2005), p. 62, vv. 87–92.

15   Derrida, *Spectres*, p. 166.

16 Bouvet, *Apparicion*, p. 64, v. 8. The locus is made significant in that its past resident does not see the current occupier as a worthy heir to this creative space: '... ce poise m'y | Quant vous en cest lieu demourez' (vv. 16–17), since the narrator has not followed Jean de Meun's example in speaking out against lapsed social mores.

17 Ibid., p. 66, vv. 99–100.

18 See Eric Hicks (ed.), *Le Débat sur 'le Roman de la rose'* (Paris: Champion, 1977).

19 Derrida, *Spectres*, p. 42.

20 Hicks, *Débat*, p. 166. 'This work deserves to be called formless chaos, ... a Proteus constantly changing shape'. English translation is my own. Gerson makes this condemnation in a Latin letter to Pierre Col which follows up on the criticisms of the *Rose* expounded in his *Traité*. I shall pursue in a future project the question of what we might call the ethics of haunting: the Augustinian debate surrounding the status of the spectre as a shape simulated by divine or by evil spirits, or as the very soul of the deceased returning to communicate with the living. This debate is mobilized notably in Crétin's *Apparition*, and may also be related to Gerson's perspective on the *Rose* continuator's *revenance*.

21 Hicks, *Débat*, p. 86.

22 Ibid., p. 66.

23 Ibid., p. 28. 'Just the day before yesterday, as if arguing in the court-room, you spoke against a dead man.' English translation is my own.

24 In *Pierre Michault: œuvres poétiques*, ed. Barbara Folkart (Paris: Union Générale d'Éditions, 1980), pp. 27–68 (p. 29).

25 It is, perhaps, important to appreciate Michault's *querelle* contribution in the context of his poetic *œuvre* since death and the sustaining of life through posthumous reputation are recurrent themes in his work. For his *Complainte*, see n. 11 above; he also composed a *Danse des aveugles*, animating a rapacious figure of Death.

26 Cf. Claude Lecouteux's reflections on the substantiality of *revenants*: *Au-delà du merveilleux: essai sur les mentalités du moyen âge*, 2nd edn (Paris: Presses de l'Université de Paris-Sorbonne, 1998), pp. 197–8.

27 Milet presents the image of women on the warpath against these writers: 'toutes oultrees | De dueil viennent vengeance querre' (*La Forest de Tristesse*, in *Le Jardin de plaisance et fleur de rethorique: reproduction en fac-similé de l'édition publiée par Antoine Vérard vers 1501*, ed. Eugénie Droz and Arthur Piaget, 2 vols (Paris: Firmin-Didot, 1910–25), I, fos 204r–24v (fo. 221r). A similarly incensed band of ladies, seeking redress against Jean de Meun in person, is depicted by Pierre de Brantôme (*Recueil des dames, poésies et tombeaux*, ed. Étienne Vaucherat (Paris: Gallimard, 1991), pp. 371–2), and the same, probably fictitious, anecdote is recounted contemporaneously by Antoine Du Verdier (*Bibliotheque d'Antoine du Verdier, seigneur de Vauprivas* (Lyons: Barthélémy Honorat, 1585), p. 679).

28 Milet, *Forest*, fo. 219v. Emphasis is my own.

29   Martin le Franc, *Le Champion des dames*, ed. Robert Deschaux (Paris: Champion, 1999), vv. 14389–91.
30   Hicks, *Débat*, p. 74.
31   Le Franc, *Champion*, vv. 11275–8.
32   Derrida, *Spectres*, p. 89.
33   Hicks, *Débat*, p. 89.
34   Michault, *Procès*, p. 58.
35   Le Franc, *Champion*, v. 12289.
36   The requirement of precise response (*negavit verbum ad verbo*) is evidenced by the early court register of the *Échiquier de Normandie* (Gustave Ducoudray, *Les Origines du parlement de Paris et la justice aux XIIIe et XIVe siècles* (Paris, 1902) p. 402), and forms part of the general forensic principle of *audi alteram partem*, decreeing that both sides of a case should be heard. This principle has its roots in the Athenian judicial oath and is attested by Aristophanes, Euripides and Demosthenes. Amongst medieval literary courts, it is enlisted by Michault's narrator when he commends Judge Raison's meticulous adherence to the code of legal practice during the trial of the anonymous misogynist 'l'Inculpé': 'sans oyr partie adverse ne voult appointier aucune chose' (*Procès*, p. 44).
37   Milet, *Forest*, fo. 220v. This careful negotiation of proprieties also arises in Gerson's *Traité*: whilst Theological Eloquence is anxious about the double bind of her discourse, 'Je pouroie cheoir ou vice que je reprens', and is eager to 'abridge' her speech, she expresses this eagerness at the same time as claiming the legitimacy of setting forth the arguments pertaining to the case: 'Si abregeray ma parole et ne diray plus que des articles contenus en la supplication de Dame Chasteté présentés par Conscience' (Hicks, *Débat*, p. 78).
38   Bloom, *Anxiety*, p. 140.
39   Le Franc, *Champion*, vv. 24161–4, 24167–8.
40   Bloom, *Anxiety*, pp. 140–1.
41   'La conjuration paraît à la fois puissante et, comme toujours, inquiète, fragile, angoissée' (Derrida, *Spectres*, p. 88).
42   See Derrida, *Spectres*, p. 209.
43   Ibid., p. 94.
44   '[L]'*être* de ce que nous sommes *est* d'abord héritage, … nous ne pouvons qu'en *témoigner*' (ibid.).
45   Ibid., p. 152.
46   *Apparicion*, p. 106, v. 763. Hanly chooses to translate this as a proverb: 'A man is only as good as his word', though it is equally possible to read the phrase literally, as I do in the present context: 'A man has value for as long as his word endures.'
47   Octovien de Saint-Gelais, *Séjour d'honneur*, ed. Frédéric Duval (Geneva: Droz, 2002), III. xii, vv. 111–12.
48   Derrida, *Spectres*, p. 144.

Chapter Three
Jodelle and Garnier: Ghost Prologues from Seneca to the Renaissance

John Nassichuk

The phantom character appears with regularity in French Renaissance tragedy, generally at the very beginning of the play. It almost always fills the role of a prologue, informing the audience of the precise context in which the characters are to appear. Tragic poets often developed episodes taken from ancient historiography, particularly Livy during the first half of the century, then Tacitus and Suetonius at the dawn of the Baroque period. For this reason, the prologue is often an essential part of the story. Such is the case, for instance, in Étienne Jodelle's *Cléopâtre captive* (1553), traditionally recognized as the first French 'classical' tragedy.[1] In this play, the dead Marc Antoine appears at the beginning and informs the spectators of what they are about to witness: he has already manifested himself to Cléopâtre in the form of a dream, and ordered that she commit suicide to avoid the disgrace of Roman captivity. This order is of particular significance in Jodelle's tragedy, because it determines in advance the events which are to follow.

The humanist poets of France also quite frequently imitate ancient tragedies, borrowing from Greek and Roman models. One such example is Robert Garnier's play entitled *Hippolyte* (1573), which contains a ghost prologue not appearing in the Greek original.[2] At the beginning of the play, Égée, the grandfather of Hippolyte, appears much in the same manner as Marc Antoine does in the *Cléopâtre captive*. Yet the two ghosts are very different in at least one fundamental respect. In Jodelle, Marc Antoine's presence constitutes a moral authority sufficiently powerful to decide the outcome of the play itself; not only does his command impinge upon the psychology of the heroine, it also clearly establishes the limits of the dramatic action. In Garnier, Égée does not exercise the same kind of dramatic authority. However, his powers of foreknowledge and moral reflection seem at least equivalent and likely superior to those of Jodelle's ghost.

The present study will examine these two plays comparatively, in an attempt to illustrate how the dramatic ghost prologue develops within the twenty-year period that separates them. While Jodelle's ghost, Marc Antoine, makes a declaration that effectively determines the events to come, Garnier creates a ghost character, Égée, whose role is less that of an authoritative prophet than of a subtle and perceptive spectator. Indeed, from Jodelle to Garnier, the ghost prologue relinquishes its power over the dramatic action which he foresees, in order to reinvest his clairvoyance in the interpretation of these events. This significant evolution of the ghost prologue, from Jodelle to Garnier, underlines the very importance of the spectral figure as an indicator of the moral and dramatic presuppositions inherent in the imitation of ancient tragedy during the second half of the sixteenth century. Such an observation is all the more significant for the relative dearth of extant prescriptive theoretical texts dating from the period. Aristotle's *Poetics*, most notably, was little known during the first half of the century.[3] Vincenzo Maggi's Latin commentary on Aristotle's fragmentary treatise was published in Venice in 1550, but does not seem to have exercised any immediate impact on the generation of the young Pléiade of which Jodelle was a member.[4]

One central aspect of the renewed consideration of Aristotelian dramatic theory during the later sixteenth century is a concern for the reception of tragic performances. Indeed, the challenge of interpretation, or of proper understanding, is explicitly presented in the prologues by Jodelle and Garnier as an essential element in the invention of classical tragedy. Ultimately, of course, proper understanding is the responsibility of the spectator who is to be aided by the work of the actors and of the poet himself. For this reason, in dramaturgy which presents ancient characters, the fundamental, ethical quality of rhetoric and action determines to a large extent the communicative effectiveness of the play. This is most certainly the presupposition fundamental to Aristotle's famous extended remarks concerning the 'effects' of a well-wrought tragedy upon the spectator.[5] In the two plays examined here, the ethically oriented discourse of the ghosts exercises a direct and determining influence upon plot structure. But the comparison of Jodelle and Garnier reveals an increasing insistence upon motifs of reception and interpretation within the play itself, or at least at the very threshold of the action as represented by the prologue. Both authors are heavily indebted, for their prologues, to the ancient model provided by Seneca in the *Thyestes* and the *Agamemnon*.

Seneca

A principal ancient model for spectral appearances in Renaissance drama is Seneca's *Thyestes*, of which the prologue consists of a long and emphatic conversation between the ghost of Tantalus and a 'Fury'.[6] Thyestes himself also appears as a ghost in the important prologue of Seneca's play *Agamemnon*, wherein he recounts the numerous crimes of the Atrides. The present section will consider these two prologues successively, beginning with that of the *Thyestes*.

It is worth noting that the first fifteen lines uttered by Tantalus, at the beginning of the play, constitute a series of questions conveying a sense of astonishment and even one of confusion. Long accustomed to the extremes of torture reserved for him in the afterlife, the ghost now wonders if this new experience – the return to Mycene – might even be the worst yet of the punishments he has known since his death. Seneca's use of the adverb *male* in verse 3 – 'Quis male deorum Tantalo vivas domos / ostendit iterum' – hints at a kind of foreknowledge, a prefiguring of the tragedy over which the ghost of Tantalus, once he is convinced by the Fury, is to preside. Tantalus' general attitude, however, seems more suggestive of bewilderment than of a determined mission conceived in the underworld.[7] 'Unto what new torment am I now delivered?' he asks. Only after having given full expression to the disorder of his thoughts does he utter, as if instinctively, a general condemnation of the House of Pelops.

The Fury, on the other hand, labours under no such confusion. She directly informs Tantalus of his task, which is none other than to fill the house with his ghostly presence. 'May profound Night return', she declares, 'and may daylight abandon the sky. Confound the Penates, bring forth hatred, murder, funereal suffering and fill the entire house with Tantalus' ('imple Tantalo totam domum'). She further informs him that she has granted him one day of liberty

– 'Liberum dedimus diem' (v. 64) – wherein he might, at least temporarily, satisfy the hunger and quench the thirst that constitute his infernal suffering. Then the Fury utters a command which has raised much critical speculation. She tells Tantalus to ensure that under his watch ('spectante te') the guests of a feast drink wine mixed with blood: 'in Bacchum cruor ... potetur'. Of course, the temporal delimitation – 'one day of liberty' – fixes in accordance with Aristotelian dramatic principle the duration of the events which are to follow. Confusion arises, however, over interpretation of the present participle ablative *spectante te* ('whilst you are watching'), since it strongly suggests that Tantalus, even though his character disappears for good immediately after the prologue, somehow remains present during the tragic feast.[8] Some critics have held that this remark proves the relative unimportance of linear time in the play, and that certain events are even simultaneous; others suggest that Seneca's Fury is speaking in figurative terms; still others have raised questions concerning the validity of the text itself. For our purposes, it will be enough to point out that the Fury's speech – and indeed her very summoning of Tantalus – is evidence of a dramatic link between the ghost's appearance and the action of the play.

The attitude of the ghost is significant in that it illustrates a state of mind radically opposed to the Senecan stoic ideal: confusion, a scattered, helpless feeling of being unable to comprehend, much less to master, the course of events as they unfold. Indeed, one of the favourite rhetorical motifs of this play, and of much of Seneca's writing, is the description of the kind of inner tranquillity which should permit even a deposed king to be contented with his lot. Thyestes pronounces just this kind of speech to his son as they go to meet Thyestes' brother Atreus who has proposed that they share the kingdom, to end their quarrel and rule together. Of course, the end of the play will reveal the profound virtue of this original sentiment to which Thyestes, tragically persuaded by his son to meet with Atreus, did not adhere. The tranquillity of the Stoic ideal appears throughout as a kind of unreachable goal. The ghost of Tantalus certainly does not exemplify it. He represents, rather, a force of evil: confused, misguided and bereft of any power of rational manipulation. In any case, he is spiritually unequal to the destiny which has befallen him and his descendants. In this sense Tantalus is quite different from the other major ghost figure of ancient tragedy, that of Polydorus who appears at the beginning of Euripides' *Hecuba*. Although Renaissance playwrights would have had relatively comfortable access to this Greek play through Erasmus' widely disseminated Latin translation, the very situation of the two Renaissance ghosts to be examined here more distinctly resembles that of Tantalus.

The Renaissance ghosts also resemble in many ways Thyestes himself, the prologue to Seneca's *Agamemnon*. Like Tantalus, Thyestes expresses a feeling of vulnerability and extreme malaise when he first appears at the beginning of this play. He also declares a firm desire to return to the underworld, since he finds the tortures of Hades far less frightening than the sight of places and objects that lead him to relive his family history. He evokes, as does Tantalus, the major pagan figures of infernal suffering, Ixion, Sisyphus, Tantalus himself, before declaring that the crimes of these condemned characters pale in comparison with those of his own family. The monstrosity of Tantalus is nothing, he says, when one considers the many evils of his descendants:

> Let us take count of all whom for their impious deeds the Cretan judge with whirling urn condemns; all of them by my crimes shall I, Thyestes, conquer. But by my brother shall I be conquered, full of my three sons buried in me; my own flesh have I consumed.[9]

This comparison is the beginning of a narrative development that constitutes the principal function of the prologue ghost. Thyestes describes a genealogy of evil that only deepens with each successive generation within the house of Pelops. The ghost figure not only communicates the general 'tone' or 'spirit' of the characters and the situation, he also situates the events of the play within a larger narrative context. Indeed, this context includes events both past and present, and even extends itself to the future: at the beginning of the play, the ghost of Thyestes reveals the destiny that awaits Agamemnon.[10]

Thyestes' calm and sinister foreknowledge is a trait that distinguishes him from Tantalus and marks the essential difference between the two ghost prologues in the plays by Seneca. Whereas Tantalus brings with him a power of evil that he seems unable to harness alone, Thyestes is remarkable for the cold prescience that animates his speech. Such a difference in the very nature of these two ghosts is indicative of a profound ambiguity peculiar to the

ancient ghost figure itself. At once an initiate of otherworldly
mysteries and a *revenant* bereft of all (or nearly all) ability to intervene directly in earthly affairs, he represents, often simultaneously,
both superhuman authority and utter powerlessness. Tantalus
possesses a power he does not easily comprehend, one which is
necessary for the Fury to accomplish what she has planned for the
house of Pelops. Thyestes, on the other hand, thoroughly masters
the events of past, present and future. Yet he communicates them
not as would an intervening agent, but rather as a passive messenger
whose status seems similar to that of a spectator.

The same question of diverse ghostly powers – the power of evil
and the power of accurate foreknowledge – remains a fundamental
preoccupation for Renaissance dramatists who invoke the figure of
the ghost prologue. Indeed, the progressive rediscovery of
Aristotle's theory of the plot makes the question of such foreknowledge a primary domain of development within the tragic genre
during this period. The following analyses will pay particular attention to the ways in which the ghosts in Jodelle and Garnier declare
their authority, through a comparison with Seneca's characters.

Jodelle

Étienne Jodelle's tragedy *Cléopâtre captive* was presented in front of
Henri II in the first months of 1553 by an impressive troupe that
included members of the court such as the poet Rémy Belleau. The
play presents an important episode in the history of Rome, adapted
from historical sources such as Livy and Plutarch.[11] In the final act,
Cléopâtre's suicide is described in some detail by the lyric choir, and
represented as a kind of moral victory over the repressive force of
imperial domination under Octavian. Cléopâtre's final gesture is
announced, by the ghost of her consort Marc Antoine, at the beginning of the first act.[12] For this reason, dramatic suspense is not the
structuring principle of the action in this five-act poetic sequence.
Indeed, action itself seems distinctly less important than the moral
portrait of the heroine. And, in so far as character development
takes precedence over dramatic action, the play itself may be
described as distinctly un-Aristotelian.[13]

Yet, even under circumstances that seem to exclude discussion of
Aristotelian influence, Jodelle's tragedy bears witness to the development of a conception of the dramatic spectator that prepares the

way for a dramatic poetry more directly informed by the *Poetics*. The principal vehicle of this development is the ghost who appears at the opening of the play, immediately after the 'prologue' addressed to Henri II. In the prologue, Jodelle explains that the excess and suffering of Cléopâtre are to serve as a moral example, as are also the understanding and clemency of Octavian. Here illustrated is the moral principle of Holy Equity ('la saincte équité'), which is presented as the fundamental requirement of rational human behaviour and expression. Avoiding excess, and following the Golden Mean, is therefore, according to the prologue, the central lesson of the play.

Such a schematic explanation as this hardly provides a sufficient interpretation of the *Cléopâtre captive*. The division of the characters into exemplary groups representing moderation (Octavian) and excess (Cléopâtre) completely neglects the psychological complexities of Jodelle's characters. Indeed, it seems as though the prologue seeks to force this complex and often ambiguous play into an allegorizing hermeneutical grid. This is perhaps the mark of a young playwright who, in making his debut as a court tragedian, hopes to avoid the sin of excessive *nouveauté*. The prologue suggests as much, insisting upon the noble antiquity of the tragic genre.[14] As if to bring some nuance to this first description of the play's action, Jodelle inserts the ghostly figure of Marc Antoine at the start of the opening act, immediately following the prologue. Marc Antoine's speech in 167 verses effectively serves as a second, and more thorough, introduction to the play. He provides a detailed narrative of the historical context, one which also illustrates and explains the principle of Holy Equity.

From the beginning of his speech Marc Antoine distinguishes himself from the ghosts in Seneca's plays, whilst borrowing something from each of them. As soon as he appears, the ghost of Marc Antoine solemnly reveals the destiny of Cléopâtre:

> *Avant que ce Soleil qui vient ores de naistre,*
> *Ayant tracé son jour chez sa tante se plonge,*
> *Cleopatre mourra ... (158–60)*[15]

Marc Antoine then explains that this spectral apparition is not a theatrical device, of which the benefit would be reserved for the spectators only. He has also just now presented himself to Cléopâtre

in a dream. Of course, there is nothing informal or haphazard
about such a rare occasion as this nocturnal visit from beyond the
grave. Marc Antoine has arrived bearing a precise message. His
words reproduce the well-known explanation of Cléopâtre's suicide
as it appears in Plutarch's *Life of Mark Antony*:

> ... *je me suis ore en songe*
> *A ses yeux presenté, luy commandant de faire*
> *L'honneur à mon sepulchre, et apres se deffaire,*
> *Plustost qu'estre dans Romme en triomphe portée (160–3)*

The warrior has uttered a command – 'luy commandant de faire' –
which the humanist poet has borrowed from one of the most
frequently consulted source-texts of the period. This authoritative
order quite definitely separates Jodelle's Marc Antoine from
Seneca's Tantalus, for the simple reason that the Renaissance ghost
lets no doubt persist regarding the moral imperative of his contribution to the events of the play. At the same time, his masterful
narrative of the plight of Marc Antoine and Cléopâtre, and his foreknowledge of Cléopâtre's death, reveal a comprehension of these
events similar to that displayed by the ghost of Thyestes. For
Jodelle's characters, Cléopâtre's suicide is dictated by the exigencies
of honour. Marc Antoine has returned as a messenger, bearing
orders to make Cléopâtre conform to this principle. The ghost's
speech reveals much about the moral code to which Marc Antoine,
Cléopâtre (and Jodelle) are determined to do justice. If honour and
humility are not necessarily incompatible, honour and public
humiliation most definitely are.

Marc Antoine's lesson to Cléopâtre is the result of his personal
experience. He recounts in some detail the events that led to his
own final humiliation. He tells the story of an immoral excess
righted by the inexorable hand of destiny. He views himself as 'a
criminal shade', now paying the penalty for the shameful events
which saw him willingly compromise the interests of Rome. It is in
part this crime against the Roman moral principle of *pietas* which
has earned him a place in the underworld:

> *Dans le val tenebreux, où les nuicts eternelles*
> *Font eternelle peine aux ombres criminelles,*
> *Cedant à mon destin je suis volé n'aguère,*

> *Ja ja fait compagnon de la troupe legere,*
> *Moy (dy-je) Marc Antoine horreur de la grand'Romme,*
> *Mais en ma triste fin cent fois miserable homme. (63–8)*

The last two lines quoted suggest a second important aspect of the moral code reflected in the ghost's speech. Sacrificing the public good for one's own private pleasure is certainly a major fault, especially in the context of late republican Rome. Just as serious, however, in the dominant ethos of late medieval and early humanist drama which to a large extent informs Jodelle's work, is the error of *intemperantia.* This is what is clearly suggested in the last two lines here quoted: instead of maintaining any kind of Golden Mean, Marc Antoine during his life moved from one guilty excess to its opposite. Once a tyrannical menace who terrorized Rome itself, he became enslaved to a woman and to his own passion. In these verses of Jodelle, a highly regarded poet at court during the middle years of the reign of Henri II, Marc Antoine describes the force which subjugated him, in terms reminiscent of the love complaints to be found in Ronsard's *Amours* published one year before:

> *Car un ardent amour, bourreau de mes moüelles,*
> *Me devorant sans fin sous ses flammes cruelles,*
> *Avoit esté commis par quelque destinée*
> *Des Dieux jaloux de moy, à fin que terminée*
> *Fust en peine et malheur ma pitoyable vie,*
> *D'heur, de joye et de biens paravant assouvie. (69–74)*

This unremitting sin – here evoked in a passage typical of Jodelle's description of love as an infernal sentiment – brought about the treachery, the flight and the misery of which the verses immediately following provide a rather long narration. At one point he tells how he repudiated his wife, Caesar's daughter Octavia, in favour of Cléopâtre. Here Marc Antoine interrupts the narration in order to declare that this mistake brought upon him the vengeance of Holy Justice or Holy Equity. Having abandoned the course of Temperance, he made himself a target of divine anger:

> *Or pour punir ce crime horriblement infame,*
> *D'avoir banni les miens, et rejetté ma femme,*
> *Les Dieux ont à mon chef la vengeance avancée,*

> *Et dessus moy l'horreur de leurs bras élancée:*
> *Dont la saincte equité, bien qu'elle soit tardive,*
> *Ayant les pieds de laine, elle n'est point oisive,*
> *Ains dessus les humains d'heure en heure regarde,*
> *Et d'une main de fer son trait enflammé darde. (113–20)*

This moral (and judiciary) principle of Holy Equity occupies the very centre of Jodelle's dramatic invention. Marc Antoine returns to claim Cléopâtre in order to end their separation and renew, literally, the integrity of their relationship. To remain separated, suggests Marc Antoine, is to put honour at risk. Also implicit in the ghost's speech, moreover, is the idea that Cléopâtre should die in order to preserve the balance of Holy Equity dictated by Fortune. Here, the ghost's role is different from that of Seneca's Tantalus insofar as it reveals a moral principle which is also a determining structural element in the play itself. In so far as he distinguishes himself from the powerful but misguided confusion of a Tantalus, Marc Antoine resembles the other Senecan ghost prologue, Thyestes. At the same time, his direct and determining contribution to the course of events in the play also distinguishes him from Thyestes.

Jodelle's ghost prologue, Marc Antoine, combines traits that figure prominently in the two Senecan ghost characters. Like Thyestes, he displays a powerful mastery of historical narrative and certain knowledge of future events. However, like Tantalus, he also possesses the power to determine the course of the future. Unlike Seneca's ghosts, moreover, Jodelle's character is the authoritative messenger of a clearly stated moral agenda.[16] His mission is to oblige Cléopâtre to protect herself from disgrace at the hands of Octavian: having committed suicide himself, he instructs her to do the same. In doing this, he evokes the principle of Holy Equity, the observation of sacred Temperance. This insistence upon the morality of temperance, of avoiding excess, serves an end that actually exceeds the goals of exemplary representation, as the hermeneutical insufficiency – or the modest aim – of the prologue seems to indicate. The play does more than simply provide a distinguishable moral *exemplum*. It also represents a significant exercise in character portraiture. Although such insistence on character development does not accord precisely with the Aristotelian notion that plot should supersede character description, it does reflect an attention to storyline in its primitive stages, in keeping with Aristotle's concession that plot and character are intimately entwined. It is precisely the primitive period in the history of French classical tragedy that Jodelle's *Cléopâtre* represents. Also worthy of note is the fact that the precise explanations brought forth by the ghost figure at the beginning of the play give evidence of a distinct preoccupation with the anticipated reception and interpretation of the action and dialogue. This formalized concern for the reaction of the spectator is to become an increasingly conspicuous trait of sixteenth-century drama, as the analysis of the ghost figure's role in Robert Garnier's *Hippolyte* will now suggest.

Garnier

At the beginning of Garnier's tragedy *Hippolyte*, the ghost of Égée pronounces a long speech which effectively situates the action of the play within a well-detailed narrative context. Garnier's challenge is different from that of Jodelle, since the primary antecedent of his play comes not from ancient historiography, but from Euripides and Seneca. His treatment of the Hippolyte theme diverges noticeably from that of his Greco-Roman models, who deploy no such ghostly figures. Indeed, despite the close imitation of Seneca's play, Garnier succeeds in appropriating the myth, and the ghost figure seems directly representative of this artistic individuality.[17] Its very presence suggests a new take on the traditional dramatic treatment of the myth. This new working of the story betrays a heightened sensitivity to the problems of reception peculiar to the reproduction of traditional themes. Garnier's ghost prologue reflects a consciousness of the spectator's presence. It constitutes an attempt at accommodating this presence even in the lines that make up the spectacle.

In general, the humanist's version of the Hippolyte story shows an increased awareness of the challenges inherent in the rewriting of ancient drama. Most notably, it produces an intensified reflection upon the probable emotional reaction to the events of the play. It is in this obvious emotional engagement that Garnier's Égée bears a distinct resemblance to Seneca's Tantalus. Égée also expresses fearful apprehension at the sight of the place where he lived and died, even indicating that he much prefers enduring the tortures of the underworld to this new encounter with the sad image of Athens:

> *Mais l'horrible sejour de cet antre odieux,*
> *De cet antre, privé de la clairté des cieux,*
> *M'est cent et cent fois plus agreable, et encore*
> *Cent cent autresfois, que toy, que je deplore,*
> *Ville Cecropienne, et vous mes belles tours,*
> *D'où me precipitant je terminay mes jours. (9–14)[18]*

One significant difference separates Égée from Seneca's ghost, for whereas Tantalus fears new sufferings (*nova supplicia*, 13–14), Égée seems to fear the memory of past tribulations. It should be remarked here that Égée generally distinguishes himself from both Seneca's Tantalus and Jodelle's Marc Antoine, by the breadth of his perspective and his proclivity for expressing sympathy. In Seneca and Jodelle, the role of the ghost figure is comparatively one dimensional. On the one hand, the trembling Tantalus serves as an instrument of evil, the symbolic origin of the sins of the house of Pelops, under the sway of the Fury. The ghost of Thyestes, on the other hand, delivers a masterful historical narration and completely foresees the coming events, but seems disconnected from them. Even in Jodelle's play, Marc Antoine's authority somewhat reduces the complexity of his role: he delivers a narration, a message which is to be obeyed, then disappears. Though he does display some tenderness toward Cléopâtre at the end of his speech, the expression of this particular trait is relatively discreet in Marc Antoine. Garnier's prologue presents a greater integration of the distinguishing features of Seneca's two ghosts.

The key element in this unique composition of character is the topic of memory. Égée tends to elevate himself above the events that he foresees, without becoming disconnected from the action. To a significant degree, he seizes upon the effects of memory induced by this return to the scene of his tragic life, as opposed to the immediate horror of the scene itself. Although his character is intimately linked with the ensuing story, his attitude resembles in many ways that of a discerning spectator. Égée is emotionally engaged in the story he recounts, but he also reasons more than the other ghosts about the conditions and the actions of the characters. For example, he interrupts his narration of the basic events early and inserts a timely *sententia*, explaining that Destiny, and not the gods, is to blame for the misery of his House:

Mais quoy? C'est le destin, c'est ce meschant destin,
Que mesme Jupiter, tant il luy est mutin,
Ne sçauroit maistriser : Jupiter qui d'un foudre
Qu'il lance de sa main, peut tout broyer en poudre. (21–4)

This sensitivity to the application of *sententiae*, which leads the ghostly narrator to weave them with discretion into the body of his story, bears testimony to the complexity of the subjective tableau that Garnier is constructing. Whereas Jodelle's Marc Antoine himself fulfils a precise causal function by ordering Cléopâtre's death, Égée seeks to provide a reason for the tragic history of his family. Marc Antoine incarnates dramatic causality, while Égée sets out to explain it. It is the fundamental complexity of this task that separates the two Renaissance ghost characters. Jodelle's ghost wholly represents (and imposes) Cléopâtre's destiny; Garnier's ghost faces the challenge of interpretation.

Égée makes use of abstract figures in order to explain both the events he has witnessed and the ones that he foresees. Destiny, according to his description, functions primarily through human agency. The narration of his family history is largely an illustration of this point. Égée first recounts the famous adventures of Thésée who, having valiantly killed the minotaur, escaped from the labyrinth with the help of a thread given to him by Ariadne. He then adds that Thésée follows this narrow escape by plundering the House of Minos and stealing away with the king's two daughters. According to Égée, this final gesture was the fatal error which determined the miserable fate of his descendants. He attributes this mis-step, not to the particular hubris of Thésée (in the way that Marc Antoine readily and solely assumes his guilt, viewing Cléopâtre as living extension of himself), but to a basic human flaw, namely the penchant for excess:

Mais ainsi qu'il advient que l'humaine nature
Insatiable d'heur convoite outre mesure,
Et jamais ne s'arreste à mediocrité,
Non bien content d'avoir ton malheur évité,
Tu brigandes Minos ... (55–9)

Such concern for the ethical principle of *mediocritas*, or the Golden Mean, seems to unite Garnier's Égée with Jodelle's Marc Antoine.

The obvious difference is that Garnier's character is not a dream figure. Égée has no mission to accomplish which is in any way pertinent to the dramatic action itself. Unlike Marc Antoine, he exercises no direct influence upon the events that are to unfold, but simply foretells, observes and philosophizes about them. This relative detachment from the dramatic constitution of the play itself translates into an increased freedom to interpret individual actions in terms of general laws.

In the midst of his narration, Jodelle's Marc Antoine noted the importance of Holy Equity and the retributive character of divine justice. Égée, on the other hand, attributes to the gods greater latitude of interpretation without abandoning this same judiciary principle. His constant explanations suggest that the divinities are no longer contented simply to redress the balance of the Golden Mean. They, and the spectator who seriously reflects upon their attitude, now require a more complex moral reasoning. Instead of applying the letter of the law, the gods, it seems, are interested more than ever by its spirit. Égée declares that they interpret Holy Equity whilst considering the relative demands of the strong and the weak:

> Les Dieux aiment justice, et poursuivent à mort
> L'homme méchant, qui fait à un autre homme tort.
> Ils tiennent le parti du foible qu'on oppresse,
> Et font cheoir l'oppresseur en leur main vengeresse. (73–6)

Here again, the ghost insists upon the peculiarly human aspect of sin and error. By thus introducing the principle of humanity as a topic of consideration, Égée clearly underlines the need for subtlety of interpretation. Indeed, the repetition of the word 'homme' in the second line quoted magnifies this point. The ghost then expresses sympathy for Thésée and for his human plight when he further exclaims:

> Que je t'en voy, pauvre homme! Hé, qu'il te falloit bien
> Entreprendre d'aller au lict Plutonien,
> Pour ravir nostre Royne! (81–3)

It is in this expression of sympathy that Égée's ghostly status acquires its full importance. At once human and no longer living among people, he occupies a median position, somewhere between the characters who are still implicated in the action and the gods who distribute divine and dramatic justice.

In many ways, this ghostly position is directly similar to that of a spectator, as the role of the spectator is constantly taken into account by Aristotle in the *Poetics*.[19] His most remarkable quality is the ability to sympathize with the tragic plight of the characters, and most notably with that of Hippolyte. For instance, when he laments the cruel destiny of his grandson, Égée adduces a similitude which provides some measure and justification of his affection. Though Hippolyte is a member of his family, Égée loves him also for reasons independent of these binding genealogical ties. He loves Hippolyte just as one might come to love any character whose actions are certain proof of virtue:

> *Or je te plain sur tout, ma chere nourriture,*
> *Et de mes ans vieillars la plus soigneuse cure,*
> *Hippolyte, que j'aime autant que la vertu*
> *Luist aimable en celuy qui s'en monstre vestu. (123–6)*

Such remarks clearly provide a more sophisticated hermeneutic key than do the comments of Tantalus in Seneca or of Marc Antoine in Jodelle. They offer guidance to the spectator (or reader) from a singularly privileged viewpoint, namely, that of the parental ghost figure who, foreseeing the development of the tragic action, anticipates also the challenge of interpretation. The terrain of this challenge is of an ethical sort. It concerns, first and foremost, the moral considerations proper to an increasingly nuanced reflection on the spirit of what truly constitutes equity.

From Jodelle to Garnier, the ghost figure evolves in a way that reflects some important aspects of French classical tragedy during the second half of the sixteenth century. In Jodelle's *Cléopâtre captive*, the ghost of Marc Antoine emerges from the dead and successfully commands the suicide of his notorious (and beloved) consort. The moral dictate at work here is that of Fortune, whose influence quite rigorously ensures the final supremacy of Holy Equity in all human affairs. Égée, Garnier's ghost, adds to this basic principle a second criterion of judgement, which is consequent to Aristotle's extended reflection on the dramatic significance of pathos in tragedy. At once emotionally engaged in the human experience of the characters and utterly detached from the causal workings of the action, Égée represents a heightened state of sophistication in the relationship between plot and character. Here, the privileged domain of Aristotelian reasoning on this relationship is one which specifically concerns the reaction and judgement of the spectator. The evolving use of the ghost prologue highlights this important nuance. Situated at the exterior limits of the tragic action, in the intermediary realm between the living and the dead, the ghost prologue also fulfils the function of a messenger. In Jodelle's play, the ghost's words inform at once the characters of the play and the spectator. In Garnier's play, their speculatively enriched information concerns only the spectator.

Notes

1 Étienne Jodelle, *Cléopâtre captive*, ed. Kathleen M. Hall (Exeter: University of Exeter Press, 1979).
2 Robert Garnier, *Two Tragedies. Hippolyte and Marc Antoine*, ed. Cathleen M. Hill and Mary G. Morrisson (London: Athlone, 1975).
3 Aristotle, *Poetics*, ed. and trans. S. Halliwell (Cambridge, MA: Harvard University Press, 1995).
4 Vincent Madius and Bartholomew Lombardius, *Vincentii Madii et Bartholomaei Lombardi in Aristotelis librum Poetices communis explanationes, Madii vero in eundem librum propriae explanationes. Ejusdem de ridiculis et in Horatii librum de Arte poetica interpretatio* (Venice: V. Valgrigio, 1550).
5 Aristotle, *Poetics*, 1449 b, 23–8.
6 Seneca, *Tragedies*, revised edn and trans. F. J. Miller (Cambridge, MA: Harvard University Press), 1987.
7 See on this topic Gordon Braden, *Renaissance Tragedy and the Senecan Tradition: Anger's Privilege* (New Haven: Yale University Press, 1985), p. 41.
8 J. Monteleone, 'Spectante te potetur (Thy. 66), un simbolo senechiano', *Latomus*, 68 (1989), 604–26.
9 Seneca, *Tragedies*, ll. 23–7, p. 7.
10 *Agamemnon*, l. 44.
11 M. Delcourt, 'Jodelle et Plutarque', *Bulletin de l'Association Guillaume Budé*, 42 (Janvier 1934), 36–52.
12 See the remarks of J. H. Greenleaf, 'L'unité de lieu dans la Cléopâtre de Jodelle', *Wisconsin Studies in Language and Literature*, 20 (1924), 62–73.
13 Aristotle, *Poetics*, 1450 a, 19.
14 Jodelle, *Cléopâtre captive*, ll. 33–40.
15 Jodelle, *Cléopâtre captive*, line nos for quotations will appear in brackets in the text.

16 See the remarks on the role of the ghost as messenger in Noël de Taillepied, *Traicté de l'apparition des esprits. A sçavoir, des Ames separées, Fantosmes, Prodiges, et autres accidens merveilleux, qui precedent quelquefois la mort des grands personnages, ou signifient changement de la chose publique* (Paris: Jean Corrozet, 1627), ch. XVIII.

17 G. Jondorf, *Robert Garnier and the Themes of Political Tragedy in the Sixteenth Century* (Cambridge: Cambridge University Press, 1969), p. 7.

18 Garnier, *Two Tragedies. Hippolyte and Marc Antoine.* Line nos for quotations appear in brackets in the text.

19 K. Eden, *Poetic and Legal Fiction in the Aristotelian Tradition* (Princeton: Princeton University Press, 1986), p. 34.

Chapter Four
Racine's Spectral Stagecraft: *Andromaque*

Joseph Harris

The final act of *Andromaque* (1667) offers one of the most dramatic and powerfully intense scenes in all of Racine's theatre. After instigating – much against his own will – the murder of Pyrrhus, king of Epirus, in an attempt to court Pyrrhus's betrothed Hermione, the unstable and melancholic Greek ambassador Oreste is aghast to see Hermione vehemently reject him. Abandoned onstage by the object of his passion, Oreste swings violently between incomprehension and despair. His close companion Pylade shortly arrives, ostensibly to rescue him, but in fact sets the seal on his mental disintegration by letting slip the news that Hermione has just committed suicide on top of Pyrrhus' corpse. Crazed by despair, Oreste is plunged into insanity. Darkness descends all around him; blood starts to gush out from the walls, preventing him from fleeing. Worse, Oreste is horrified to see the murdered Pyrrhus now standing, incomprehensibly, once again before him, apparently alive but bathed in blood. When Oreste lashes out at the apparition, it is swiftly ushered to safety into the ghostly arms of Hermione; the two dead figures now engage in an embrace they had never shared while living, apparently putting aside their various differences simply to spite Oreste. Finally the ghosts of the murdered couple stand aside to reveal an apparition more horrific still: that of the snake-headed Furies, goddesses of remorse and vengeance. Overcome by this succession of supernatural beings, Oreste collapses.

Yet, we, the audience, can see nothing of this. The ghostly Hermione and Pyrrhus, like the monstrous Furies, are nowhere to be seen. From our (perhaps disappointingly objective) perspective, the only souls onstage are Oreste himself, his increasingly distressed companion Pylade and a small gathering of soldiers. The disparity between this stark reality and the violence of Oreste's fevered imagination could scarcely be more bathetic. This chapter proposes to offer a fuller appreciation of Racine's thematic, dramatic and psychological treatment of ghosts in this final scene by reading Oreste's ghostly visions alongside a variety of related early modern theatrical texts. As I shall argue, Racine's dramatic evocation of ghosts both mobilizes and reworks ideas about illusion, belief and audience engagement raised by authors ranging from Corneille to the theatre theoreticians d'Aubignac and Dubos.

Despite its dramatic power, the visual and psychological impact of the final scene of *Andromaque* is surprisingly easy to overlook for those simply reading, rather than watching, the play. As was the dramatic convention, there are no explicit stage directions; all the key action of the scene is contained and reflected in the spoken word. Yet the absence of stage directions does not mean that this scene contains no drama. Far from it; indeed, the scene allows the actor playing Oreste a physical freedom unequalled elsewhere in Racine's theatre. The scope for physical movement and facial expression here is vast, rivalling even (albeit in a tragic mode) the *lazzi* of Italian comedy. Owing to the need both to evoke and to interact with these invisible apparitions, the scene is a notoriously demanding one for an actor – indeed, the role of Oreste allegedly caused its first performer, the great actor Zacharie-Jacob de Montfleury, a ruptured blood vessel which cost him his life.

Yet, while the scene poses demanding constraints on its actors, it also requires a particular mindset of its readers and spectators. A few years before *Andromaque* was first performed, Molière had demanded of his readers 'des yeux pour découvrir dans la lecture tout le jeu du théâtre',[1] and, as this chapter will argue, Racine's theatrical invocation of ghosts in this final scene requires a similar act of imaginative visualization both of the readers of Racine's text and of his spectators. The dramatic impact of Oreste's ghostly visions has rarely attracted the attention it deserves, even in explicitly theatrical readings of Racine's works; even David Maskell's astute study lists only six references to the play's final scene in his index, none of which explores the dramatic potential of Oreste's final movements.[2] When critical attention has been paid to this scene, it is Oreste's visions of the Furies, rather than the ghosts of Hermione and Pyrrhus, that tend to take centre stage, not least because the former have the more striking precedents in classical theatre.[3] Here I intend to redress the balance, arguing that ghosts play an important role in the dramatic, psychological and symbolic fabric of *Andromaque*, as indeed of seventeenth-century theatre more generally.

Immaterial as they are, the ghosts Oreste encounters are only the most tangible of a succession of literal and metaphorical phantoms that populate *Andromaque*. Both the play and its characters are haunted by a past that is never truly exorcized.[4] For most of the play's main characters, the Trojan War is at once a traumatic scene of bloodshed and a repository of role models which the young characters are expected both to imitate and to rival; the main characters of the play are all 'latecomers',[5] haunted by the demands of parents (Achilles, Helen, Agamemnon) whose death or absence only confirms their symbolic power.

One of the most present ghosts in the play is that of Andromaque's husband, Hector. Both Andromaque and her confidante Céphise frequently allude to Hector as if he were still alive, even in sentences which explicitly acknowledge his death: 'Pensez-vous qu'après tout ses mânes en rougissent?' (l. 986); 'Allons sur son tombeau consulter mon époux' (l. 1048). Death, it appears, is not necessarily the end of one's existence in *Andromaque*. Commentator Emily R. Wilson has recently argued that a certain strain of tragedy relies less on death itself than on what she calls 'overliving' – the sense that death never comes at the right time.[6] This theme of outliving one's allotted death plays a persistent role within the poetic fabric of *Andromaque*, most notably in the curious formulation applied to Hector's and Andromaque's young son Astyanax as 'un enfant qui survit à sa perte' (l. 877). Originally believed dead because of a substitution of children, Astyanax represents the possibility of the rebirth of the Trojan cause, the possibility that the suppressed past will be brought back to life. Yet Astyanax, the most tangible remains of Hector, never appears onstage and seems to partake in the same ghostly partial existence as his father.

Hector and his son are not the only ghostly occurrences in a play whose characters can be haunted even by the living. Indeed, Georges Mary has demonstrated how one particular image – that of the blood-drenched Pyrrhus – is key to the 'système imaginaire' of the tragedy.[7] As Mary argues, all four main characters are beset by this image, although its significance varies: while the memory of Pyrrhus as the bloody murderer of Hector drives an insuperable wedge between himself and Andromaque, it is the sight of Pyrrhus' body butchered by the Greeks that drives both Hermione and, in its last apparition, Oreste to instability and remorse. In a sense, then, Oreste's final ghostly vision of Pyrrhus has been stalking the stage long before the real Pyrrhus actually dies; it is this image that haunts the interactions between the characters onstage, anticipating both the king's murder itself and Oreste's descent into madness and hallucination.

With this network of thematic and psychological precedents, Racine thus takes care to foreshadow, and hence to motivate, Oreste's final ghostly visions on a number of levels. Before exploring the ending of *Andromaque* in more detail, however, it is important to reconsider Racine's dramatic treatment of ghosts within its wider historical and theatrical context; as we shall see, other writers of the time raise important questions about illusion and belief that shed light on Racine's own stagecraft. It is not surprising if some thinkers are drawn to the 'ghostly' nature of theatrical representation. If, like writing in general, ghosts are associated with 'a certain secondariness or belatedness',[8] then this play of presence and absence is perhaps particularly striking in a genre which uses the human body in order to bring historical or mythological figures back to life. In her study of onstage ghosts, Monique Borie claims that 'à travers la figure du fantôme, c'est toute une définition du théâtre comme entre-deux du visible et de l'invisible ... qui se trouve mise en jeu'.[9] The indeterminate, 'entre-deux' position of the ghost is suggested by its various uses as theatrical metaphor in seventeenth-century France. While the theatre theoretician d'Aubignac refers to actors as the 'fantômes vivants' of the kings and princes they represent,[10] for Molière it is the dramatic characters themselves who are 'des fantômes proprement'.[11]

Officially, unlike its Renaissance predecessor, French theatre of the so-called 'classical' age had little time for ghosts. As Emmanuelle Hénin has amply demonstrated, however, the ghost retains a powerful metaphorical presence in seventeenth-century theatre theory despite its unpopularity onstage.[12] Yet despite Hénin's claims, ghosts tend to take second place in much early modern theatrical thought to other supernatural metaphors, and particularly to the rhetoric of magic and illusion. Even the period's most striking evocation of ghosts as theatrical metaphor involves a magician. In Pierre Corneille's *L'Illusion comique*, a distraught father, seeking news of his fugitive son Clindor, consults a powerful wizard who, rather than simply telling Pridamant what has happened to his son, chooses to have Clindor's life re-enacted before him. As the wizard Alcandre explains,

> *Sous une illusion vous pourriez voir sa vie,*
> *Et tous ses accidents devant vous exprimés*
> *Par des spectres pareils à des corps animés;*
> *Il ne leur manquera ni geste ni parole. (ll. 149–54)*

Corneille thus draws a compelling and evocative analogy between the theatre and magic, both of which trade in illusion. Yet the fact that Alcandre explicitly refers to the ensuing performance in such terms should not suggest that he is simply a trickster; indeed, while the performance itself may be considered illusory, Alcandre's ability to summon '[des] fantômes vains' (l. 218) to enact it is testimony to his magical powers. In other words, Corneille presents his ghosts as emphatically real, at least within the world of the play.

Yet ghosts do not simply provide the medium of the inner play (that is, the performance of Clindor's life as presented to Pridamant); they are also evoked on another level within *L'Illusion comique* or, to be more correct, within Pridamant's misreading of the inner play. In the final act, Pridamant is horrified to see his son die, stabbed by one of his rival's men; momentarily forgetting that what he is watching is not happening in real time, Pridamant begs Alcandre to save his son's life. After offering a few trite words of consolation, Alcandre stages a veritable *coup de théâtre*, lifting the background curtain to reveal Clindor and his companions all counting money on a table. As becomes clear, this final act has all been a double illusion; Clindor and his companions have become actors, and the death Pridamant witnessed was part of a theatrical performance. Significantly, however, Pridamant himself takes a while to grasp the significance of what he sees, and is initially uncomprehending:

> PRIDAMANT
> *Que vois-je? chez les morts compte-t-on de l'argent?*
> ALCANDRE
> *Voyez si pas un d'eux s'y montre négligent.*
> PRIDAMANT
> *Je vois Clindor: ah! dieux! quelle étrange surprise!*

Je vois ses assassins, je vois sa femme et Lyse!
Quel charme en un moment étouffe leurs discords,
Pour assembler ainsi les vivants et les morts? (V. 5. 1611–16)

So Pridamant momentarily compounds this already doubly illusory situation with a third level of representation. Rather than recognizing the truth, he imagines that Clindor is still truly dead, and thus a ghost, mingling inexplicably with the other characters. What Pridamant sees, then, is one of Alcandre's 'fantômes vains' playing the ghost of Clindor. Yet it is also worthwhile considering Pridamant's final question here: the 'charme', the wondrous enchantment that can bring together in harmony the living and the dead, implies Corneille, is that of the theatre. Only the theatre, with the unreality it can confer even upon death, can provide a rational or plausible explanation for the apparent cohabitation of the living and the dead.

In effect, Alcandre here explains away the apparently supernatural sight, relocating it into the realm of the comprehensible and the everyday. Yet by debunking the apparent presence of ghosts within the inner play, Alcandre also threatens to expose the fictional underpinnings of Corneille's own plot, which of course relies on the supposition that supernatural phenomena do indeed exist. After all, the very fact that *L'Illusion comique* can be staged at all requires, and thereby proves, that Alcandre's magic powers can be replicated by non-magical means. Any apparently supernatural occurrence which cannot be achieved through illusion cannot, of necessity, be replicated onstage (unless, of course, the theatre troupe is lucky enough to contain a resident sorcerer ...).

A good eighty years after Corneille's play, the Abbé Dubos would return to the theatre-ghost analogy, albeit with a rather different agenda:

> *Or il est vrai que tout ce que nous voyons au théâtre concourt à nous émou-*
> *voir, mais rien n'y fait illusion à nos sens, car tout s'y montre comme*
> *imitation ... Nous n'arrivons pas au théâtre dans l'idée que nous y verrons*
> *véritablement Chimene et Rodrigue. Nous n'y aportons point la prévention*
> *avec laquelle celui qui s'est laissé persuader par un Magicien qu'il lui fera*
> *voir un Spectre, entre dans la caverne où le Phantôme doit aparoître. Cette*
> *prévention dispose beaucoup à l'illusion, mais nous ne l'avons point en*
> *venant au théâtre.[13]*

Despite some superficial similarities – the presence of the magician, the cavern – Dubos's use of the spectre is quite the opposite of what we find in *L'Illusion comique*. Indeed, given the direction of his argument, the cavern to which Dubos alludes is reminiscent less of Alcandre's 'grotte obscure' (l. 2) than of Plato's famous cave, whose occupants take the projected shadows they see on the walls for reality. In Corneille's play, the spectre provides the vehicle through which something real (Clindor's life) can be represented, while for Dubos the spectre is the very archetype of what does not exist and what thus can exist only as an illusion or representation.

For Corneille, then, the spectre is the *means* of representation, while for Dubos it is representation's *object*. Yet for Dubos the spectator's perception of the ghost is facilitated by the conjuror's powers of persuasion even before the ghost is summoned. That is to say, the existence of the ghost lies for Dubos as much in the magician's attempt to render the spectator's mind susceptible to external influence as it does in the illusion itself. Yet we do not go to the theatre expecting to see unmediated reality, insists Dubos, and there is no conjuror attempting to convince us of the reality of what we see. This is essentially what happens to Pridamant in Corneille's play, the crucial difference being that Pridamant is not interested in seeing ghosts for their own sake but, rather, seeks to know his son's fate. Despite this, the trickery at work in both cases is still comparable; both Pridamant and Dubos's hypothetical spectator are persuaded by the magician, before they even set foot into the grotto, to attribute reality to what they see (whether this be Clindor's death or the ghost itself).

So Dubos both underlines and undermines an analogy between the theatre and the conjuror's ghost. The key difference resides in the spectator's initial mindset. Indeed, when read together, Dubos's example and *L'Illusion comique* suggest another reason why the theatrical representation may seem to partake of the spectral. By entailing a similar play of presence and absence as the ghost, the theatre poses important questions of belief (*croyance*) – a term which plays a key, if disputed, role in seventeenth-century theatrical theory. For some thinkers, the spectator is expected to 'believe', albeit provisionally, that what they see is actually taking place in front of them – or at least to suspend their disbelief for the duration of the play. For others, the audience must be able to believe that the play is a faithful rendering of a historical occurrence, as one might believe a historical source. It is because of the tight relationship between theatrical belief and *vraisemblance* – in effect, a work's aesthetic ability to evoke belief – that it is ultimately irrelevant to ask whether audience members of the time would really have believed in ghosts. Whatever the extent of popular belief in ghosts, an educated seventeenth-century theatre audience could not normally be expected to add the necessary amount of credence when confronted with ghosts onstage.

As these examples suggest, the ghost poses problematic questions of belief that parallel those of the theatre. What happens, then, when both come into conjuncture and we have ghosts represented onstage, as in *Andromaque*? Or, to reformulate the question: to what extent are we expected to believe that the ghosts Oreste sees are actually present? A third (and final) example of the period's reflection on the play of presence and absence in the theatre does not deal with ghosts as such, but does help to answer these questions. Corneille's contemporary and critical rival d'Aubignac, often held as one of the great theorists of 'neoclassicism', has a very literalistic notion of theatrical representation. One of the founding tenets of d'Aubignac's theory is that, while there is an insurmountable theoretical gulf between theatrical representation and what it represents, the theatre should imitate real life so closely that everything onstage should correspond directly to the reality it represents; one consequence of this is that the supernatural is, for the most part, banned from the stage. Within this literalistic framework, however, d'Aubignac is sometimes surprisingly free in his tastes. For example, in his description of the rhetorical device of apostrophe – the act of addressing someone or something physically absent – he advocates a very similar technique to that which Racine would use in *Andromaque*. Apostrophe, he claims, is particularly suited to the theatre:

Elle suppose toujours présente, ou une véritable personne, quoiqu'absente en effet, ou une fausse personne, qui ne l'est que par fiction, comme est la Patrie, la Vertu, et autres choses semblables; car elle les suppose si bien présentes, que celui qui discourt, leur adresse sa parole, comme si véritablement il les voyait: ce qui est tout à fait Théâtral; attendu que cela fait deux personnages où il n'y en a qu'un, l'un visible, et l'autre imaginaire; l'un qui parle, et l'autre à qui il semble qu'on parle: Or quoique la feinte soit connue, néanmoins comme c'est un effet de l'emportement de l'esprit de l'Acteur, elle emporte avec elle l'imagination de ceux qui l'écoutent.[14]

Although he elsewhere harshly condemns such devices as asides and monologues as transgressions of *vraisemblance*, d'Aubignac here embraces the play of absence and presence evoked by apostrophe as 'entirely theatrical'. With this formulation d'Aubignac implies that such make-believe lies at the very heart of the theatrical enterprise. If carried out successfully, this device will sweep the spectators off their feet, leading them into an exhilaratingly liminal state which will engage their imagination. For d'Aubignac (and for contemporaries such as Chapelain), the spectator's imagination is typically understood as the capacity to imagine that the scene presented is in fact real. Here, however, d'Aubignac's spectator, instead of being a passive consumer of the scene, is expected to engage creatively with it, projecting a further presence onto the stage while remaining aware of its fictionality.

Within the constraints of an ostensibly literalistic and objective mode of representation, then, apostrophe allows d'Aubignac an 'entirely theatrical' way in which to evoke the vagaries of subjectivity and passion. In a sense, Racine's play takes the device of apostrophe to an extreme; Oreste not only speaks to the murdered Pyrrhus and Hermione, but also sees – and even attempts to attack – them.

Although the ghosts in *Andromaque* can be seen as motivated on levels both supernatural and psychological, Racine ultimately steers us towards the latter explanation. On one level, the ghostly re-appearance of Hermione and Pyrrhus is certainly in keeping with conventional thought on phantoms. Traditionally, ghosts are often understood to arise when some aspect of the death, burial or mourning process has not been carried out successfully; ghosts typically cannot be put to rest until some wrong has been righted, and unavenged murder is precisely one of these 'wrong' types of death. Yet Pyrrhus' murder appears as 'wrong' for reasons beyond the purely ethical. Above all, it is also a botched job; Pyrrhus was not even killed by Oreste, but by Oreste's men. As Oreste admits to Hermione, in amongst the tumult of Pyrrhus' murder, 'je n'ai pu trouver de place pour frapper' (l. 1516). As a result, Pyrrhus dies not out of personal vengeance, as Hermione has expressly demanded (in lines 1269–70) but, rather, for political reasons; the Greeks are driven to the murder by Pyrrhus' defiance in embracing the political interests of the Trojans.

Pyrrhus' death is thus at least doubly 'out of place'. Yet, although the conditions surrounding his death may thus be propitious for some ghostly reappearance, Racine takes care to locate matters more firmly on the psychological terrain of Oreste's disintegrating subjectivity. Indeed, Racine presents Oreste's madness as being not simply a matter of distorted perception (his hallucinations), but extending far deeper. There is no apparent logic behind Oreste's actions in this scene; in M. J. Muratore's evocative summary, 'like a mad script-writer out of control, he, too, constructs incoherent scenarios characterized by aesthetical lawlessness. The dead come back to life; violence is enacted on the stage; the taboo against physical contact is broken.'[15] Yet this madness is anticipated and thematically justified by a succession of episodes which offer Pyrrhus' and Hermione's ghostly reappearances a psychological and symbolic motivation.

In order to appreciate the full poetic significance of Oreste's ghostly visions, we need to consider his descent into madness more generally. So firm and stable a reference point has Hermione been to Oreste's world-view and value system that when she turns against her previous command and defiantly rejects him, Oreste's entire sense of reality is shaken to the core:

> *Que vois-je? Est-ce Hermione? Et que viens-je d'entendre?*
> *Pour qui coule le sang que je viens de répandre?*
> *Je suis, si je l'en crois, un traître, un assassin.*
> *Est-ce Pyrrhus qui meurt? et suis-je Oreste enfin? (ll. 1565–8)*

In a matter of lines, Oreste slips from feeling that Pyrrhus' death has been stripped of all motivation to doubting whether it even took place. Hermione's will provides such a strong imperative for Oreste's behaviour that her sudden volte-face robs even death of its objectivity. Within a few lines, the identities of all three main characters have been put into question; since Oreste can no longer trust the evidence of his senses or his inner convictions, the main characters' identities start to become detached from the material beings who until now have been presumed to embody them. The next step towards utter madness for Oreste is when he learns, almost by chance, of Hermione's suicide. Oreste's announcement that he intends to follow Hermione and expiate his crime prompts a brief misunderstanding in which Pylade, already aware of her death, infers that he wishes to commit suicide. Hermione's death seems to share a similar uncertainty to that of Pyrrhus. In a tragic inversion of

the 'false death' device so beloved of comic and tragicomic playwrights (including the Corneille of *L'Illusion comique*), Hermione is
believed alive when she is in fact dead, and this mismatch between
subjective belief and objective truth also foreshadows her ghostly
reappearance at the end.

Oreste's reason, then, has lost its anchor in reality. Identities have
become uprooted from their owners, and the objectivity of death
itself has been cast into doubt: both, again, fitting preconditions for
the appearance of ghosts. Yet it is not simply that the deluded
Oreste has visions of figures who are not present; he seems also to
be oblivious to the presence of those who are present, such as his
friend Pylade. Indeed, in his delusions Oreste now even sees the
murdered Pyrrhus standing in front of him, still bleeding from the
attack:

> ... *Quoi? Pyrrhus, je te rencontre encore?*
> *Trouverai-je partout un rival que j'abhorre?* (*ll. 1629–30*)

Faced with this vision of Pyrrhus, Oreste draws his sword and
attempts to strike the ghost, exclaiming 'Tiens, tiens, voilà le coup
que je t'ai réservé' (l. 1632). It may even be that he is lashing out at
his friend, since it is only after Pylade speaks that Oreste notices
Pyrrhus' presence.

Despite his failure to hit the ghostly Pyrrhus, Oreste's behaviour is
nonetheless 'striking' in another sense. In reality, of course, Oreste
had never wanted to harm Pyrrhus; when offered the chance to
relive the scene, however, he has no such scruples or regrets.
Indeed, Oreste's madness thus manifests itself both in his hallucinations and in his response to them. Just as before, however, Oreste
does not actually manage to strike Pyrrhus – in this case because a
vision of Hermione appears to whisk him out of harm's way:

> *Mais que vois-je? A mes yeux Hermione l'embrasse!*
> *Elle vient l'arracher au coup qui le menace?* (*ll. 1633–4*)

In reality, of course, Pyrrhus felt no love for Hermione at all, but in
Oreste's fevered mind their spirits are united for all eternity to
mock and torment him. Again, the ghostly vision bears little resemblance to the reality it purports to represent. This time, though, the
seeds of this image may have been planted in Oreste's mind by

Hermione's earlier threat that she would murder both Pyrrhus and herself and thus yoke their destinies together forever (ll. 1244–8). Hermione's impossible dream thus becomes a taunting source of despair for Oreste.

It is at this point that the Furies, the goddesses of vengeance, now appear behind the happy couple. This is not, of course, the place to discuss the full symbolism and dramatic potential of the Furies, although the latter in many ways parallels what we have already seen with the ghosts. In effect, Racine here grafts the ending of the more famous episode of his protagonist's life – his murder of his mother Clytemnestra and his subsequent torment – onto his own plot, thus either collapsing the two episodes into one or at least giving the audience a foretaste of Oreste's later descent into madness.[16] More importantly, however, Racine's Oreste – unlike his classical precedents – finally refuses to succumb to the Furies, and turns back to his ghostly vision of Hermione. In a final display of both defiance and despair, Oreste proclaims to the Furies that they have less power to torture him than the cruel object of his love:

> *Mais non, retirez-vous, laissez faire Hermione:*
> *L'ingrate mieux que vous saura me déchirer;*
> *Et je lui porte enfin mon cœur à dévorer. (ll. 1642–4)*

Oreste collapses, and Pylade encourages his men to carry him off to safety, warning that he might reawaken in the same furious disorder.

Despite its hyperbolic terms, Oreste's final, desperate move is to reject the supernatural justice system of the mythological world in favour of one that takes place on an essentially human plane. Indeed, for Revel Elliot nothing better illustrates 'le caractère moderne de certaines parties d'*Andromaque*' than Oreste's final submission to Hermione.[17] Yet Oreste's rejection of the supernatural in favour of the human is echoed on another level, since throughout this whole final scene Racine himself repudiates supernatural motivations for the onstage action in favour of human, psychological ones. By not having the ghosts (or the Furies) played by real-life actors, Racine refuses to give any credence to supernatural explanations, while still allowing the ending to fit within its traditional mythological framework.

Racine thus reworks the traditional myth to highlight both Oreste's fragmented state of mind and – I would argue – his symbolic

position within the play. *Andromaque* ends with this powerful image of
Oreste flailing around, trying to strike at figments of his imagination.
This final scene thus emphasizes both Oreste's vulnerability and his
distress; he is both totally alone, utterly unaware of his friend's presence, and yet constantly beset by his memories and figments of his
own imagination. In fact, this final image provides a neat visual
summary of Oreste's position throughout the play. Being at one end
of the 'chain' linking the four lovers, he has precious little control
over events, and indeed his own behaviour as the play progresses
rarely has the effect he intends. The murder of Pyrrhus is a case in
point; Oreste obeys Hermione's orders and has Pyrrhus killed, but
meets nothing but fury and despair for doing so. He engineers the
murder and feels guilty for it, but he does not actually manage to
strike Pyrrhus. Throughout the play, then, Oreste never really
connects with or has any impact on any of the other characters, and
this final image of him thrashing around, chasing shadows, offers a
stark visual shorthand for his position.

As the ending to *Andromaque* suggests, Racine constantly takes
liberties with our expectations. Rather than being confronted with
the reality of his actions in a moment of anagnorisis or revelation,
Oreste ends up falling prey to a ghastly vision. The ambivalent status
of the spectres allows Racine to play with conventions of *bienséance*
by conjuring up physical violence onstage without transgressing the
taboo on bloodshed. The Furies may appear as a nod towards
mythological tradition, but Racine implicitly locates them on the
same psychological and hallucinatory plane as the ghosts that
precede – and ultimately supersede – them. By refusing to give any
ontological status to the ghost, Racine thus embroils his spectator in
a complex play of belief and unbelief which mirrors that of the
theatre more generally. It is precisely through spurning the more
expressionistic technique of literally representing Oreste's own
inner demons onstage that Racine manages to call upon and
engage his spectator's – and indeed his reader's – imagination as a
necessary supplement to the onstage action. Yet Racine's spectral
dramaturgy in this scene also implies a realization that, whatever the
suggestions of Corneille, Molière, d'Aubignac and Dubos, the ghost
cannot be pinned down quite so easily to the theatrical medium.
The processes of imaginative visualization that Oreste's ghostly
visions encourage in his audience are, after all, more familiar to us
from reading written texts than from watching plays. Ironically,

then, despite being one of the most dramatic and theatrical moments in all Racine's works, the final scene of *Andromaque* is itself haunted by its own ultimately textual origins in the written word.

Notes

1 Molière, 'Au lecteur' of *L'Amour médecin*, in *Œuvres complètes*, ed. Georges Couton, vol. II (Paris: Gallimard Bibliothèque de la Pléiade, 1971), p. 95.

2 David Maskell, *Racine: A Theatrical Reading* (Oxford: Clarendon Press, 1991).

3 See, for example, Revel Elliot, *Mythe et légende dans le théâtre de Racine* (Paris: Lettres Modernes, 1969), p. 59 n. 17. A more directly relevant theatrical precursor for the theme of ghosts can be found in Eraste's visions of the underworld in Corneille's comedy *Mélite*; see Armand Helmreich-Marsilien, 'Un inspirateur paradoxal du tragique racinien: Corneille comique', *Australian Journal of French Studies*, 2 (1965), 291–312, and Simone Dosmond, 'Folie d'Eraste, folie d'Oreste', in Jean-Louis Cabanès (ed.), *Littérature et médecine*, vol. II (Bordeaux: Université Michel de Montaigne Bordeaux III, 2000), pp. 149–55.

4 See, for example, Louise K. Horowitz, 'The second time around', *Esprit Créateur*, 38, 2 (summer 1998), 23–33.

5 Roland Racevskis, 'Generational transition in *Andromaque*', *Dalhousie French Studies*, 49 (winter 1999), 63–72 (p. 63).

6 Emily R. Wilson, *Mocked with Death: Tragic Overliving from Sophocles to Milton* (Baltimore/London: Johns Hopkins University Press, 2004).

7 Georges Mary, 'La Folie d'Oreste ou l'écart minime à l'équilibre', *Poétique*, 98 (1994), 171–80 (p. 175).

8 Peter Buse and Andrew Stott (eds), *Ghosts: Deconstruction, Psycho-analysis, History* (Basingstoke: Macmillan, 1999), p. 8.

9 Monique Borie, *Le Fantôme, ou le théâtre qui doute* (Arles: Actes Sud, 1997), p. 22.

10 D'Aubignac, *La Pratique du théâtre*, ed. Hélène Baby (Paris: Champion, 2001), p. 127.

11 Molière, *L'Impromptu de Versailles*, sc. 4 (in *Œuvres complètes*, vol. I).

12 Emmanuelle Hénin, 'Fantôme et *mimèsis* à l'âge classique: la théorie hantée', in Françoise Lavocat and François Lecercle (eds), *Drama-turgies de l'ombre* (Rennes: Presses Universitaires de Rennes, 2005), pp. 229–45.

13 Jean-Baptiste Dubos, *Réflexions critiques sur la poésie et sur la peinture* (Paris: Jean Mariette, 1719), I, pp. 620–1.

14 D'Aubignac, *La Pratique*, p. 476.

15 M. J. Muratore, 'The pleasures of re-enactment in *Andromaque*', *Dalhousie French Studies*, 24 (spring–summer 1993), 57–70 (p. 67).

16 Commentators are generally agreed that Racine's Oreste has not yet

committed the double murder of Clytemnestra and Aegisthus; see C. J. Gossip, 'Oreste, *amant imaginaire*', *Papers on French Seventeenth-Century Literature*, 20: 39 (1993), 353–67, p. 356.

17   Elliot, *Mythe et légende*, p. 62.

Chapter Five
Les Misérables:
the Shadowlands of Epic

Fiona Cox

Dieu donne aux morts les biens réels, les vrais royaumes.
Vivants! vous êtes des fantômes;
C'est nous qui sommes les vivants![1]

Les Misérables is a haunted work. Ghosts crowd around its vibrant
and archetypal protagonists, such as the exuberant urchin
Gavroche, the inexorably principled police inspector Javert and the
Christ of the nineteenth-century poor, Jean Valjean. In many
instances these ghosts are simply different aspects of the main characters. For example, when Jean Valjean must renounce his identity
as the saintly M. Madeleine and adopt once more his hated and
ignoble name, Jean Valjean, Hugo observes that: 'C'est ainsi que ce
fantôme qui s'était appelé M. Madeleine se dissipa à Montreuil-sur-
mer.'[2] Again and again Valjean reinvents himself as the various
selves he inhabits are forced to dissipate, and throughout the book
this process is marked by the series of aliases and pseudonyms by
which he is known. Ultimately he functions as Everyman, but this
entails forfeiting a permanent sense of identity and becoming as
substanceless as no one, a point that Hugo emphasizes at the end of
the book where he depicts Valjean's gravestone from which the
name is effaced.[3] Towards the end of the book Valjean observes to
Marius: 'Un nom, c'est un moi', highlighting the presentation of
himself as an empty cipher, as he adopts one new name after
another.[4] In his critical work Hugo presents this insubstantiality as
the necessary reverse of the literary archetype, observing that:

> *Un type ne reproduit aucun homme en particulier; il ne superpose exactement à*
> *aucun individu; il résume et concentre sous une forme humaine toute une*

famille de caractères et d'esprits. Un type n'abrège pas; il condense. Il n'est pas un, il est tous. Alcibiade n'est qu'Alcibiade, Pétrone n'est que Pétrone, Bassompierre n'est que Bassompierre, Buckingham n'est que Buckingham, Fronsac n'est que Fronsac, Lauzun n'est que Lauzun; mais saisissez Lauzun, Fronsac, Buckingham, Bassompierre, Pétrone et Alcibiade, et pilez-les dans le mortier du rêve, il en sort un fantôme, plus réel qu'eux tous, don Juan.[5]

On this reading the literary archetype embodies a host of characters who all take substance from him/her as they pass like ghosts through the text. Jean Valjean is never a single person; he is an arch-criminal, but also an archetypal father and archetypal mother to Cosette. In his guise as M. Madeleine he is a version of the saintly bishop M. Myriel; as Ultime Fauchelevent he becomes brother to the convent gardener, Fauchelevent; as hero of Hugo's Bible of the nineteenth century he is Christ; as hero of Hugo's epic of nineteenth-century France he is a French Dante, plumbing a new French underworld. In interpretations such as Claude Lelouch's *Les Misérables* (1995) we see him also as a Second World War hero, helping Jews to safety. The potential for such intertextual embodiment is infinite since, as Everyman, Valjean also embodies the readers of the text who are asked to empathize imaginatively with Jean Valjean, to learn what he has had to learn.

This chapter will argue that this boundless proliferation of ghostly characters and of intertextual ghosts is central to Hugo's aim to write the epic of infinity. Hugo's resolve to write an epic that will surpass all previous epics, an epic that will therefore offer us the most complete vision to date of human understanding, depends in part on his ability to eliminate hell on earth and to create a social utopia. Yet this ambition is undermined throughout the book. In his Preface Hugo observes:

Tant qu'il existera, par le fait des lois et des mœurs, une damnation sociale créant artificiellement, en pleine civilisation, des enfers, et compliquant d'une fatalité humaine la destinée qui est divine ... tant qu'il y aura sur la terre ignorance et misère, des livres de la nature de celui-ci pourront ne pas être inutiles.[6]

However, the end of the book makes it clear that the cycle of misery is bound to continue as Valjean is finally effaced within his unmarked grave, while the villainous Thénardier sets off for America to make his fortune in the slave trade. The continuing relevance of the book, its capacity to spawn endless rereadings, depends on its failure to map out a human paradise.[7] In analysing this paradox at the heart of *Les Misérables* I shall argue that Hugo's digression on convent life, far from constituting a negligible aside, in fact provides a key to understanding Hugo's vision of his epic project and its links with the identities of his protagonists and readers.

Hugo sets out his epic agenda in detail:

> *Faire le poème de la conscience humaine, ne fût-ce à propos d'un seul homme, ne fût-ce à propos du plus infime des hommes, ce serait fondre toutes les épopées dans une épopée supérieure et définitive. La conscience, c'est le chaos des chimères, des convoitises, des tentatives, la fournaise des rêves, l'antre des idées dont on a honte; c'est le pandémonium des sophismes, c'est le champ des batailles des passions. À de certaines heures, pénétrez à travers la face livide d'un être humain qui réfléchit et regardez derrière, regardez dans cette obscurité. Il y a là, sous le silence extérieur, des combats de dragons comme dans Homère, des mêlées de dragons et d'hydres et des nuées de fantômes comme dans Milton, des spirales visionnaires comme chez Dante. Chose sombre que cet infini que tout homme porte en soi et auquel il mesure avec désespoir les volontés de sa vie!*
>
> *Alighieri rencontra un jour une sinistre porte devant laquelle il hésita. En voici une autre devant nous, au seuil de laquelle nous hésitons. Entrons pourtant.*[8]

This passage is Hugo's rewriting of the episode from Dante's *Inferno* where Dante encounters the shades of his own poetic ancestors – Homer, Ovid, Horace and Lucan. While Dante is ostensibly humbled and delighted to be in their presence, he does not allow the reader to forget that his own epic surpasses all of their works because he is the only one to be working in the Christian tradition. Likewise, Hugo points out that his own work which focuses on the lowliest of men is, in fact, the definitive epic. As such it has absorbed and transfigured the ideas of his predecessors – the battles of Homer, Milton's hellish cluster of ghosts and Dante's visionary circles. Hugo follows in the footsteps of Dante, but underpins his epic with existential crisis. For any individual to weigh up the actions of their life, the secrets of their hearts, is to contemplate a darkness shrouded by silence and enveloped by despair. Dante shrank from the gates of hell and now Hugo's readers must shrink from Valjean's spiritual conflict as he decides between denouncing himself as Jean Valjean, thereby saving Champmathieu but ensuring that he himself will return to the galleys, or keeping quiet and retaining his position as M. Madeleine, thereby forfeiting his soul. Both options lead to a version of death. The integrity of his soul transforms the return to the degrading galleys into a heavenly option; the dishonesty of allowing another to suffer in his place would transform his privileges as mayor of Montreuil into a hellish sham.

Just such a reversal of fates is also experienced at the threshold of the Petit-Picpus convent to which Valjean unwittingly escapes with Cosette in order to flee from Javert and where he ends up living as Ultime Fauchelevent for several years. It is here that Hugo inserts his meditations on convent life, meditations that offer a key to understanding the whole book, as Butor recognized when he argued that the convent episode was one of the 'arias sémantiques' which 'nous donnent l'élément qui rend intelligible une "énigme" du récit'.[9] The first description of the convent likens it to a tomb, and indeed Valjean must become as a ghost as he feigns death and is removed from the convent in a coffin in order to gain legitimate re-entry. Furthermore, like Dante who wakes from a dream disorientated in the heart of a dark wood, Valjean also is disorientated and forced to recognize that he is not dreaming. Both characters are at the start of a spiritual quest:

> *Où était-il? qui aurait jamais pu imaginer quelque chose de pareil à cette*
> *espèce de sépulcre au milieu de Paris? qu'était-ce que cette étrange maison?*
> *Édifice plein de mystère nocturne, appelant les âmes dans l'ombre avec la voix*
> *des anges et, lorsqu'elles viennent, leur offrant brusquement cette vision épou-*
> *vantable, promettant d'ouvrir la porte radieuse du ciel et ouvrant la porte*
> *horrible du tombeau.*[10]

From the start Hugo emphasizes the fact that the convent is a place of death steeped in shadows, filled with silence: 'un silence où l'on ne recueillait rien, pas même des soupirs, une ombre où l'on ne distinguait rien, pas même des fantômes'.[11] This 'demi-jour de cave' is the light inhabited by so many of the *misérables*.[12] The nuns share the same half-light as Fantine who cannot afford to light her home, the light known by Jean Valjean in the galleys and by Marius who lives in self-imposed straitened circumstances. But it is in the convent episode that this light that is not light, this 'darkness visible'[13] is evoked most extensively.

The reason for this is made clear when Hugo articulates the *raison d'être* of convent life: 'Idéal, absolu, perfection, infini: mots identiques'.[14] Infinity is the subject matter of Hugo's epic and infinity is the object of the nuns' contemplation, so that readers have perhaps taken Hugo too literally when he apologizes for inserting his digression and states that it is not pertinent to the subject matter of the book: 'que le lecteur nous permette encore une petite digression, étrangère au fond de ce livre, mais caractéristique et utile en ce qu'elle fait comprendre que le cloître lui-même a ses figures originales'.[15] The Petit-Picpus convent episode has, indeed, received little critical attention, and yet it presents in a microcosm the fundamental themes of the work as a whole:

> *Ce livre est un drame où le premier personnage est l'infini.*
>
> *L'homme est le second.*
>
> *Cela étant, comme un couvent s'est trouvé sur notre chemin, nous avons dû y pénétrer. Pourquoi? C'est que le couvent, qui est propre à l'orient comme à l'occident, à l'antiquité comme aux temps modernes, au paganisme, au bouddhisme, au mahométisme comme au christianisme, est un des appareils d'optique appliqués par l'homme sur l'infini.*[16]

The convent episode allows Hugo to analyse the nature of infinity and to recognize that there is more than one infinity. When he speculates,

> *En même temps qu'il y a un infini hors de nous, n'y a-t-il pas un infini en nous? ces deux infinis ne se superposent-ils pas l'un à l'autre? Le second infini n'est-il pas pour ainsi dire sous-jacent au premier? n'en est-il pas le miroir, le reflet, l'écho, l'abîme concentrique à l'autre abîme?*[17]

he extends St Paul's observations that 'now we see through a glass, darkly; but then face to face'.[18] The daily life of the nuns entails a constant recognition of the fleetingness of human life in the face of the divine mystery that will dispel the shadows, and throughout the Petit-Picpus episode Hugo depicts the nuns as ghostly figures, suspended between their earthly life and the hope of a paradise to come, while they meditate upon the nature of infinity.

At first sight it seems difficult to see how these nuns, who have chosen a life detached from the world, could have anything to do with the protagonists of *Les Misérables* whose lives are so grounded in the world. And yet Jean Valjean's life is extensively mirrored in convent life. Just as his entry into the convent is symbolized by death, so too is theirs: 'La prise de voile ou de froc est un suicide payé d'éternité'.[19] Furthermore, within the convent walls there is a female version of Jean Valjean, a woman with no past, no knowable family history, a woman who commanded respect but who passed through convent life as if she were dead:[20]

> *Vers cette époque donc, il y avait dans le couvent une personne mystérieuse qui n'était pas religieuse, qu'on traitait avec un grand respect, et qu'on nommait Madame Albertine. On ne savait rien d'elle sinon qu'elle était folle et que dans le monde elle passait pour morte … Elle avait une étrange grâce spectrale. Là où elle entrait, on avait froid. Un jour, une sœur, la voyant passer, dit à une autre: 'Elle passe pour morte.' – 'Elle l'est peut-être,' répondit l'autre.[21]*

The description is rich with echoes of Jean Valjean's passage through life.[22] For much of his life he was believed to be dead. At one point his death is even announced in the newspapers. Time and again he undergoes experiences that equate to a figurative death – the drowning as he fell in the sea after saving his fellow convict, the false burial at the Petit-Picpus convent and the descent into the sewers with Marius. Even when he is known and recognized by those around him he is still depicted as dead. In the famous tableau which presents Marius, Valjean and Javert as 'le cadavre, le spectre et la statue' it is Jean Valjean who is the ghost, a ghost who 'semblait fait d'ombre'.[23]

Throughout the book Hugo has emphasized that Jean Valjean is not only inhabited by shadows, but lives among shadows and in this also he resembles the sisters. Within a book whose explicit aim is to remedy the dystopias on earth he gives us a vision of the ideal community:

> *Ils sont vêtus de grosse laine ou de grosse toile. Pas un ne possède en propriété quoi que ce soit … La cellule est identique pour tous. Tous subissent la même tonsure, portent le même froc, mangent le même pain noir, dorment sur la même paille, meurent sur la même cendre … Il peut y avoir un prince, ce*

prince est la même ombre que les autres. Plus de titres. Les noms de famille
même ont disparu … Ils se disent l'un à l'autre mon frère.[24]

This vision both meets the demands of the Sermon on the Mount
and transfigures the hardships that Valjean endured as a convict.
The nuns share equally brutal living conditions but, whereas the
convicts are treated as subhuman and sink into the mire, the nuns
have a mutual recognition of their humanity and transform their
hellish conditions into a utopia. Not only does Hugo offer a vision
of perfect equality in this depiction, but he also remedies the
damage perpetrated upon individuals by their families.

The rupturing of family ties within *Les Misérables* has been extensively analysed in critical works, as has the theme of the disappearing
family. By emphasizing the importance of fraternity Hugo is also
reminding the reader of Jean Valjean's renaissance under the
bishop's recognition of him as a full human being, as a 'frère'. Under
Valjean's gaze, too, the sisters become configured as humans rather
than as ghosts: 'A force d'attention et de pénétration, il était parvenu
à remettre de la chair dans tous ces fantômes, et ces mortes vivaient
pour lui.'[25] And yet this ideal community, one that comes closer to
perfection than any other society on earth, is also one that consistently turns its gaze towards the shadows. Part of the reason for this is
that the nuns, like Jean Valjean, are haunted by the selves they used to
be. The crux of convent life is the vanquishing of self, a process that
involves the endless murderings of one's past selves:

> *Quant à nous, nous respectons çà et là et nous épargnons partout le passé*
> *pourvu qu'il consente à être mort. S'il veut être vivant, nous l'attaquons, et*
> *nous tâchons de le tuer.*
>
> *Superstitions, bigotismes, cagotismes, préjugés, ces larves, toutes larves*
> *qu'elles sont, sont tenaces à la vie, elles ont des dents et des ongles dans leur*
> *fumée, et il faut les étreindre corps à corps et leur faire la guerre, et la leur*
> *faire sans trêve, car c'est une des fatalités de l'humanité d'être condamnée à*
> *l'éternel combat des fantômes. L'ombre est difficile à prendre à la gorge et à*
> *terrasser.*[26]

It is part of the human condition to be engaged on a perpetual
quest to vanquish the ghosts of the past and, as the nuns experience
most intensely the human condition viewed from the perspective of
infinity, it is natural that the imagery of haunting and shadows
pervading *Les Misérables* should be found most strongly here.

That this is the case is indicated by the fact that Jean Valjean himself described his arrival at the convent as the most terrifying experience of his life. Since Hugo has already shown that Valjean experienced the horror of the galleys twice, and has undergone the Gethsemane experience of the *affaire Champmathieu* he is ensuring that we too are chilled by the spectres of the convent. It is the figure of the prostrate nun that so disturbs Valjean:

> *Cela était étendu à plat ventre, la face contre la pierre, les bras en croix, dans l'immobilité de la mort. On eût dit, à une sorte de serpent qui traînait sur le pavé, que cette forme avait la corde au cou.*
>
> *Toute la salle baignait dans cette brume des lieux à peine éclairés qui ajoute à l'horreur.*
>
> *Jean Valjean a souvent dit depuis que, quoique bien des spectacles funèbres eussent traversé sa vie, jamais il n'avait rien vu de plus glaçant et de plus terrible que cette figure énigmatique accomplissant on ne sait quel mystère inconnu dans ce lieu sombre et ainsi entrevue dans la nuit. Il était effrayant de supposer que cela était peut-être mort, et plus effrayant encore de songer que cela était peut-être vivant.[27]*

It is the shock of recognition that terrifies Valjean so much. He too straddles the threshold between the living and the dead; he too inhabits this twilight world. In his analysis of *Les Travailleurs de la mer* Brombert observes that: 'Increasingly Hugo seemed haunted by the belief that poetic vision depends on the dangerous intimacy with evil, that God and the artist join in a theology of shadows.'[28] In this instance Valjean may not be in proximity with evil, but he is looking at a scene that suggests a violent death, even suicide. For a man who walked through the world as a 'passant' and who is consistently defined as a ghost it is understandable that this apparent spectacle of annihilation should unfold his deepest terrors.

That Valjean's arrival at the convent demands of him a descent into the underworld of personal insecurities and fears is indicated by the frequent allusions to Dante in this digression. The importance of Dante to *Les Misérables* generally has been well attested,[29] but as yet insufficient attention has been paid to Hugo's clear invocations of Dante in the convent episode, although these provide further evidence of the importance of this apparent digression to his understanding of his epic ambitions. Like Dante, who wakes from a dream disorientated in a dark wood, at the threshold of the convent Valjean has lost all bearings and has to force himself to recognize that he is not dreaming. Both characters are embarking upon a spiritual quest. When Hugo describes Dante's project in *William Shakespeare* (1864), his treatise on poetic genius published only two years after *Les Misérables*, he draws heavily upon the imagery that he used to depict the Petit-Picpus convent: 'Architecture inouïe. Au seuil est la brume sacrée. En travers de l'entrée est étendu le cadavre de l'espérance. Tout ce qu'on aperçoit au-delà est nuit.'[30] The moment is a recreation of Valjean's moment of terror at the threshold of the convent. Like Dante, Valjean finds himself in a place bordering both heaven and hell:

> *Cette existence claustrale si austère et si morne, dont nous venons d'indiquer quelques linéaments. Ce n'est pas la vie, car ce n'est pas la liberté; ce n'est pas la tombe, car ce n'est pas la plénitude; c'est le lieu étrange d'où l'on aperçoit, comme de la crête d'une haute montagne, d'un côté l'abîme où nous sommes, de l'autre l'abîme où nous serons; c'est une frontière étroite et brumeuse séparant deux mondes, éclairée et obscurcie par les deux à la fois, où le rayon affaibli de la vie se mêle au rayon vague de la mort; c'est la pénombre du tombeau.[31]*

This site of transition is Janus-faced, is shadowed both by the past and the future, by life and death. It is in just such a place of limbo that Hugo situates the heart of his poetic enterprise: 'la poésie a deux oreilles, l'une qui écoute la vie et l'autre qui écoute la mort'.[32] For Dante these shadows are expelled by an emergence into Paradise but, on Hugo's reading, he fails to take his readers with him; we are left, like Virgil his guide, in the shadows: 'Du reste, qu'importe à Dante que vous ne le suiviez plus! il va sans vous. Il va seul, ce lion. Cette œuvre est un prodige. Quel philosophe que ce visionnaire! quel sage que ce fou.'[33] It suits Hugo's poetic ambition to deny Dante's ability to bring his readers into Paradise, since it allows him to take up where Dante left off. In his discussion of Dante in *William Shakespeare* there are moments when he seems to be speaking as much of *Les Misérables* as of Dante. Once again the protagonist is depicted as a 'passant' in an epic peopled by ghosts: 'Malheur à celui des vivants sur lequel ce passant fixe l'inexplicable lueur de ses yeux' and 'Dante a construit dans son esprit l'abîme. Il a fait l'épopée des spectres.'[34]

Hugo too has constructed a world that shows us Hell and Purgatory, a world that posits the promise of a Paradise founded by and through humanity. But like the world of Dante, Hugo's world is inhabited by ghosts whose stay on earth is fleeting and who leave few discernible traces when they depart; and whereas Dante was able to unfold for us his vision of Paradise, Hugo can only project the failure of his ambition. Time and again he shows us how the cycle of misery is set to continue. Thénardier steps out of the pages of *Les Misérables* to deal in the slave trade in America. Towards the end of the book Valjean is forgotten and abandoned by his adopted daughter and son-in-law, both of whom he rescued. Even his grave is neglected – the rain has worn away the inscription, leaving it blank.

However, if we accept Hugo's ambition to write a Bible for the nineteenth century and read *Les Misérables* in the light of the Book of Revelation, whose author John shares his name with Jean Valjean, it is clear that individual redemption is achieved through an acceptance of anonymity:

> *He that hath an ear, let him hear what the Spirit saith unto the churches; To him that overcometh will I give to eat of the hidden manna, and will give him a white stone, and in the stone a new name written, which no man knoweth saving he that receiveth it. (2:17)*[35]

Valjean's biblical forefather promises a cycle of blank stones awaiting the inscriptions of the names of those who attain eternal life; *Les Misérables* depicts the blank gravestone of Everyman. A further Proustian reading of this blank gravestone enables us to see it not only as Valjean's tomb, but as a site accomodating the ghosts of readers who have visited the text: 'Un livre est un grand cimetière où, sur la plupart des tombes on ne peut plus lire les noms effacés.'[36] Not only is *Les Misérables* haunted by ghosts in the form of its characters, who are 'passants', but it is also inhabited by the countless shades of its readers and by the other books that resonate within its pages. Furthermore, Jean Valjean's blank gravestone looks beyond Proust's observation to Simon's presentation in *Les Géorgiques* of the crumbling gravestone that offers a concrete image of the disintegration of writing. Our passage on earth will be marked by nothing more than an epitaph which becomes progressively more effaced and meaningless:

L'idiot, donc, agenouillé dans l'herbe trempée, insensible à la pluie, à la boue,
le visage épanoui, radieux, montrant du doigt sur la pierre grenue et rongée
l'inscription, l'épitaphe … lisant au fur et à mesure que son doigt suivait les
lettres alignées MARIE ANNE … puis grattant la pierre de l'ongle, effritant
les écailles jaunes des lichens, disant HASSEL … la fin du nom tout à fait
effacée.[37]

These twentieth-century meditations on the blank gravestone, asserting the impossibility of stabilizing a final, coherent meaning, add further resonances to Hugo's ambition to write 'une espèce d'essai sur l'infini'.[38] Such intertextual proliferation helps to ensure that both reader and protagonist are left 'au bord de l'infini', straining for glimpses of the world beyond and straddling the threshold between life and death.

When Dante attempted to show his readers a land beyond death he showed us visions that we cannot possibly understand, according to Hugo: 'En s'élevant il s'idéalise, et la pensée laisse tomber le corps comme une robe; de Virgile il passe à Béatrix; son guide pour le ciel, c'est la poésie. L'épopée grandit encore ; mais l'homme ne la comprend plus.'[39] Hugo, too, is depicting a work that eludes human control, that has acquired its own life, but he is also pointing to the function of the author. Etymologically 'authors' are those 'qui augent', who extend or add to the work of their predecessors. By the end of the book it is clear that this supreme epic, this Bible of nineteenth-century France, is in fact far closer to the self-conscious questioning of the *nouveaux romanciers* than to Dante's self-sufficient circle of perfection.[40] In Hugo's hands Dante's epic has grown into *Les Misérables,* has taken the shape of a book that can offer only the hope of a future paradise to its readers who, in the meantime, must wait in the shadowlands of doubt and uncertainty.

Notes

1   Victor Hugo, 'Quia pulvis es', *Les Contemplations* (Paris: Gallimard, 1973), p. 140.
2   Victor Hugo, *Romans 2 – Les Misérables* (Paris: Robert Laffont, collection Bouquins, 1985), p. 234.
3   See Georges Piroué on the collapse between being someone and being no one:

> Le mot 'personne' dans son double sens serait peut-être la meilleure
> fiche d'identité pour définir ce Dieu et cet homme face à face. A savoir

nullité et désignation, dilution et densité, effacement et localisation; rien dans l'ordre du positif, tout dans l'ordre du potentiel. Un balancement qui va de la phrase 'Ce n'est personne' à la phrase 'C'est une personne.' (in *Victor Hugo ou les dessus de l'inconnu* (Paris: Denoel, 1964), p. 206.)

4   *Les Misérables*, p. 960.
5   Victor Hugo, 'William Shakespeare', in *Œuvres critiques* (Paris: Robert Laffont, collection Bouquins, 1985), p. 335.
6   *Les Misérables*, p. 2.
7   See Kathryn Grossman, *Figuring Transcendence in Les Misérables – Hugo's Romantic Sublime* (Carbondale/Edwardsville: Southern Illinois University Press, 1994):

This preface situates Hugo's book at the center of a dialectic between the historical persistence of institutionalized hell and the advent of an age where his vision of a better world would be obsolete, if not useless. From one perspective, this would seem to be the highest achievement to which his work could aspire. From another, it would signify that the novel carried the germs of its own self-destruction, a paradoxical will to non-existence. (p. 5)

8   *Les Misérables*, p. 175.
9   Michel Butor, 'Victor Hugo romancier', *Répertoire II* (Paris: Minuit, 1964), pp. 215–42; p. 218.
10 *Les Misérables*, p. 366.
11 Ibid., p. 381.
12 Ibid., p. 380.
13 Milton, *Paradise Lost*, I, 63 (New York: Norton, 1993), p. 10.
14 *Les Misérables*, p. 411.
15 Ibid., p. 398.
16 Ibid., p. 403.
17 Ibid., p. 409.
18 Corinthians 13: 12.
19 *Les Misérables*, p. 411.
20 Grossman also points out that,

In rejecting the need for possessions or, at the end, for a personal niche, Valjean resembles the inhabitants of the Petit-Picpus convent. Like his fictive existence, the life of this order, now about to 'fade away' (378; 's'effacer') in the memory of a few elderly women, evaporates without a trace. Saintly stories and histories seem destined to suffer the same fate – the *évanouissement*, the disappearance of Léopoldine. (*Figuring Transcendence*, p. 165)

21 *Les Misérables*, p. 392.
22 Piroué observes that, 'Cet homme existe à peine. Je veux dire que, sur le plan de l'existence, il est presque toujours absent. Il se crée en s'annulant; il s'impose en se niant. Ses disparitions successives sont les avatars de son indiscutable présence' (*Victor Hugo*, p. 43).
23 *Les Misérables*, pp. 1032 and 1031.
24 Ibid., pp. 407–8.
25 Ibid., p. 421.

26 Ibid., p. 406.
27 Ibid., p. 366.
28 Victor Brombert, *Victor Hugo and the Visionary Novel* (Cambridge, MA: Harvard University Press, 1984), p. 168.
29 In particular, see Brombert, *Visionary Novel*; Fiona Cox, 'The dawn of a hope so horrible: Javert and the absurd', in James Hiddleston (ed.), *Victor Hugo – Romancier de l'abîme* (Oxford: Legenda, 2002), pp. 79–94; and Grossman, *Figuring Transcendence*.
30 *Les Misérables*, p. 277.
31 Ibid., p. 413.
32 Hugo, 'William Shakespeare', p. 322.
33 *Les Misérables*, p. 278. At the end of his magisterial work on Hugo's poetic vision Jean Gaudon depicts him as a modern Dante, but points out that although Hugo's poetry is illumined by divine light it is also pervaded by emptiness: 'cet immense poète, qui est notre Dante; un Dante moderne, sans théologie, sans Virgile pour le guider au royaume de l'ombre, mais dont l'œuvre est tout illuminée par ce rêve qu'il a osé faire d'un poème béant' (*Le temps de la contemplation: l'œuvre poétique de Victor Hugo des Misères au Seuil du gouffre* (1845–1856) (Paris: Flammarion, 1969), p. 410). Brombert also depicts Hugo in these terms: 'Hugo clearly conceives of himself as a modern Dante' (*Visionary Novel*, p. 118).
34 *Les Misérables*, pp. 278 and 277. See also Hugo's poem 'Écrit sur un exemplaire de la *Divina Commedia*', *Les Contemplations*, p. 125.
35 For a discussion of the influence of Revelations on *Les Misérables*, see Fiona Cox, 'Money and identity in *Les Misérables*', in Sarah Capitanio, Lisa Downing, Paul Rowe and Nicholas White (eds), *Currencies – Fiscal Fortunes and Cultural Capital in Nineteenth-Century France* (Bern: Peter Lang, 2005), pp. 121–32.
36 Marcel Proust, *À la recherche du temps perdu*, ed. Jean-Yves Tadié, 4 vols (Paris: Gallimard, Bibliothèque de la Pléiade, 1987–9), vol. IV, p. 482. For a resonant and illuminating discussion of these issues see Timothy Raser, *The Simplest of Signs: Victor Hugo and the Language of Images in France 1850–1950* (Newark: University of Delaware Press, 2004):

> Like vampires or the undead, works of art take the life of those they touch. Thus, a 'spirit', visiting the earth, enables a sculpture to respond to the reader's gaze, but also, and more importantly, it enables the reader to discover the sculpture. It is not just Ruskin who resurrects the sculpture, or Proust who resurrects Ruskin, or the reader who resurrects Proust: it is also Ruskin who is resurrected in his reading of the sculpture, and the reader who is resurrected by reading Proust. Only print can reproduce this resurrection: the multiplication of readers occasioned by publication, together with the durability of stone, permits the chance encounter of a reader and a text. Many stones go unread; many would-be readers find no texts; on occasion, however, a text finds a reader and both come to life. (p. 99)

37 Claude Simon, *Les Géorgiques* (Paris: Minuit, 1981), pp. 162–3. Jean Duffy persuasively links this imagery in Simon to Poussin's *Et in Arcadia Ego*.

Furthermore this description culminates with a passage which I would interpret as a literary reworking of Poussin's *Et in Arcadia Ego*. Here, the narrator's guide stoops to point out the inscription on the tomb, an inscription that has been partially obliterated by the lichen growing on the stone, and which the 'idiot', like Poussin's shepherd, has to trace out slowly with his finger. (*Reading Between the Lines – Claude Simon and the Visual Arts* (Liverpool: Liverpool University Press, 1998), p. 231)

38 Letter to Frédéric Morin copied by Hugo. Cited in Victor Hugo, 'Dossier des *Misérables*', *Chantiers* (Paris: Robert Laffont, collection Bouquins, 1990), p. 749.

39 *Les Misérables*, p. 277.

40 See Grossman, *Figuring Transcendence*. 'The text thus represents both Hugo's response to his patrimony and his legacy to the future by offering a prototype of the modern prose epic.' (p. 12)

Part II

Modern Ghosts

Chapter Six
Spectral Texts, Spectral Images: *L'Usage de la photo* as Haunted Text

Lynsey Russell-Watts

In their study *Ghosts: Deconstruction, Psychoanalysis, History*, Peter Buse and Andrew Stott comment on the 'unfashionable' nature of their topic compared to the then contemporary rage for aliens and conspiracy theories, but remark that 'Chances are, ghosts will make another comeback'.[1] Any such concern with outmodedness is here subject to a twofold dissipation: while the existence of the present volume speaks to the topic's return to fashion,[2] it can be argued that, in relation to photography and psychoanalysis at least, ghosts never really went away, or, perhaps, never stopped 'coming back'. Annie Ernaux's *L'Usage de la photo* (2005), co-authored with her erstwhile partner, Marc Marie, can be seen as a perfect illustration of the shared concerns of the ghostly and photography, for it revolves around questions of memory, pastness, death, loss, mourning and the trace, and evokes dichotomies of presence/absence, true/false and real/imaginary. Indeed, photography and haunting are frequently drawn together; in modern French literature, we can find plenty of instances where a photograph actually becomes that which haunts a text, as in the case of the absent photo.[3] A similar association can be traced between psychoanalysis and the spectral. The focus of psychoanalysis on the history of the subject, on buried memories, on what we could term the haunting of the subject by her unconscious, underpins its implicit relation to the ghostly. In a similar vein, psycho-analysis acts in this present essay as a latent influence, inseparable from the concerns evoked above, rather than as an explicit theoret-ical focus. It will, however, enable a consideration of the possible therapeutic outcomes both of producing a text such as Ernaux and

Marie's and of engaging with it as a reader/viewer. With the photograph as with the ghost, the decidability and interpretation of its
status and meaning is a multilayered process, resting not just on what
is apparently given to be seen, but also on the viewer and what she
believes is seen, and wants or needs to see. Adding the extra complexities of the reading experience to the viewing one serves only, as I
shall argue is demonstrated by Ernaux's text, to intensify the relationship with the ghostly in the case of the photo-textual. Certainly,
though echoing concerns which regularly form part of Ernaux's
work (autobiography, relationships between men and women, the
memories of her parents), *L'Usage de la photo* worked on me as a
reader in a different and more profound way than her other texts
have done. In part, then, examining this text through the optic of
haunting is an attempt to sketch out and account for the possible
ways in which the reader too can be grabbed – or haunted – by this
text. However, before going on to examine *L'Usage de la photo* and the
questions raised by the formal and thematic hauntings therein, I
want first to provide a framework for this examination by briefly
considering the notion of haunting as theoretical concept.

   The notion of textual haunting does not, as is demonstrated by
Jacques Derrida and critics working from his theorization of
hantologie,[4] necessarily presuppose or imply the presence of the
supernatural or, more specifically, and at risk of sounding
oxymoronic, the actual, substantial presence of a spectral figure. A
haunted text, then, does not have to be one which obviously or
explicitly contains or deals with ghosts. If we focus on haunting as a
metaphor for intertextuality and/or the textual unconscious, there
is of course a degree to which all stories are in some way ghost
stories. As Avery Gordon writes in her book *Ghostly Matters*, 'To write
stories concerning expulsions and invisibilities is to write ghost
stories'.[5] Of course, this demands that we question the usefulness of
a seemingly universal category. What I want to explore here is
whether the notion of haunting can open up something in this text
that might otherwise be hidden, whether it allows connections to be
made between apparently disconnected points of interest. Through
considering haunting in its specific relation to and manifestation in
Ernaux and Marie's work, I hope to demonstrate that it can be
differentiated both from a concept restricted only to those texts
dealing openly in the supernatural and also from one potentially
banal in its general applicability. *L'Usage de la photo*, I would argue,

provides a perfect opportunity for such a conception of haunting: not subject to visitation by ghosts as such, nor obviously dealing in the fantastic, it nevertheless – as a text which is fundamentally hospitable to ghostliness – lends itself to a notion of textual haunting. So, to expand on Gordon's 'expulsions' and 'invisibilities', other features can be included in the notion of the ghostly: echoes, repetitions and returns; intrusions; attempts to deny or arrest death or loss; and the sharply haunting occurrences of the uncanny. What these allow us to do is to conduct a type of archaeology of the text, uncovering layers of creation, meaning and interpretation which might otherwise remain buried. Reading *L'Usage de la photo* through the broad metaphor of haunting, then, serves to enable rather than to confine the reading of the text, since its multiple levels of interconnection are made evident and the text is thereby allowed to resonate within and beyond itself, within and beyond the reader.

This idea of 'resonance' itself recalls Fredric Jameson's intelligent engagement with Derridean hauntology in his 1999 essay, 'Marx's purloined letter', in which he describes the effect of the ghostly as being to call into question the 'density and solidity' of the 'living present'[6] – it is 'what makes the present waver' and is where 'the object world … shimmers like a mirage'.[7] So, resonant, wavering, shimmering, vibrating, vacillating, the present around us becomes, with an awareness of and openness to spectrality, something far more multilayered, multifaceted and complex than we are often ready to acknowledge. This is further compounded by the photo-textual nature of *L'Usage de la photo*, since, as we shall go on to consider further, photography itself, in its enactment of the ghostly dialectics of presence and absence, reality and imaginary, truth and fiction, sits – like the ghost – on the borderline between them. As Gordon, who evokes such layered, resonant, shimmering qualities in her theorization of complex reality and personhood, writes: 'The photograph is involved in the ghostly matter of things and not surprisingly, since the wavering quality of haunting often hinges on what sign or image raises the ghost and what it means to our conscious visible attention.'[8] The photo-text, then, would seem almost necessarily to have a haunted aspect, to be a place in which the resonant, vacillating nature of reality can be apprehended. Where the present analysis differs from the theoretical position of Jameson is in the potential allowed to such a resonant present. In his Derridean-inflected analysis, Jameson argues that hauntology 'serves to underscore the very uncertainties of the spectral itself, which promises nothing tangible in return; on which you cannot build; which cannot even be counted on to materialize when you want it to'.[9] Though accepting the slippery or even, at times, deceptive nature of the spectral, it might not be fair to say that nothing at all can be built upon it. Rather than a flat, solid building surface, what we have instead is a multidimensional, shimmering, wavering present, which offers a density and complexity of thought, emotion and experience. Thus, in a departure from what could be termed the more nihilistic and bleak aspects of Derridean theory, it is possible to build a positive textual relationship on and with the spectral through an experiential and individual engagement with *L'Usage de la photo*.

Written in collaboration with a former partner, Marc Marie, *L'Usage de la photo* consists of an opening prologue and untitled opening chapter, written by Ernaux alone, followed by fourteen co-authored photo-textual chapters. Each co-authored chapter begins with a black-and-white photograph (the only coloured photo in the Gallimard edition is to be found on the wrap-around advertising strip), which provides it with its title (for example, chapter eleven is headed 'Bruxelles, hôtel des Écrins, chambre 125, 6 octobre'). The photograph is then followed with a text by Ernaux and then one from Marie. All dated, the photographs cover a period of just under a year, from March 2003 until January 2004, and follow the course of the authors' relationship and Ernaux's simultaneous treatment for breast cancer. The photographs generally take the form of pictures of Marie's and Ernaux's clothes, left as they were discarded just before lovemaking, though other images occasionally feature.[10] The photographs are not particularly beautiful or artistic but depict everyday objects in everyday settings, albeit in abandoned, ghostly form. This somewhat flat style echoes Ernaux's 'écriture plate'[11] and leaves the principal source of aesthetic value to lie in the interaction of text and photo. Ernaux's segments of text always begin with a description of a photograph, corresponding to the one we have in front of us, but then evoke the time of writing and/or the time of taking the photograph, as well as the memories, thoughts and feelings it recalls and the responses it engenders. Marie's text generally lacks this description, but then branches out in a similar way to, if often in different directions from, the preceding text by Ernaux.

In many ways, *L'Usage de la photo* seems to cover ground already explored by Ernaux in earlier texts. Narratives of loss and bereavement, of grief and mourning, particularly in relation to her parents, play a significant role in Ernaux's *oeuvre*, as does the concurrent concern with the trace and preservation.[12] Indeed, by Ernaux's own admission, 'all her writing is motivated by the same desire to save, to preserve'.[13] Equally, given the increasingly autobiographical mode of her work, the involvement of herself and her own life in this text is not a new development. Thus, in such self-implication, ghosts of real or imagined, past or present selves can be seen as an implicit and integral part of Ernaux's writing. This autobiographical aspect has before extended even to more intimate details: as Lyn Thomas points out in relation to *Passion simple* (1992), Ernaux is concerned with the 'question of the representation of the erotic, and of the link between the experience of sexual passion and literature'.[14] Neither are images of herself as an old woman or the contemplation of her own mortality entirely uncharted territory, as these are a feature of *La Femme gêlée* (1981), *Journal du dehors* (1993) and *Je ne suis pas sortie de ma nuit* (1997). Even the use of photography is not a completely new endeavour, since descriptions of photographs appear in *La Place* (1984), *Une Femme* (1988) and *La Honte* (1997). However, in spite of these similarities, there are several immediately striking ways in which *L'Usage de la photo* can be figured as a new departure in Ernaux's work. The open collaboration, which here extends to co-authorship, seems to divide this text from the rest of the Ernaux corpus, particularly given its concern with its authors' personal history. Moreover, the physical presence of photographs, where in Ernaux's previous work they have been only described or referred to, also sets this photo-text apart from the earlier, purely textual, work. Through its exploration of Ernaux's experience of cancer, *L'Usage de la photo* grapples in a far more explicit way with the author's own mortality and thus with her future trace, her potential ghost. Indeed, all of these distinguishing features intensify the text's possibilities for ghostly echoes. Where on one level the presence of the visual record, as well as the 'corroborating testimony' from another witness/participant, seem to give this text a new way of laying claim to documentary status, both the co-authorship and the photographs will be demonstrated to be part of that which most directly brings this text into the realm of the ghostly. Of course, the very fact that we are reading this text, with its reassuring framing

devices, ensures that we are aware that the worst did not come to
pass for Ernaux; so, in fact, what this text confronts us with is the
ghost of a ghost.

At the beginning of the text, Ernaux explains the genesis of the
project, which began with a photograph Ernaux took one morning
of the shoes and clothes abandoned in the hallway the night before.
Though this, she tells us, was the first time it occurred to her to take
a photograph, she had, since the beginning of the relationship,
been troubled by the tidying away of their things, because 'J'avais
l'impression de supprimer la seule trace objective de notre jouis-
sance'.[15] Marie, Ernaux tells us, then confessed to having a similar
desire to make a photographic record of these 'traces' of their relationship, after which they continued to take the photographs. The
idea to accompany them with text came several months later, by
which time certain rules governing their practice had been set out:
namely, in relation to the photographs, that they would not alter
any of the arrangements of clothing that were photographed – what
we have here is, apparently, 'really reality'. In the same way, their
written contributions, produced at the end, once fourteen photos
had been chosen, would not be shared until the end of the process,
again maintaining a semblance of spontaneity and reality in their
textual responses. Indeed, it is not until the end of the book that
Ernaux tells us that she is about to receive Marie's texts and admits
to some trepidation, but we learn nothing about her reactions when
this actually happened, or of any negotiations or recriminations
which followed. It is not clear when the decision to publish the
photographs and text was taken, or the effect of this on any editorial
decisions, but that such an editorial process did indeed take place is
evident from the start, even though it is not explicitly acknowledged
or discussed. Ernaux tells us that the fourteen included photos are
chosen from a much larger collection: 'M. effectuait généralement
plusieurs prises de vue de la scène, avec des cadrages différents
pour saisir la totalité des choses éparpillées sur le sol.'[16] So, what we
have here is not the 'totalité' of their lives at that point but, rather,
some edited highlights. Textually, the unacknowledged sorting and
editing is immediately apparent from the fact that Marie's texts,
which always follow Ernaux's, never duplicate the work of
describing the photograph that hers have already done.

There are several levels on which this photo-text can be experienced as haunted, whether formal, thematic, or in the inextricable

entwining of the two. The spectre of death is ever present in the text, whether this be the imagined deaths of the protagonists, the actual deaths of those close to them, or, indeed, the death of their relationship. Significantly for this text which tells the history of a love affair, eroticism is immediately connected with death. More importantly, it is bound up in the interplay of life and death, the realm of the ghostly: the epigraph, taken from Georges Bataille, reads 'l'érotisme est l'approbation de la vie jusque dans la mort'.[17] This association of eroticism and death at the outset, which remains a compelling feature due both to the subject matter of the text and to the form of its telling, encourages us to interrogate their relation. Indeed, the trappings of eroticism – the discarded lingerie of the photographs – increasingly seem to evoke death, both because of their lifeless, abandoned state, but also because of the accompanying texts, which tell of the growing coolness of the relationship. As Ernaux points out, her discarded underwear comes more and more to resemble some sort of ideal of seduction, eroticism and femininity, rather than standing as a marker of true passion: the clothing becomes 'Rien d'autre que les accessoires de plus en plus commercialisés et banalisés du théâtre érotique intime'.[18] Paradoxically, then, the more the relationship becomes drained of actual eroticism, the more the participants attempt to raise the ghost of passion spent, with recourse to the accoutrements of a somewhat hackneyed vision of desire. What we find in this text is, then, a female body and sexual relationship haunted by the pressure of its cultural surveillance, haunted by a drive to femininity and desirability.[19]

The interplay of life and death is central to the relationship between Marie and Ernaux, given the treatment for breast cancer which Ernaux was undergoing during the time of their relationship, a disease which is a continual haunting presence in the text. This returns abruptly at certain moments, for example in the formal intrusions into the text, such as the inclusion of factual, technical or statistical information relating to breast cancer, occasional square-bracketed interjections or somewhat out-of-place footnotes.[20] Equally abrupt is the fashion in which Ernaux admits first telling Marie about her illness. As Marie writes: 'Durant plusieurs mois, nous ferons ménage à trois, la mort, A., et moi. Notre compagne était envahissante … Envahissante mais impuissante à *atteindre* notre amour … Et puis, la mort est toujours là.'[21] At various points,

Ernaux alludes to or discusses the experience of facing up to the possibility of her death, which hovers throughout the text: 'comme naguère pour les signes de la jalousie, je voyais ceux de la mort écrits partout'.[22] Additionally, she recounts the attempt to buy herself a plot in the cemetery as well as the experience of visiting Marc's grandparents' grave, where 'j'ai imaginé mon nom à la place, sur la pierre. Je le voyais très bien mais ce n'était pas réel', a moment which can certainly be seen as one of uncannily vacillating reality in the text.[23]

The actuality rather than the possibility of death is further evoked in the textual presence of the authors' dead mothers (though fathers are not utterly absent — one of the cameras used, we are told, to belong to Marie's father).[24] Indeed, an association between the maternal and the spectral can be distinguished more generally in Ernaux's *oeuvre*. Thomas identifies instances of Ernaux connecting the mother with white roses and of seeing the mother as a figure of death, as a 'big, white shadow' or 'the white woman'.[25] The evocation of death comes through describing the somewhat haunted and haunting activity of clearing out Marie's mother's house and selling it after her death. Marie tells us:

> *J'ai conservé, comme A. avec les effets de sa propre mère, une robe, un chemisier, un foulard, des bas, dans un sac qu'il m'arrive d'ouvrir, juste, par le biais de l'odeur – mélange de bois brûlé, de renfermé et d'eau de Cologne à la lavande – pour ce plaisir triste d'être replongé, brutalement, dans le temps où elle était là.*[26]

Ernaux amplifies the ghostly potential of this description by telling us how, in helping Marc go through his mother's things, she has the feeling not only that, though she never met her, she knew Marc's mother, but also that Marc's mother now knows her.[27] To extrapolate the uncanny power of this to the reading-viewing relationship, we are now required to ask of ourselves the extent to which we get to know Ernaux in going through her intimate things, and, thereby, the extent to which she gets to know us: what does it say about us that we are reading this intimate account, raiding the drawers of this relationship? Apart from in these recounted visits to empty, even haunted, houses, the spectre of the mother is most substantial in Marie and Ernaux's trips to Brussels, which remain located in the space of death. The hotel they stay in on their first visit is the same that Marie stayed in on a visit to Brussels whilst mourning his recently deceased mother, and, coincidentally, the same one that Ernaux visited just before her own mother died, lending that city a somewhat haunted aspect in *L'Usage de la photo*.

Significantly for a text located in the space and time of a relationship, the end of that relationship – since it is one which is always already over – is also a ghostly figure in the text, and is something to which Brussels is equally important. From early on there are allusions to the incipient ending; for example, after the first trip to Brussels, which constitutes only the second photo-textual chapter of the book, Marie tells us that Ernaux says to him: 'Le bonheur de Bruxelles, c'est fini.'[28] It is also at this point that Ernaux's insecurities, fears and jealousies – ghostly factors which in themselves threaten the relationship – become apparent: she suspects Marie of going to phone his former partner, when he actually goes to buy flowers, though, as she points out, refusing to allow the ghost of suspicion to evaporate, 'il avait peut-être téléphoné *et* acheté des fleurs'.[29] The second trip to Brussels (in chapter eleven of fourteen) would seem to spell the imminent end of the relationship. Its photograph,[30] for the first time, represents neither a post-coital scene nor discarded clothing, and, in the course of her accompanying text, Ernaux recounts the effect on her of a comment of Marie's – 'd'un seul coup, c'était comme si on ne se connaissait pas'.[31] In the next photograph, tellingly, there is nothing of his visible, an absence of the trace on which they both feel compelled to comment in their accompanying texts.

The recurring absence of traces, in this text which seems to be trying so hard to concretize and capture them, becomes a striking theme, but also a key formal aspect, of *L'Usage de la photo*. There are allusions to the spectrality of the protagonists themselves, in their project, in their relation to each other and in the siting of that relation between life and death – in the 'grandes vacances du cancer'[32] – as here, for example, where Marie compares himself and Ernaux to 'des fantômes en apesanteur, des spectateurs accidentels'.[33] The most remarkable absence, however, is perhaps their bodily absence from the photographs, in which neither Marie nor Ernaux ever appear. This absence is further foregrounded in the prologue, where Ernaux describes a photograph of Marie which we are not shown and for which he provides no text: here, he is triply absent – bodily, visually and textually. Incidentally, this also forms the first occasion of many in the text where allusion is made to a 'missing' photo, to one we are never shown. Of course, these missing photos themselves become extra-textual, ghostly absent-presences which serve to haunt writer, text and reader. This dialectic of presence and absence, familiar and uncanny, which is made explicit here, but in which all photographs, particularly after Barthes, can be seen to engage, sites the photograph in a movement between indexical force and symbolic significance.[34] The photograph, like the ghost, is located on a wavering borderline.

This ghostly power of the photographs in *L'Usage de la photo* is strengthened by the photo-*textual* nature of the project. The relation of text to photo is arguably not as innovative or free floating as it is, for example, in the work of photo-textual narrative artist Sophie Calle, since here the relationship between text and photo is one of supplementation. The photographs alone, it seems, are not enough, as Ernaux writes: 'Comme si ce que nous avions pensé jusque-là être suffisant pour garder la trace de nos moments amoureux, les photos, ne l'était pas, qu'il faille encore quelque chose de plus, de l'écriture.'[35] However, the texts, in their own divergences, do not, in fact, simply explain the photographs, fixing their meaning and thus delimiting their possible resonances, but, rather, bring into being the possibility of multiple memories, fantasies, responses and departures. The addition of text, rather than seizing the trace the photographs missed, serves only to dissipate this trace even further, to elaborate further layers of haunting, making the reading reality waver even more. Ernaux's and Marie's texts, indeed, can be seen to haunt one another: despite the differences in their memories and perspectives on events, there are moments of uncanny convergence, for example in echoed vocabulary or shared associations.[36] And, just as the texts engage in mutual hauntings, so the relation in which the photographs and texts stand to one another can be figured as a spectral one. The texts escape and surpass the photographs, making evident the ghostly presence of the blind field, but neither are the photographs entirely controlled and contained by the texts. The photographs' relation to the reader-viewer is a potentially disturbing one because of the uncanny power of their spectral depictions of empty domesticity, ghostly evocations of presence-absence and their embodiment of a kind of sterile, dead eroticism (what we have here are the remnants, not the thing itself, and the remnants further removed by being photographed). Thus, in trying so hard to stall or fend off death, they succeed only in creating more ghosts, in making absence and loss all the more present. Rather than a trace of presence, these photographs tend more towards a ghostly embodiment of absence and loss, of irretrievable anteriority and of the impossibility of the complete return to a past moment. More than anything, then, what is evoked is the problematic of the ghostly missed encounter, echoed in the relation of text to text, of photo to text, in the reality we are asked to perceive. The existence of any original, 'untainted' reality is itself called into question by the nature of the project: can such apparent impetuousness in ripping off one's clothes before sex *always* be spontaneous, even once it becomes a repeated action destined to be documented? And, just as the dressing and undressing must have happened in the knowledge that the result would be photographed, Ernaux and Marie wrote knowing that their text would be shared, both facts which must have had an impact on the moment of photographing or writing. Therefore, in the same way that the photo-text is haunted by the ghost of its project, by the temporal confusions of being overly concerned with the what-will-have-been, so the reader-viewer is haunted by the unseen, unspoken facets of the project, by the selecting, ordering, editing and negotiation, which must have happened but which go largely unacknowledged and undocumented.

Ultimately, for Ernaux and Marie, the photographs lose their power and the project fails, as they are forced to realize the impossibility of arresting decay, loss and death: Ernaux writes, 'Paradoxe de cette photo destinée à donner plus de réalité à notre amour et qui le déréalise. Elle n'éveille rien en moi. Il n'y a plus ici ni la vie ni le temps. Ici je suis morte.'[37] Once the end of their relationship is imminent, the attempt to preserve it is also doomed. However, these photo-texts only ever portray reality – and it is a spectral, multi-layered, resonant reality – in a highly questionable way for the reader-viewer. It is thus paradoxically possible that at the moment they lose power for Ernaux, they become most hauntingly powerful for us: rather than a ghostly representation of life, they become a substantial representation of the spectre of a love affair. A wavering reality, thus, does not equate to a meaningless reality but, rather, one which enacts a complication of meaning, which demands a personalization of interpretation. Indeed, precisely what this photo-text does is encourage our own intervention, as Ernaux writes: 'nous y voyons justement ce qui n'est pas représenté: ce qu'il s'est passé avant, pendant, et juste après'.[38] Or, even, we see what we imagine or project has happened, which may not be the same as what Ernaux or Marie remember, or what actually happened. This text, therefore, which seems so concerned with seizing visual and textual traces, turns out to be far more about absence than presence. Its empty photographs do not succeed in narrating one history but, rather, document the process of trying to pin down something which was always already ghostly and ungraspable. The trace that remains is that of the attempt to catch hold of a phantom, rather than being a fragment of the essence of the thing itself.

The metaphor of haunting, then, allows us to consider the ghostly intrusions of photo into text, text into photo, text into text, photo-text into the reader-viewer's experience; it provides a framework in which we can place and examine the multilayered interactions between text, photo and reader in *L'Usage de la photo*. Though exploring territory familiar to us from Ernaux's other work, the photo-textual form of this work enacts levels of haunting not apparent elsewhere, levels which allow the text to resonate more intensely with its reader. Far from shutting down imaginative inter-pretation, as visualization of the textual is sometimes accused of doing, the inclusion of these empty, depersonalized photographs of the everyday allows the inscription of the viewer into the text in a deeper way. We are called upon here as reader and as viewer, as witness but also as potential agent: this could be our home, our clothes, our love affair, our photos, and so our feelings, memories and associations. Identifying processes of haunting in these layers permits the visual and textual reality with which we are faced to shimmer and resonate, whilst our impulses to capture and preserve and to fend off death are called into question. In short, we must consider what happens to us and what we are aiming to achieve in writing, photographing, reading or viewing. Enabling this textual archaeology can, in turn, enable a more intense, but more positive, reading relationship, one which allows the reader to develop his or her own shimmering, resonant, spectral encounter with the text. These troubling hauntings, as well as proving potentially therapeutic for Ernaux, writing and working through her experience of cancer, can also be seen to invoke the reader's own ghosts and, thus, to compel a self-examination and working-through parallel to that of the author.[39] Therefore, the mutual hauntings of the reading and writing processes confront us with a reading relation in which we must play an active part: as Gordon argues, 'you have no other choice but to make things up in the interstices of the factual and the fabulous, the place where the shadow and the act converge'.[40] Haunting, then, comes to provide a clarifying optic for viewing the many layers of this text, helping us to unpick both its internal workings and the complexity of the individual reading encounter with it. Rather than burying the text under obfuscating generalities, the ghostly uncovers its specificities. Thus, read through the metaphor of haunting, *L'Usage de la photo* becomes increasingly a ghost story, as the metaphor builds up force, takes on substance and becomes itself an illuminating and enabling spectral presence.

Notes

1   Peter Buse and Andrew Stott, *Ghosts: Deconstruction, Psychoanalysis, History* (Basingstoke: MacMillan, 1999), p. 1.
2   This is not the only example of a current interest in ghosts: see also Mark Alizart and Christophe Kihm (eds), *Fresh Théorie II* (Paris: Éditions Léo Scheer, 2006), Colin Davis, '*État présent*: hauntology, spectres and phantoms', *French Studies*, 59, 3 (July 2005), 373–9, and Jean-Bertrand Pontalis, *Traversée des ombres* (Paris: Gallimard, 2003), to choose from several possible examples.
3   I am thinking here of instances of missing photos (of photographs absent, lost or imagined which play a founding role in the text), which can be found, notably, in the work of Roland Barthes (*La Chambre claire*, 1980), Régine Detambel (*Album*, 1995), Marguerite Duras (*L'Amant*, 1984), Anne-Marie Garat (*Photos de familles*, 1994), Hervé Guibert (*L'Image fantôme*, 1981), Patrick Modiano (*Dora Bruder*, 1997) and Marie Nimier (*La Reine du silence*, 2004). They are, of course, also a feature of some of Ernaux's earlier texts, such as *La Place* (1984) or *Une Femme* (1988), and, as shall be discussed more fully later, the first chapter of *L'Usage de la photo* is missing its photo.
4   While this essay will not provide a detailed discussion of Derrida's concept of *hantologie*, readers wishing further expansion could consult, *inter alia*, Jacques Derrida, 'Fors: Les mots anglés de Nicolas Abraham et Maria Torok', preface to Nicolas Abraham and Maria Torok, *Le Verbier de l'homme aux loups* (Paris: Flammarion, 1999, first published 1976), pp. 7–73; and Michael Sprinker (ed.), *Ghostly Demarcations: A Symposium on Jacques Derrida's 'Specters of Marx'* (London/New York: Verso, 1999); as well as Davis, '*État présent*'. Indeed, though there has not been space for a fuller discussion of it here, further exploration of Abraham and Torok's work on transgenerational communication and the spectrality of psychic inheritance could prove fruitful here, given the force of the ancestral spectres in the text, which we shall go on to examine in relation to the maternal figure.

5   Avery F. Gordon, *Ghostly Matters: Haunting and the Sociological Imagination* (Minneapolis/London: University of Minnesota Press, 1997), p. 17.
6   Fredric Jameson, 'Marx's purloined letter', in Sprinker (ed.), *Ghostly Demarcations*, pp. 26–67 (p. 39).
7   Ibid., p. 38.
8   Gordon, *Ghostly Matters*, p. 102.
9   Jameson, 'Marx's purloined letter', pp. 38–9.
10 The photograph dated 6 October, for example, shows a lightbulb covered with a makeshift shade – a flannel wash-glove over a tumbler – while that of 5 April documents the objects knocked from Ernaux's desk in the course of lovemaking. That of 10 March contains aspects of both types: it shows a hotel room in morning-after disarray, where clothes are only some of the objects visible.
11 See Lyn Thomas's useful full-length study of the writer, *Annie Ernaux: An Introduction to the Writer and Her Audience* (Oxford/New York: Berg, 1999), p. 38.
12 This concern for developing and leaving traces is discussed by Thomas in *Annie Ernaux*, p. 178, where we can also see that the creation of images as a trace of a sexual relationship has an antecedent in Ernaux's work in *Fragments autour de Philippe V* (see Thomas, *Annie Ernaux*, Appendix 1, pp. 177–9, for a complete, though translated, reproduction of this text).
13 Ibid., p. 24.
14 Ibid., p. 18.
15 Annie Ernaux and Marc Marie, *L'Usage de la photo* (Paris: Gallimard, 2005), p. 9.
16 Ibid., p. 10.
17 Ibid., p. 7.
18 Ibid., p. 137.
19 Many thanks to Shirley Jordan for allowing me to read an unpublished paper in which she makes this point.
20 A number of footnotes appear in Ernaux's contributions to the text, mostly in the first sections of the book, but also at the end. Although there is one which comments on the use of the term 'argentique' to describe pre-digital cameras, they relate mostly to aspects of her experience of cancer treatment. One example, discussing the wearing of wigs, reads: 'À vrai dire, davantage un signe, celui du cancer, comme le foulard, celui de la religion islamique. D'où l'abandon de l'un et de l'autre comme purs accessoires de mode féminine, qu'ils ont été jusqu'à la chimiothérapie et au développement de l'islam' (Ernaux and Marie, *L'Usage de la photo*, p. 37). As for the square-bracketed comments, several of them appear in the first two-thirds of the text. Their status is unclear, but they seem to constitute later additions to the text, for example, as here:

> J'ai longtemps vu traîner un *Madame Figaro* où figurait sur la couverture une fille aux seins nus sous une robe en voile. Il y avait écrit en gros caractères OSEZ LA TRANSPARENCE! En France, 11% des femmes ont été, sont atteintes d'un cancer du sein … Trois millions de seins

couturés, scannerisés, ... irradiés, reconstruits ... Il faudra bien oser les montrer un jour, en effet. [Écrire sur le mien participe de ce dévoilement.] (Ernaux and Marie, *L'Usage de la photo*, p. 84.)

21   Ibid., p. 76.

22   Ibid., p. 26. The other ghost evoked here is that of *L'Occupation* (2002), where jealousy is a key theme.

23   Ibid., p. 111.

24   Ibid., p. 11. Of course, as mentioned above, the lives of Ernaux's parents, her relationships with them and mourning for them form the basis of other works, namely *La Place* (1984), *Une Femme* (1988), *Je ne suis pas sortie de ma nuit* (1997) and *La Honte* (1997), so the importance of these 'family ghosts' connects us not only to Ernaux's own life, and to similar experiences the reader may have had, but also to the textual ghosts of these other books.

25   Thomas, *Annie Ernaux*, pp. 94–5.

26   Ernaux and Marie, *L'Usage de la photo*, p. 95.

27   Ibid., p. 73.

28   Ibid., p. 42.

29   Ibid., p. 36; Ernaux's italics.

30   It is the first photograph described in n. 10 above.

31   Ibid., p. 120.

32   Ibid., p. 55.

33   Ibid., p. 77. This is the text's only explicit reference to 'fantômes'.

34   Of course, in Barthes (*La Chambre claire: Note sur la photographie* (Paris: Cahiers du Cinéma/Gallimard/Seuil, 1980)), the principal way in which a ghostly power could be attributed to the photograph would be through the *punctum* operating in tension with the *studium*, a dialectic alluded to by Gordon (*Ghostly Matters*, p. 105–8) in her reading of the haunting powers of photography. Further exploration would certainly be possible of the ways in which Ernaux and Marie seem to invite such discussion at several points.

35   Ernaux and Marie, *L'Usage de la photo*, p. 12.

36   Compare, for example, their texts accompanying 'La chaussure dans le séjour, 15 mars', where Marie's boot is said to 'piétine' Ernaux's bra (ibid., pp. 45 and 48), or the echoed image in 'Dans le bureau, 5 avril', where the game 'Mikado' is recalled for both of them in the spilled pencil pot (ibid., pp. 63 and 66).

37   Ibid., p. 146.

38   Ibid., p. 95.

39   Ernaux's use of writing as therapy is discussed in Thomas, *Annie Ernaux*, pp. 42–3, where she also suggests (pp. 129–30), from her analysis of readers' letters, that it has some therapeutic benefit for them, as well as being a potentially challenging process: 'Ernaux's writing can be disturbing, as well as beneficial' (p. 130).

40   Gordon, *Ghostly Matters*, p. 197.

Chapter Seven
Sans soleil and the Ghost of the Image

Jean-Xavier Ridon
Translated by Suzanne Dow

In his analysis of photography in *La Chambre claire*, Roland Barthes clearly establishes the link between what is represented in the photographic image and the notion of the ghost.[1] In looking at a photograph, the viewer is confronted with the realization of a 'Cela a été'[2] in which a moment from the past is referenced and which the photograph has set down on paper. One of the three 'pratiques' that Barthes discerns in the act of photographing, in addition to those of *Operator* and *Spectator*, is that of the *Spectrum*, which he defines in the following terms:

> *Et celui ou cela qui est photographié, c'est la cible, le référent, sorte de petit simulacre, d'eidôlon émis par l'objet, que j'appellerais volontiers le Spectrum de la photographie, parce que ce mot garde à travers sa racine un rapport au 'spectacle' et y ajoute cette chose un peu terrible qu'il y a dans toute photographie: le retour du mort.*[3]

The photograph thus offers up to the viewer's gaze an object that already belongs to the past, but which can come back to haunt the present at any time from the moment at which it draws and holds our gaze. What photography shares with the ghost is its fundamental characteristic of referencing an absence – what I am seeing here no longer is – but which it brings into being through what Susan Sontag calls a 'pseudo-presence'.[4] In this we can recognize the traditional image of ghostliness – namely that of a being no longer with us, who therefore always confronts us with her or his absence, a void, but who goes on haunting the present through an insubstantial manifestation of her or himself. This being is therefore there without being there, since her or his presence takes us back to a time now gone by. The ghost is thus always a trace of an object or person now disappeared, whose imprint is left behind on the flow of time. Elsewhere Barthes and Sontag establish a distinction between the cinematographic and photographic image based on the opposition between the movement of one and the immobility of the other. Of this, Sontag writes: 'Photographs may be more memorable than moving images, because they are a neat slice of time, not a flow.'[5] And yet we can clearly detect in Sontag's very hesitation the fact that the moving image itself, and in spite of the form of reactualization that it implies, also reproduces the spectral dimension – that is, this moving image also refers to a time when the camera captured an image in order to fix it in a mode of representation that is destined to remain unchanged. The relationship to the ghost and to death is similar, despite the illusion of life rendered by the movement.

It is this cinematographic spectre that I would like to analyse in this essay. Indeed, Chris Marker in his 1986 film, *Sans soleil*, elaborates his film's reflection on cinema, memory and travel, taking as his starting point a scene filmed in Iceland, of three children walking on a hill, and which, the film's narrator tells us, represents for him an image of happiness:

> La première image dont il m'avait parlé, c'est celle de trois enfants sur une route, en Islande, en 1965. Il me disait que c'était pour lui l'image du bonheur, et aussi qu'il avait essayé plusieurs fois de l'associer à d'autres images – mais ça n'avait pas marché.[6]

The entirety of the film is from this point onwards haunted by this preliminary image of a moment lost in time that the narrator seeks to offer up exactly as he experienced it at the moment at which it was captured on film. He is thus attempting to reactualize this scene by reproducing the feeling of happiness with which it is associated for him. One of the questions that Marker's film asks is that of knowing how to summon the ghost, which is to say what it would take to endow these images with their full significance. In terms of cinematographic language, Marker wonders how to connect this moment with other images that could restore its original meaning. As we can see from this, the image of the ghost is inseparable from a reflection on memory, which manifests itself in two distinct forms.

First, the filmed scene as object represents the memory of a moment that each screening will serve to reactualize. This is the cinematographic image working at the level of the document, where an imprinted image, regardless of the medium, and whoever the viewer might be, will always reappear as self-identical. In this sense, the documentary image bears direct relation to the idea of witnessing and truth. On the other hand, there is also the memory of the person who lies behind the recording of this image or scene that confronts us with a mental, subjective image which is itself not fixed. Indeed, this subjective memory follows the dynamic belonging to the phenomenon of forgetting that distances the image from the moment when it was imprinted, and which has aroused the memory. Here I am attempting to distinguish between the ghost as an objective document of a past which fails to speak to us in the absence of a reading (a gaze), and the ghost as a form of haunting of a past moment within a subjectivity. What Marker is interested in is indeed this latter form of haunting, rather than engaging in any act of 'témoignage'. His film calls to be read as an attempt to bring together these ghosts, these traces that the narrator has accumulated in the course of his travels to Japan, in Africa, and in the Cape Verde, so as to elaborate a reflection on the relationships between memory and the image. In this sense, one of the questions raised by the film is that of finding out how to link the visual traces of past moments in such a way as for the cineaste's experience to take on meaning. The film is looking for an uneasy balance to be struck between the necessity of bearing witness and the desire to express the subjective traces that the images have left behind in their wake, and where I would locate the dimension of the ghost. In essence, Marker is trying to lend meaning to these few images by which he is haunted.

The ghost may be a presence that does not speak on its own. As a silent and spectral presence, whoever perceives it will project onto it her or his own fears and uncertainties as to the reality of this presence, but also her or his anxieties surrounding death and the inexorable march of time. The meaning attributed to the ghost thus depends very much on the nature of the gaze directed towards it. Transposed onto the level of the recorded images of the documentary film, it is generally the gaze of the film-maker that comes to order the images presented, and thus that gives them a particular orientation and meaning. And yet, in *Sans soleil*, Marker, even as he remains master of his own film, is looking for a means to avoid imposing a definitive meaning on his images, attempting to leave them an interpretive margin so that they might haunt all the more the memory of the viewer.

The ghost and the interstice

One of the primary techniques used by Marker to effect this opening up of the meaning of the documentary image is to create at times a split between the film's commentary and the image. The commentary is not always an explanation of the image, and nor is the image always an illustration of the commentary. This becomes clear at the moment at which, after the vision of the three children in Iceland, there appears the image of an American fighter plane on an aircraft carrier that seems to take the viewer back to the Vietnam war. And yet the relationship between these two images is never explained. In the same year as *Sans soleil* was released, Chris Marker published a book entitled *Le Dépays* containing text and images dealing with the representation of Japan. In his notes for the reader, Marker makes the following statement, which may also be applied to the relationship between text and image in *Sans soleil*:

> *Le texte ne commente pas plus les images que les images n'illustrent le texte.*
> *Ce sont deux séries de séquences à qui il arrive bien évidemment de se croiser*
> *et de se faire signe, mais qu'il serait fatigant d'essayer de confronter. Qu'on*
> *veuille donc bien les prendre dans le désordre, la simplicité et le dédoublement,*
> *comme il convient de prendre toutes choses au Japon.*[7]

If I take haunting here as a form of reference that runs between one linguistic element and another, Marker then effects two kinds of dissociation: the first between commentary and image that no longer directly correspond, the second between the meaning of the perceived images and what the film-maker is trying to make them say. One question we may therefore ask here is whether or not the ghost always bears a logical relation to the space it haunts. Does haunting not come from a form of dissociation between the ghost and its location, which would be the cause of a certain failure of understanding? The site of the ghost is after all the interstice, the in-between: it belongs to one world but appears in another, it represents a dead person, but one whom it presents as living. On a more metaphorical level I would also locate it in this significatory uncertainty generated by Marker.

The ghost and fiction

This uncertainty pertaining to the images presented in the film is pushed still further by the fact that it is Marker himself as cineaste and author of the film who enters into a movement of spectralization. Indeed, Marker seems to want to become the ghost of his own film, at once present and rendered absent by a certain difficulty entailed in identifying or locating him. As Barbara Lemaitre and later Catherine Lupton have suggested, one of *Sans soleil*'s characteristics is the multiplicity of voices found within it.[8] The most important voice in terms of presence, given that it is the one that makes up the greater part of the film's commentary, is that of a character named Sandor Krasna. Krasna sends letters addressed to a woman which are read to us, and it is these readings aloud of Krasna's letters that constitute the majority of the commentary. Nothing, moreover, is ever revealed about the identity of Sandor Krasna, whose name we learn only when it appears in the closing credits. On a first viewing of the film, Krasna's letters are therefore read with the author remaining shrouded in anonymity; all we know here is that someone is speaking. The film sets up a gap between the female recipient of the letters and Krasna, which the letter-writing reinforces with the frequent repetition of the phrase 'Il m'écrivait' within the commentary. The two narrative agents simultaneously draw us into the realm of fiction. Sandor Krasna is a film-making traveller who can be considered Marker's double who sets himself up as the author of *Sans soleil* given that it is his name that appears in the credits under the heading 'composition et l'image'. Krasna's name also appears in the credits as the author of the letters that are read out. Marker thus places a question mark over the reality of Krasna's identity, who seems to hover somewhere between reality and fiction. The addressee of the letters within the film takes the form of the voice of actress Florence Delay, whose voice-over reading of the letters apprises us of their content. Once again, Marker here forces us to make the distinction between the voice we hear and the possible identity of the letters' addressee(s). We might well wonder at the reasons behind Marker's introducing this narrator's voice, when Marker could just as well have read or commentated the film's images. The most obvious answer is that this enables him to fictionalize the voice of documentary itself. These fictionalizations of the various narrating agencies create a certain distance between Marker's project and documentary proper. Within what is conventionally understood as documentary, the author of the film is usually the one who puts his name to the commentary. Furthermore, even when it allows others to speak through interviews or other documents, documentary offers narrative voices that are immediately identifiable. These voices become the guarantee for the veracity of the document produced, by lending authority to the information provided.

Through such practices, Marker becomes the ordering, ghostly presence who is at once present and difficult to locate. Marker thus distances himself from a form of authority that would impose a definitive meaning upon the images presented. He introduces an element of floating within the image, whose meaning can take a number of different directions. The ghost is thus here directly linked to the idea of fiction, by participating in a fictionalization of reality. At the same time, the ghost enables a form of disappropriation to the extent that the visual memory that it offers is no longer attached to a single subjectivity. Thus Marker puts in place a spectral subject who leaves more room for the images' possible meanings. Still following the metaphor of the ghost, the subject has to spectralize itself so as to give back to the ghost of the recorded image a possible voice. In this sense, Marker himself has to give back a form of visibility to what had thus far remained hidden.

Making the visible invisible

Indeed, at several points in the film the narrator apprises us of his desire to represent forms of invisibility. He speaks, for example, of the 'dropouts' of the Japanese economic system, those failed individuals who have not proved able to find their place within Japanese society and who end up turning to alcohol for solace:

> *Comment prétendre représenter une catégorie de Japonais qui n'existe pas? Oui, ils sont là, je les ai vus à Osaka se louer à la journée, dormir à même le sol, ils sont voués depuis le Moyen Âge aux tâches malpropres et ingrates, mais depuis l'ère Meiji rien officiellement ne les distingue et leur nom véritable, les Etas, est un mot tabou, imprononçable. Ils sont des non-personnes, comment les montrer sinon sous la forme de non-images?*[9]

But of what might a 'non-image' consist? For even as these people have no name, they are altogether real and literally haunt the streets of the cities of Tokyo and Osaka. What we are dealing with here are ghosts who represent a space of invisibility but within the order of representation. They are not represented in order that they might better be forgotten, as if they were the incarnation of the bad conscience of a society that exploits them without knowing what to do with them. Marker thus wants to give these forgotten individuals their place, to offer them a space of representation that becomes a sign of acknowledgement of their existence. The spectralization of the subject also enables this, namely an act of giving body to a form of social repression. Thus the ghost of an unsaid or hidden reality is transformed into an image by the film-maker's gaze. It is thereby integrated into the memorial space of cinematographic representation and thus participates in the element of ghostliness that is part of any image – that is, Marker prevents it from disappearing altogether. Here I would distinguish between two forms of ghost: a ghost, on the one hand, that represents a form of negation on the part of a society that does not want to confront its own problems and which is therefore invisible in a form of unsaid; and a ghost, on the other, that constitutes the passing of this invisibility into the film-maker's gaze and which therefore finds a space of representation that will prevent its disappearance.

The ghost's gaze

In wanting to restore a certain autonomy to the ghost, Marker also attempts to give it back a gaze. Indeed, the ghost is not only someone or something to be looked at and interpreted, but is also in possession of a gaze of its own. This is observable from the very first scene with the three children in Iceland. The children present themselves full-square to the camera and smile. The narrator returns several times to this idea of an 'égalité des regards', which he had already discovered in the Japanese 'dropouts': 'J'ai payé la tournée au bistrot Namidabaski: ce genre d'endroit permet l'égalité des regards.'[10] These moments are those when the gaze that he directs at others with the camera is returned by the others themselves, and the narrator seems to await these moments when he becomes the object of others' attention. One such example is the exchange of gazes that he describes between himself and a woman

at the market at Bissau in Cape Verde, and which he relates to a
game of seduction:

> *C'est sur le marché de Bissau au Cap-Vert que j'ai retrouvé l'égalité du
> regard, et cette suite de figures si proches du rituel de la séduction: Je la vois –
> elle m'a vu – elle sait que je la vois – elle m'offre son regard, mais juste l'angle
> où il est encore possible de faire comme s'il ne s'adressait pas à moi – et pour
> finir le vrai regard, tout droit qui a duré 1/25 de seconde, le temps d'une
> image.*[11]

What we have here is a moment of recognition between a subject
and his object. In being looked at, however, the cineaste opens up
to the possibility of himself becoming an image. And yet, as we can
see from watching the film, this 'égalité du regard' will not be
directly offered, since in order for this to occur the woman being
filmed on the marketplace would have had to have been given a
camera herself which would have given us an image of Marker. In
the absence of this image, Marker is allowed to escape his own
representation – in this sense, and in spite of his desire to spectralize himself, he retains mastery over his text/film.

There are, however, moments of dispossession of the gaze and
where the narrator-director is not the only master of his vision.
These moments are not only linked to the emergence of the gaze of
others but to the very power of images which, in their own way, have
a certain capacity for inversion. The narrator notes this with respect
to the posters he sees around Tokyo representing cartoon characters: 'et ces visages géants dont on sent peser le regard – car les
voyeurs d'images sont vus à leur tour par des images plus grandes
qu'eux'; or when he watches images flashing across his television
screen: 'Mais plus on regarde la télévision japonaise plus on a le
sentiment d'être regardé par elle.'[12] Here, though, the inversion of
the gaze is not the sign of a mutual recognition as in the meeting of
two gazes, but the narrator's increasing awareness of being himself
an image in a world of images. The omnipresence of images breaks
down the boundaries between reality and its representation and the
risk that Krasna realizes he is running is that of being dispossessed
of his own vision – just as he occasionally has the feeling of being
dispossessed of his own dreams: 'Je commence à me demander si ces
rêves sont bien à moi, ou s'ils font partie d'un ensemble, d'un gigan-
tesque rêve collectif dont la ville toute entière serait la projection.'[13]

The danger that Krasna discovers, and which concerns our modern world, is of finding oneself inhabiting a world populated only by ghosts, in a place where all individuals would be transformed into an image, immediately integrated into a form of representation, with no more referential relationship to the real world itself than this. At the same time as adding to Barthes's analysis the idea that images also look at us, Marker here denounces the limits of a virtual world, or what Baudrillard would term a world containing only semblances, a hyperreality with all direct relation to the world and to objects lost. Thus, to take photographs is also to be taken by them, to open oneself up to the possibility of being dispossessed by what they have to show us and which exceeds the photographer's original intention. The ghost would thus lose its coherence by losing what most allows it to signify, namely its memory.

Indeed, Marker shows us that in order for the ghost to retain this capacity to look it must above all be linked to a memory – to memory as a return to the context where the photographic image was taken, but also to the memory of the person who took it. And, yet, the defining characteristic of memory is never to be self-identical. In opposition to the image that represents a moment fixed in time, the memory is caught in a mechanism of change that is part of the dynamics of forgetting. As our narrator notes: 'Les mémoires doivent se contenter de leur dérive, de leur délire. Un instant arrêté grillerait comme l'image d'un film bloqué devant la fournaise d'un projecteur.'[14] The ghost must not be fixed in time or space but be caught in a dynamic of remembrance that presupposes its becoming different from itself.

Thus, in order for the ghost to become truly significant for Marker, it must not simply be put back in its original context, at this first moment when it became inscribed within the traveller's subjectivity, but be linked to other ghosts that will make it speak differently. It is within this associative process, in the way in which the film's images begin to haunt one another, that they succeed in elaborating their own meaning whilst simultaneously suggesting this space of the invisible that remains within the realm of that which can never be represented, but which the film's images constantly suggest.

Notes

1   Roland Barthes, *La Chambre claire, Œuvres complètes*, III (Paris: Seuil, 1993).

2   In his article 'Rhétorique de l'image' (1964), Barthes writes: 'la photographie installe, en effet, non pas une conscience de l'être-là de la chose (que toute copie pourrait provoquer), mais une conscience de l'avoir-été-là' (in *Œuvres complètes*, I (Paris: Seuil, 1993), p. 1424).

3   *La Chambre claire*, p. 1114.

4   Susan Sontag, *On Photography* (London: Penguin, 1973), p. 16.

5   Ibid., p. 17.

6   Commentary of *Sans soleil*, published by the cinema review, *Trafic*, 6 (spring 1993), (Paris, POL), p. 79. All references are to this edition.

7   Chris Marker, *Le Dépays* (Paris: Herscher, 1982). This text has no pagination.

8   Barbara Lemaitre, 'Sans soleil, le travail de l'imaginaire', in Philippe Dubois (ed.), *Théorème 6, Recherches sur Chris Marker* (Paris: Presse Sorbonne Nouvelle, 2002). All essays within this volume are recommended reading, each giving a detailed analysis of the various aspects of Marker's work. See also Catherine Lupton, *Chris Marker: Memories of the Future* (London: Reaktion Books, 2005).

9   *Sans soleil*, p. 88. Elsewhere, Marker talks about the people of Cape Verde, whom everyone has forgotten, he says, and whom he characterizes in these terms: 'Peuple du rien, peuple du vide, peuple vertical' (p. 86).

10 Ibid., p. 80.

11 Ibid., p. 85. Elsewhere in the film, Marker says of the photographic gaze: 'Franchement, a-t-on jamais rien inventé de plus bête que de dire aux gens, comme on l'enseigne dans les écoles de cinéma, de ne pas regarder la caméra?' (p. 80)

12 Ibid., pp. 82 and 83.

13 Ibid., p. 87.

14 Ibid., p. 90.

Chapter Eight
Spectres of Substance: François Ozon and the Aesthetics of Embodied Haunting

Andrew Asibong

A persistently spectral dimension of existence, a dimension endowed with a palpable power to invade and infect real life, hovers over the cinematic universe of French film-maker François Ozon (born 1967), no matter with which genre the film in question is loosely aligned. In his existential drama *Le Temps qui reste* (2005), a young photographer is dogged by ghostly apparitions of himself as a child, together with the ever-nearing spectre of his own imminent death from an implacable cancer. In his psychological portrait of the contemporary marriage relation *5x2* (2004), the reversed-narrative time structure creates an effect whereby the couple is haunted throughout the film by the future death of their fragile love. In the thriller *Swimming Pool* (2003), a female crime writer is policed at a distance by the spectral authority of her absent publisher and lover. In Ozon's musical melodrama *8 femmes* (2002), eight women spin hysterically around the barely perceptible presence of the apparently dead father and master of the household, a shadowy Papa who rules more despotically from the murder-bed than he ever did when alive. In the film-maker's sombre analysis of mourning and melancholia *Sous le sable* (2001), a female academic is regularly visited by the perhaps imaginary ghost of her inexplicably missing husband. In the modern-day fairy tale *Les Amants criminels* (1999), a fleeing murderous teenage couple are captured by an ogre-like woodsman who forces them to cohabit with the dug-up, wide-eyed corpse of the boy they have just killed. In Ozon's comedy of transgression *Sitcom* (1998), a mother and her two teenage children are bewitched by the bewilderingly unresponsive father of the family and his magical pet rat, before being eventually confronted by the rat's malevolent ghost, metamorphosed into gigantic form and conflated with the soul of the father himself. In the hour-long exercise in menace *Regarde la mer* (1997), a diffident young mother is literally enchanted by a mysterious, coercive and invasive young female traveller who appears to have crawled out of the grave itself, a ghoulish creature who will ultimately butcher her and abduct her child. In the short family melodrama *La Petite Mort* (1995), a young photographer is subjugated by his own desire to capture traces of paternal death and onanistic ecstasy on film, to generate solidly photographic panoplies of orgasmic ghosts. And in Ozon's graduating film, the fourteen-minute piece *Victor* (1993), an awkward young man is haunted by his gruesomely present dead parents, whom he has himself recently killed, and with whose cadavers he sleeps nightly.

Ozon's world is brimming over, then, with ghostly entities of all shapes and sizes. His ghosts tend to arise as deathly clusters of trauma, emotion and authority, outlandish invaders into the apparently controlled universe of the hypersensitive protagonists, simultaneously fear- and desire-inducing creatures that simply will not be laid to rest. Sometimes, as in *Sitcom*, the ghost-figure emerges in the context of a preposterous eruption of fantastical transformation within the narrative. Elsewhere, as in *Sous le sable*, the ghost that at first appears genuinely supernatural eventually becomes reducible within the narrative's logic to a nebulous amalgamation of neurosis and psychosis within the protagonist. And, in a film like *5x2*, there is no true, graspable ghost to speak of, just an unbearable sensation of a horror already witnessed but always *à venir*, which settles over the viewer after the first few minutes like an obscene and oppressive shroud. My purpose in this essay is to wrestle with Ozon's omnipresent ghosts, to tease them out where they are less visible, to stand them next to one another, and accordingly to assess how crucially different their operation is from film to film. These ghosts all seem to emerge from the same place, from that cave of the unconscious, the unspoken and the unrepresented that seems to give birth to the vast majority of Western culture's spectres. Their diverse means of expression from film to film, however, has serious implications for the extent to which a given film can be said to work as an exorcizing machine. From my rapid opening survey of Ozon's remarkably prolific output over the last decade or so, a pattern can be discerned. In the more recent films, spectrality, as a rule, is an insubstantial, evanescent, abstract affair, the characters never quite making contact with the haunting presences that nevertheless structure their lives, fears and desires. The further back in the filmography we move, however, the more concrete, horrific and upsettingly tangible the films' hauntings become. The living characters (and fascinated spectators) are forced, as we go back towards these earlier films, into an increasingly promiscuous (at times unthinkable) cohabitation with the ghost figure. I want to explore (looking backwards) the implications of Ozon's gradual progression from embodied, all too disgustingly corporeal spectres in his early films towards the weightlessness of purely abstract hauntings in the more recent work. The move seems to have become synonymous with a critically acclaimed coming-of-age widely considered to have thankfully supplanted Ozon's youthful need to provoke at any cost. I want to suggest, however, that Ozon's 'de-horrifying' of his cinematic spectres may be interpreted as, in many senses, a retrograde move in both aesthetic and ethical terms.

Le Temps qui reste opened in France in November 2005 to generally admiring reviews. The film's sombre tracking of the last few weeks on Earth of the dying young photographer Romain (Melvil Poupaud) is certainly masterful in its creation of a constant tone of unremitting misery. More than a little reminiscent of the bleak 1963 Louis Malle film *Le Feu follet* (right down to its use of a resplendent Jeanne Moreau in cameo), the film is structured around a series of essentially failed encounters between Romain and various others, both real and spectral. From the film's opening sequence of Romain furiously photographing a pair of vacantly, vapidly ungraspable models, Ozon offers us little hope for Romain's capacity, in this life at least, to bridge the ever-widening chasm between himself and fellow humans, living or dead. Within this film's universe, everywhere, at the heart of every relation, sewn into every circumstance, lurks the certain impossibility of sustained or successful intimacy between individuals. Romain tears at his sister's attempts at love with a lupine ferocity, and rejects his dewy-eyed German boyfriend's emotion with equally perplexing wrath. With his gruff, guardedly tender, bearded father, the painfulness of the relation is more difficult to describe: in the one protracted scene the two men have together the dynamic is simultaneously loving, disappointed and full of a disquieting longing. Later, the film seems to set up the possibility of something more promising offering itself to Romain in the form of the love of his aged, solitary, irresponsible grandmother (played by Moreau), an apparently more acceptable living presence only because she too, as Romain brutally puts it to her, 'va bientôt mourir'. Even her offer to stay with him until the end is rejected by our hero, however, in favour of absolute solitude. The shadowy unreality of the inarticulate, childless, married couple with whom Romain has sex, and for whom he fathers a potential baby, presents itself as one more possibility for relation, but one which is, again, not really viable: they are only interested in each other and the new foetus, and he, Romain, is going to die in any case.

As out of Romain's reach as all these humans (and there are others: his doctor, his boss, a man glimpsed in the backroom of a sex club) are the various ghosts that increasingly posit themselves throughout the film as one final potential source of relation. These spectres sporadically reveal themselves to Romain and the spectator as fleeting ambassadors of a foreclosed dimension. The apparitions of little boy Romain and his little girl sister, little boy Romain and a little boy friend and, most relentlessly and most hauntingly, little boy Romain all alone, hint at the poignant (remembered? fantasized?) potential for ephemeral communion, yet remain either oblivious to the adult Romain's nostalgic gaze or, in the case of the lone child, are able only to stare back kindly but impenetrably. *Le Temps qui reste* goes beyond Malle's *Feu follet* in its existential nihilism, then, presenting its isolated protagonist with a wider ontological range of encounters, but with apparently no possibility of satisfying rapport, whether sexual, familial or spiritual. The film's dancing phantoms of the past will not, in the manner of those encountered by the old professor of Bergman's *Wild Strawberries* (1957), lead to something like enlightenment and communication with the living, but will remain ungraspable and destined to remain mockingly out of reach. Living sisters, mothers, fathers, employers, lovers, doctors, grandmothers and strangers are on the same bleakly unapproach-able continuum as the spectral entities structuring Romain's radically alienated unconscious. The overwhelming shadow of rapidly approaching death itself will not be tamed, not in this film at any rate, by either protagonist's or spectator's insight into the world of the living, the dead or anything in between. The spectres compound the gap separating Romain from his various others; they merely haunt. In the film's final moments the tousle-haired Romain-ghost-child will skip ruefully away, and Romain himself will die with only the setting sun for company.

Le Temps qui reste and its depressing dynamic of a frustrating, fruit-less, insubstantial pseudo-haunting, destined to isolate an already 'on-the-edge' protagonist once and for all from all possibility of interaction with either the living or the dead, continues a cycle of abstractly spectral films begun in 2001 with Ozon's first bona fide critical and commercial success, *Sous le sable*. In this film Charlotte Rampling's middle-aged English academic Marie ends up, like Romain, alone on a beach, chasing a far-off and tantalizingly out-of-reach male shape. Whilst the phantom figure remains obscure in these final frames, the spectator is in little doubt as to its identity. Marie has been haunted throughout the film by the laconic appar-ition of her inexplicably missing husband Jean (Bruno Cremer). Unable truly to touch him when he was with her in life, she is no more easily able to gain access to the phantom that returns to her. Before Jean's disappearance, early scenes of the couple eating plain pasta in silence and going straight to sleep at bedtime suggested the essentially non-communicative nature of an otherwise comfortable-looking marriage, a suspicion confirmed by our later discovery of Marie's ignorance of Jean's diagnosed clinical depression. When, post-disappearance, the *revenant* Jean comes back to Marie in her Paris apartment, he is as frustratingly distant as ever he was, content merely to watch Marie in her ˙bed from the doorway and to exchange brief banalities with her at breakfast before she goes to work. The monosyllabic, inexpressive ghost of the husband fails, then, to push things forward in the way creatures from another dimension so often do in supernatural dramas, and seems to exist in the film as quite simply a dull perpetuation of his fat, bored and rather boring living self.[1] The actual function of this intangible cipher, we slowly realize, is to structure and perpetuate Marie's failure to engage with the new sexual and professional opportun-ities around her. Brutally rejecting the apparently genuine courtship of handsome, intelligent and highly promising suitor Vincent (Jacques Nolot), retreating from her well-meaning friends and increasingly uncommunicative with her students, Marie flees human connection with an ever-sharpening anxiety. And, exactly as with Romain, it is to the inhabitants of an evanescent spirit world

that she looks for solace and whom she demands as the only acceptable partners in communion, but who prove utterly unwilling or
unable to be touched.

As with almost all of Ozon's films, the protagonists of both *Le
Temps qui reste* and *Sous le sable* are forced by their phantoms into a
state of stasis and stagnation.[2] Prevented from developing relations
with other living characters because of their obscure conviction that
only the spectral ones are worthy of consideration, they find not
only that these spectres are utterly unfulfilling partners but also that
they refuse to disappear precisely because they cannot be truly
confronted. Towards the end of *Sous le sable* Marie is given the
chance to stare Jean in the face, as it were, to see, feel, touch and
smell the horror of him, his disappearance and the tragedy of his
intangibility when he was her husband. All she has to do is accept
that the badly decomposing cadaver the police have placed before
her is in fact what remains of Jean. She refuses. This refusal is, in a
way, shared by the film itself. Ozon's camera never shows the
monstrous heap of rotting flesh lying on the table, and contents
itself merely with recording Marie's sharp intake of breath as the
body bag is opened. A scene that might have served as a kind of
violent and disgusting shove onto a new plane of understanding,
Marie being forced towards the revelation of Jean's equivalence
with a pile of putrefaction, is stopped in its tracks, leaving Marie
nowhere to go but the beach. And there she remains until the film's
close, chasing after a ghost that will not be caught, but that will
prevent her ever from relating to anyone or anything else.

In Ozon's recent films, isolated characters such as Romain and
Marie seem unable to shake off a melancholic attachment to the
shapes and shades of fantasy. Marie's refusal to break her haunting
by Jean through acknowledging the undeniable fact of his monstrous
corpse provides, though, the key to understanding how exorcism
(or therapy) in the world of Ozon's cinema might potentially work.
There is always the *possibility* of the character successfully pene-
trating the spectre to reveal the monstrous mess lying beneath it, a
revelation that would, we may be sure, free both character and spectator to relate in new and unforeseen ways to the world around
them. It is just that in these recent films such revelation is somehow
obstructed. In *5x2* (2004), the chronologically reversed narrative,
relating five key moments in the relationship between Marion
(Valéria Bruni-Tedeschi) and Gilles (Stéphane Freiss), from the day

of their divorce to the moment they fall in love some years earlier, orchestrates a framework which enables the putrefaction at the heart of the fantasy to be glimpsed, in brutal fashion, at the film's start: Gilles will rape Marion in the hotel room where they naively believe their love can have a pleasant post-divorce coital send-off. Because of the film's backwards time structure, however, that monstrous mess of a revelation will remain inaccessible to the characters and, as the film proceeds, it simply weighs down the spectator with a dull, deathly ache. Ironic sprites of romantic fantasy (the rapturous musical interludes of Paolo Conti or The Platters, the sublime slow-motion wedding dance sequence and, of course, the picture-postcard setting sun on the deserted Italian beach where the final frame leaves a younger Marion and Gilles to their fate) waltz away with that ache, their mockingly conjoined figures allowing us no transcendence whatsoever of their oxymoronic haunting.

This recent cycle of *Le Temps qui reste*, *Sous le sable* and *5x2* are all structured, then, around ghostly entities that the living protagonists cannot access, harness, plug into, confront. These ghosts are ungraspable in nature and expression: the will-o'-the-wisp of an irrecoverable, romanticized childhood in *Le Temps qui reste*, the haunting myth of companionship beyond abandonment in *Sous le sable* and the fantasy of love's young dream in *5x2*. On each occasion, the ghost in question is subtly linked to the protagonist's desire for an impossible endorsement by a blandly patriarchal social imaginary, and will lead the subjugated protagonist a wretched dance that will culminate in all three cases on Ozon's locus of predilection: by the ocean, on the beach of half-death and delusion. In no case will the spectres' monstrous undersides (respectively: the non-negotiable Real of death, the impossible silence of loss and the abjection of rotted love's limitless capacity for humiliation) offer themselves up to either protagonist or spectator as survivable illumination.

The melancholia exuded by these films is moving and masterful. Each is a highly intelligent, exquisitely crafted piece of European art-house cinema. But it is in that slightly hackneyed, catch-all phrase that the problem lies. Ozon's recent (and, significantly, increasingly acclaimed) cinema reeks more of those existential cinematic blueprints of radical emptiness left behind by Antonioni in 1960 than of the fascinatingly, perplexingly 'over-full' filmic paradigms set up by Ozon himself in the mid-1990s. By increasingly dwelling on the impalpable (and thus seemingly non-negotiable) spectral fallout of essentially realistic protagonists and landscapes condemned to a limbo of anguished neurosis, the potential of Ozon's cinema for the creation of something truly and fantastically *progressive* is in danger of being eroded. In Ozon's earlier cinema, however, we find an apparently unabashed willingness to explore the possibilities of going to meet a tastelessly embodied spectre. The result is a cinema of singular aesthetic dynamism and violently thera-peutic value.

When a film dares to violate its viewer by impinging itself upon the senses rather than the intellect, it usually achieves this violation through recourse to one of the so-called 'body' genres: horror, melodrama and pornography. These genres can be argued to be intrinsically corporeal in that they act directly upon the viewer's body, often forcing him or her to bypass judgment, reflection and analysis in favour of less voluntary responses such as sweating, weeping or genital seeping. English-language film criticism, particu-larly in the wake of Gilles Deleuze's two groundbreaking *Cinéma* volumes, seems increasingly interested in the implications of films apparently worthy of serious critical consideration which neverthe-less simultaneously exploit the corporeal aesthetic typical of 'low' or 'trash' art.[3] In *The Cinematic Body*, a survey of the effect and affect of film-makers as diverse as Romero, Fassbinder, Bresson and Warhol, Steven Shaviro argues for a cinema capable of shattering the viewing subject's sense of self with the sheer excess of its sounds and images. It is, Shaviro suggests, only when 'we are no longer able to separate ourselves, no longer able to put things at the proper distance and turn them into objects' that the psychoanalytic para-digm of cinema as a kind of spell through which the viewing subject vainly attempts to cover up his or her primordial lack may be surpassed.[4] Shaviro, heavily influenced by Deleuze, is putting forward a case for the cinematic experience being more than an inevitable symptom and reinforcement of the human subject's allegedly constitutive fantasies but, rather, a potentially unprece-dented encounter from which the viewer emerges both shattered and transformed.[5] Laura U. Marks, in her book *The Skin of the Film*, similarly (albeit using a very different cinematic corpus) pushes for a conception of cinema as something potentially exceeding existing models of a static and utterly knowable psychic disposition, leaving

behind the realms of both readable subjectivity and the strictly
audio-visual for the uncharted territory of a 'haptic' cinema. Haptic
cinema, according to Marks, will seek to represent the dimensions
of experience that elude both realist and psychoanalytic discourse,
and to deploy its flickering screen images not in the viewer's
predictable entrancement and quasi-hypnosis, but in an unprecedented, palpable and transformational *touching*.[6]

This is precisely the bold aesthetic step taken by the denoue-
ments of most of Ozon's earliest films. Their tendency to escalate
towards moments of unprecedented affect does not function as
gratuitous shock for shock's sake. Instead, the absurdly 'out of the
blue' viscerality of their later sequences serves to jolt both spectator
and haunted protagonist out of a shared state of neurotic stasis and
stagnation, pushing both that one step beyond which Ozon's more
recent films and their protagonists find so impossible. An abrupt
aesthetic shift of gear is wedded to a psychic breakthrough for both
characters and narrative, with the result that the entire filmic experience is mimetic of something approaching visually, psychically and
physically experienced Revelation.

I have tried elsewhere to rehabilitate Ozon's first two feature-
length films *Sitcom* (1998) and *Les Amants criminels* (1999), largely
dismissed by public and critics alike as jejune attempts to *épater la
bourgeoisie*. I have argued that the two films orchestrate, just when we
think both narrative and protagonists have nowhere left to go and
are doomed to a perpetual haunting by spectres of their own
making, the sickening intrusion of a monstrous, all too solidly fleshy
spectre, clearing the way for the propulsion of narrative, protagonist and spectator alike into a new space of being beyond haunting.[7]
In *Sitcom* this passage into climactic obscenity is brought into effect
by the mild-mannered scientist father Jean's possession by the ghost
of the rat, metamorphosing into a true monster which can finally be
killed by his unhappily haunted family. In *Les Amants criminels* the
new level, the space where haunting and neurotic addiction to
transgression may potentially end, is inaugurated by the film's mid-
way transformation into fairy tale and the arrival of an 'ogre'
determined to make the teenage protagonists confront (and eat)
the ghost-cadaver-remnant of their murderous behaviour. These
outrageous hinge-points of (already faintly absurd) films are fasci-
nating, disgusting, ridiculous, but their aesthetic significance
cannot be dismissed. They mark the point at which a basic situation

of haunting, a dynamic common to all Ozon's cinema, is ruptured by something even more fantastical – a flesh-and-blood ghost. Confronted with the fleshy contours of the hairy, flailing, sickeningly present embodiment of a pseudo-authority that has been silently haunting everybody since the start of the film, these films' protagonists (and we too) are pushed forward into an unthinkable state of sensory, bodily stimulation, from which we all emerge *different*. The moment when the rat-ghost of *Sitcom* or the 'ogre' of *Les Amants criminels* emerges functions in the films' logic as a flash of radical excess, dramatically altering the terms and conditions of a haunting the characters have started to take for granted. And, as far as the spectator is concerned, the moment is a puncture, an assault, a penetration that forces him or her either to laugh in contempt or – and I think this is a more worthwhile reaction – simultaneously to retch and reflect. In following these films in their shift from abstraction and allusion to obscene embodiment, the metaphor of a haunting by a patriarchal Law we can never satisfy no matter what we do becomes suddenly, disgustingly real. And, as the characters themselves are forced to realize, when a situation is revealed as real, there is nothing one can do but confront it or be consumed by it.

This aesthetic and narrative paradigm (the dramatic shift from a generalized and purely allusive haunting to an unexpected encounter near the film's climax with an improbably ghoulish embodiment of deathly authority itself) is one Ozon rehearses twice more after *Les Amants criminels*. Both *8 femmes* (2002) and *Swimming Pool* (2003) can be understood as interesting, if ultimately less effective or affecting, attempts at the same kind of two-tiered dynamic of haunting.[8] It is in key sequences of early shorts, however, that the abstract haunting/embodied ghost dynamic can be illustrated most clearly. Here, the radically new relations enjoyed by the protagonists in the aftermath of the unprecedented hinge-moment suggest, in no uncertain terms (if we take the films seriously, of course) the urgent social and ethical imperative for the revelation, at any cost, of the fleshy ghost lurking beneath the abstract spectre.

The fourteen-minute *Victor*, Ozon's graduating piece from the film school FEMIS, relates the path from haunting to exorcism of a young man who, before the opening credits have even started, shoots both his parents, preferring this course of action to admitting something apparently unspeakable about himself to them. Rather than killing himself, burying them or running away, Victor simply hangs around the family house with the cadavers, playing with them, masturbating in the garden whilst they slump in the swings next to him, eating his dinner, licking his plate and burping in their presence, comically unsure ('Pardon!') as to what extent the opinion and censorious judgment of dead parents have any currency. In fact, Victor is haunted more by his now inevitable inability to say or do anything that will provoke any kind of response from his parents (whether praising or condemnatory) than by anything as banal as guilt. The sense of Victor's entrapment within a nightmarishly static parental haunting is conveyed throughout the film by multiple images and tropes of stillness and stagnation. Before the opening credits begin, before Victor's murder of the parents even, the screen is taken up with various still photographs of the adult Victor squashed between his stiff and stony-faced parents, frozen in perpetual immaturity. Throughout the film, photographs in frames surround Victor in his bedroom and that of his parents, their seemingly watchful motionlessness echoing the immobile yet ongoing influence of the parents' dead bodies (the rigor mortis of which is, predictably, exploited to comic effect). The garden is filled, like the front drive of Cocteau's *Orphée* (1950), or the chateau grounds in Resnais's *L'Année Dernière à Marienbad* (1961), with stiff, timeless, unapproachable statues. And the old gardener to whom Victor repeatedly turns for reassurance and advice simply spouts the same, unchanging, enigmatic refrain, an impenetrable riddle that, like the psychic blockages of neurosis itself, refuses to bend, shift or melt towards something resembling communication.

This haunting by a rigid set of unchanging and apparently unchangeable structures seems set to last Victor's entire life. But the aesthetics of Ozon's early cinema insist on the puncture of the haunting by a fantastical, embodied, literally moving appearance of ghostliness. In this film, the violent intrusion and its propulsion of film, protagonist and spectator towards a new level of experience occurs when Victor is in the middle of playing in bed with the parent-cadavers as though they were a pair of giant dolls, manipulating their hands and genital areas in a frenzy of compulsive 'acting out'. Suddenly, Victor (together with the terrified viewer) is quite shockingly *assaulted* by the momentarily revived mother and father. The parents, wide-eyed and filling the screen with their dead-alive faces, jerk upwards to castigate – at last! – Victor for his inappropriate behaviour. For a few terrible seconds the world established so

far in the film is turned upside down. A rapid montage of photographs of Victor as a huge, grotesque adult baby in his parents' arms
flashes across the screen; infantile screams are heard from nowhere.
The sheer aesthetic *excess* of the moment is paramount. The rising
up in bed of the zombie parents, their arms outstretched, their
dead, shouting voices ('Qu'est-ce que tu fais encore, Victor?') crush-
ingly, nauseatingly strident, is all somehow *more* obscene and *more*
preposterous than all that has gone before in a film which already
contained more than its share of obscenity and preposterousness.
But this aesthetic gear-change is also wedded to a narrative-psychic
breakthrough: Victor has at last, through a psychotic lurch towards
the realm of the fantastic, been able to see and hear the hitherto
still, silent, spectral parents as horrifying, angry, vengeful ghosts.
The moment is a truly disruptive one, pushing both Victor and the
spectator through into a new space, just as we were all, shockingly,
getting used to the haunted space into which we had slipped.[9] The
new space into which we are pushed is one of radical, unprecedented movement, movement which demands that we shout,
scream, somehow declare the horror that has previously been
silenced and normalized. For, once declared, we can trample on
that horror. And this is precisely what the wily maid (the first of
several Jeanne Moreau-like chambermaids in Ozon's cinema) does,
when she bursts into the room to comfort the screaming Victor,
treading on the cadavers with the joyous (and quintessentially
Ozonian) announcement: 'Ils sont morts! Vous les avez tués!'.

    In this space of new horror and new movement, something like
genuinely new relations with both oneself and others may be
constructed. In *Victor* these new relations are characterized, perhaps
simplistically (but this is, after all, only a fourteen-minute film), by
exciting new interactions, simultaneously social and sexual. With
the maid and her male lover, within whose shared embrace (in a
scene that immediately follows the parent-zombie moment) Victor
is 'born again', our hero simultaneously enjoys his (we presume)
first sexual experience, regressing to a near-foetal state, seemingly
allowed wondrous access to the Freudian primal scene on lucid,
conscious, adult terms. His subsequent halting and silencing of the
old gardener's perennial refrain with a masterful, loving hug,
together with his eventual ability to leave the house and catch the
metro, where we leave him in the final frame (to the strains of
'Sometimes I Feel Like A Motherless Child'), signal with

unashamed clarity the new terms of existence and communication the parent-zombie moment appears to have allowed.

Ozon's early cinema is one that is rapturously fixated on the moment at which our everyday hauntings may be given a shape so unexpected, so solid and so dynamic that we are either annihilated by them or roused to ride and surpass them. These instances of dynamism, optimism (parodic only if one wishes it so) and messy corporeality are extremely invigorating in the context of the often anaemic, nihilistic and solipsistic French cinema Ozon's films increasingly resemble. The substantial aesthetic and emotional difference between the recent *Le Temps qui reste* and the short *La Petite Mort* (1995) is overwhelming, all the more so given their remarkable narrative similarity (young gay photographers are torn between angry, purely self-centred futures or giving in to the possibility of new relations with those around them). Where the 2005 film leaves Romain alone and dying on the beach, unreconciled with his sister, unable to speak to his father and contemptuous of his lover, the earlier short again uses an out-of-place, quasi-fantastical sequence to propel the protagonist from a stagnant haunting by his dying father's indifference towards rebirth and potential communion with his sister, boyfriend and father's memory. In *La Petite Mort*, the embodiment and injected dynamism of the suddenly embodied haunting depends not on a ghost-rat nor on zombie-parents but on the development of a new, 'magical' relation to photography, to the old, stagnant image of the monstrous haunter and to the old, stagnant image of the self as haunted.

Sudden exposure to the quasi-fantastical reality of one's haunting in monstrously embodied form does not always work for Ozon's early protagonists, of course. Notably, in what may be his master-piece, *Regarde la mer* (1997), the heroine fails to perceive the embodied ghost as such in time, and is consequently swallowed whole by it. By and large, though, the further back we move in Ozon's cinematic trajectory, the closer we get to the possibility of exorcism, salvation and therapy, usually facilitated by a brush with an unprecedented embodiment of ghostliness. Reading Ozon backwards in this way, from a present quagmire of cynicism and solitude, towards the long-past potential for something radically, concretely puncturing and new, may be compared to the reverse motion of the film *5x2* itself. Like that film's hapless protagonists Marion and Gilles, Ozon appears to have wandered, for the time being, at least, off a once-resplendent path of solidly spectral hope.

Notes

1   Consider, for example, ultimately therapeutic haunting narratives as different as the classic Dickens novel *A Christmas Carol*, the neglected Val Lewton film masterpiece *The Curse of the Cat People* (1944) and the recently departed American television series *Six Feet Under* (2001–5).

2   Tragically hilarious scenes such as one in *Sous le sable* where Marie sits elegantly sipping Coke in a crowded Macdonald's, or one in *5x2* where Marion sits rigidly in a packed nightclub whilst zombie-like revellers leap to Whigfield's 'Saturday Night', have a wonderful metonymic function in Ozon's depiction of contemporary situations of sickening paralysis.

3   Gilles Deleuze, *Cinéma*, vol. 1, *L'Image-Mouvement* (Paris: Minuit, 1983) and vol. 2, *L'Image-Temps* (Paris: Minuit, 1985).

4   Steven Shaviro, *The Cinematic Body* (Minneapolis/London: University of Minnesota Press, 1993), p. 47.

5   The psychoanalytic paradigms extolled by the journal *Screen*, with its emphasis on lack, division and imaginary suture, are increasingly abandoned or radically reworked (cf. Žižek's repeated focus on the Lacanian real) to emphasize cinematic excess, over-fullness, that which precisely cannot be symbolized but which pushes spectator towards encounters with the sublime. See also C. Plantinga and G. M. Smith (eds), *Films, Cognition and Emotion*, (Baltimore/London: Johns Hopkins University Press, 1999) for a critique of the capacity of some psychoanalytic approaches for coming to terms with the hugeness of *feeling* in the spectator.

6   See Laura U. Marks, *The Skin of the Film: Intercultural Cinema, Embodiment, and the Senses* (Durham/London: Duke University Press, 2000).

7   See Andrew Asibong, 'Meat, murder, metamorphosis: the transformational ethics of François Ozon' in *French Studies*, 59, 3 (July 2005), 203–15.

8   The characters of *8 femmes* finally progress to the climactic revelation of the absent, silent, haunting Papa as undead, all-too-present, monstrous mess. Meanwhile Sarah, the crime writer of *Swimming Pool*, eventually abandons the dimension of hackneyed murder fantasy, performed for a silently judgmental lover-publisher, for an unprecedented series of violent actions that simultaneously reveal that benevolent controller as horrific tyrant and leave Sarah utterly indifferent to him.

9   Compare this with Patrick ffrench's analysis of the potentially ethical significance of moments of motion within an overall context of stillness, in 'The memory of the image in Chris Marker's *La Jetée*', *French Studies*, 59, 1 (January 2005), 31–7.

Chapter Nine
'Reiterature', or the Haunting of Style in the *Portrait de Jacques Derrida* by Hélène Cixous[1]

Frédéric Regard
Translated by Suzanne Dow

'Fantôme que je suis, je prends des photos fantômes de fantômes.'[2] I would like to put this autobiographical statement from Hélène Cixous to work around her *Portrait de Jacques Derrida en jeune saint juif.*[3] In this latter text, Cixous takes as her material no more of Derrida's life than what he himself had said about it in an autobiographical text published ten years earlier: the *Portrait de Jacques Derrida* is, indeed, conceived as a commentary on Derrida's 'confessions', which he called his 'Circumfession', and which itself consisted in a meditation made up of fifty-nine 'periods', or periphrases, written in at the foot of the theoretical essay that Geoffrey Bennington had devoted to him at the time.[4] Hélène Cixous, at the instigation of her publisher, Michel Delorme,[5] decided to offer up to the reader nine extracts from the 'Circumfession', annotated and surlined in her hand, in coloured pen (red, blue or black), and it is these 'periods' alone, surlined in Cixous's hand, that will concern me here.[6] The biographical portrait does not then work over the life, understood as a series of verifiable anecdotes, but over fragments of autobiographical sketches, or fragments of self-narration. I would like to put forward the idea that this portrait is thus inscribed under the sign of a felicitous and positive haunting that sees the spirits readily invited to make themselves heard, as if the ghost were a sort of guest. The matter at hand is no more, no less, than a question of writing style: the nine acts of surlining indeed work to show how this haunting sets in motion the loosening of Derrida's tongue, or, to borrow Hamlet's term, throws it 'out of joint', so as to find its ghosts, its spectres. These spectres are welcomed not as the deadly repressed of Derrida's tongue, but as its survival force,[7] just as much as the event that germinates, that 'fait terre' in that of Cixous.[8] It is this operation that I will be calling 'reiterature'.

Cixous's critical operation is very much related to a ritual, as defined by Lévi-Strauss in *La Pensée sauvage*. Also known as 'magical thought', 'wild thought' was characterized by 'a belief' consisting in making of the visible world the sign of a 'secret arrangement' staged by this ritual. The ritual would thus operate in much the same way as what is now termed in French 'bricolage', given that the ritual would go to work on 'second-hand' signs (Lévi-Strauss here uses the English term).[9] It is from a similar 'science of the concrete', as Lévi-Strauss describes it, that this work of surlining seems to proceed. For example, period 8 of 'Circumfession', surlined and annotated in red in the *Portrait*, reveals a 'secret arrangement' of Derrida's writing, which is made both intelligible and operational by the surlining effected by Cixous's second hand; it seems that a hidden determinism, namely the play of the a, i and y (the vowel sounds), be they seen or heard, of Derrida's real first name – 'Jacky' – is at work in 'Circonfession'.[10] To write such a portrait of Derrida would thus be to 'bricoler', or 'cobble together', a signifying system from such residues of construction formed into a repertoire. The function of Cixous's ritual of surlining would be to cobble together this phantom meaning, tracing itself out unbeknownst to Derrida. And, yet, this is not to say that this unconscious of Derrida's writing would be the truth of the confession. When the work bears on period 1, the letters, syllables, words or groups of words surlined in red raise up a series of questions in the margin that show how the method of surlining does not allow Cixous to find the message of the statement, its hidden truth; on the contrary, the recipient of the message gets lost in the addressee's grammar: 'lui qui?', 'ma mère? ou Dieu ou bien lui? ou elle?'.[11] To be Derrida's friend, to live and write as close to him as can be, to be able to paint the most intimate portrait of him there is, is to allow the return of a world of indecision, where there is no intervention from conceptual syntheses to fix the postures of identity.

The ritual of surlining thus introduces no radical distance between the manifest 'I' of Cixous and the supposed 'you' or 'he' of

Derrida. To place oneself within the intimacy of Derrida's gesture, to live with Derrida's ghosts, is to deny oneself this view-from-above of hermeneutic violence, a kind of 'overhang' that the procedure of underlining usually signifies. When the hand surlines the corpus, when the feminine second hand weds the work of the first, masculine hand, presents and is present to it, the body becomes one with the other body, the critic incorporating herself into the text, incorporating the corpus into herself. This is how we might construe the way in which the question of 'Jewishness' ironically traverses these pages.[12] This ritual of surlining – a ritual that seeks to circumscribe little bits, tiny morsels, of writing – should indeed be thought as a sort of magical circumcision. Within this perspective, the work of the second hand might consist in circumscribing, in circumcising, these little shreds of red flesh, these tips-of-the-tongue, in such a way, fore-sure, as to cut them away, but also, and at the same time, to sew them back. For these 'foretastes' are no sooner circumscribed than they are reinscribed in the margin, but also within the text, within the corpus: the whole point of the surlining is to retrace, to reinstate, that which has been cut away with the red pen. The work of the second hand thus operates as a positive circumcision that does not splice away, but that augments this presence, that finds life yet in Derrida's text, that makes of the spectral remains the key to the survival of Derrida's text. It is thus not so much a case for Cixous of circumscribing – that is to say of drawing a line around, of delimiting, marking out, containing – but of *con-scribing* Derrida, in the sense of not only responding to the secret injunction of Derrida's writing, of responding to the spectre's call, but also of writing in Derrida's place, as his ghostly double, as his ghost writer, even as Cixous's intervention does not chronologically precede Derrida's text. Cixous reads Derrida as her contemporary, as a guest writer, as if she were inviting herself along to the 'Circumfession' ceremony, as if an active participant in this 'Circonfession'.

A few words ought to be said about the visual dimension of the work. For the ritual of surlining does not only seek to have us understand and hear the ghost. Rather, as period 8, reworked in Cixous's hand, shows, to colour in a vowel, to transfuse the letter into the margin, to subtract it from the impersonal typography of the edited and printed book, to draw it out anew in one's own hand, to 'feminize' it, then, is also to *see* the ghost and to offer him up to the gaze of the other – literally, to 'phantasize him'. These eyes – those of

Cixous, our own as readers – see these remains of construction, open themselves up to these dancing images, make out these trickles of blood, contemplate the corpus's hidden vein. Derrida's likeness, the most faithful of his portraits, is therefore to be found right here, on these nine pages, which function like the pictures within the text, put here in place of those photographic portraits that any avid reader of biography is so eager to find. The annotated text replaces for Cixous the photographic impression of the man in life. On these nine pages is drawn out the secret photo of Derrida, his spectral image, his phantasy. And, yet, what this curious layout tells us is also that the portrait, even as it belongs to the domain of the visual, is no less of that of writing, of writing and commentary. It is for this reason that on page 110 of the *Portrait* we find reproduced at last, also in facsimile, an autograph of Derrida's (a closer look at which reveals that what we have here is an unpublished draft of 'Circumfession', a handwritten extract given as a genetic fragment of period 54). This illustration, this image, is the last in Cixous's *Portrait*, and features as its crowning moment. This last page does not function, however, as a revelation, a final unveiling of Derrida's portrait. In substituting for the traditional photographic portrait of the author the reproduction of an autograph, extracted, excised, from the Derrida archives, Cixous rather invites the reader to grasp the resemblance, the similarity, the consanguity, between these two exercises in handwriting – her own and that of Derrida. Telling the difference between Cixous's work and that of Derrida, between the Cixous and Derrida archives, is all the more difficult for the fact that this text illustrates how far Derrida always-already sought to circum-scribe his own text, which is to say to auto-deconstruct, to auto-divide, to auto-spectralize himself. The nine micro-portraits by Cixous are thus in the image of the only self-portrait by Derrida: to draw Derrida's portrait is to reproduce Derrida, which is to say to offer up to the reader's gaze a text in deconstruction, at deconstruc-tion's most intimate moments.

If the exposure of Derrida's text is not conceived without the intervention of the feminine hand that passes back over the letter in order to bring back its colour, that offers up the letter to be seen as if freshly drawn, to look for a chronology, an order of precedence, a hierarchy of operations, becomes an exercise in futility.[13] If surlining, as distinct from underlining, can in no sense be conceived as a reading-from-above, an anachronistic reading, it is because surlining as it is practised here is inscribed within the spectral intimacy of writing. The second hand does not seek to underline the cryptic or esoteric aspect of the text, whose true message might be waiting to be unveiled; the eye of the second hand guarantees a sur-view, a sur-vival, a sur-crescence of the life of the text as it is, without overtaking it, without taking over from it, with no *after-text*. All we need to do is look at it, to open our eyes. The ghost of Derrida's text is not *hors-texte*, it is the text, to the letter, in the body of the letter. But the ghost does not, for all that, exist absolutely; it needs a spectator – that is to say the work of reading, as well as that of the interlocution. Derrida's spectre could not be offered up to the reader's gaze were it not for Cixous's operation of reiteration. We should thus grant this practice of surlining a real pragmatic force: the surlining invites itself into the text, makes of itself a guest writer, in order to summon the ghost, the spectre, in order to invite him to come, to bring out the text's lifeline. All of this also means not that the spectre is there, waiting to manifest himself, but that it is constituted by the reading, by Cixous's gaze-touch, as the lineage, the text's new lineage, born of the meeting between the text's spectre and its posthumous ghost-writer. From the very first example in period 16, we can see how the letters surlined in the body of the text, either in red or blue, are in a sense 'exalted' in the upper or lateral margins, where they form a line of black ink, which is also the new line of Derrida's text.[14] The phrases 'Elle y arrive', 'A la fin Elie arrive', or even 'qu'arrive Elie!' constitute so many statements from Cixous, and yet are also the offspring of Derrida's text. It is as if Derrida's text were secreting its own yet-to-be-said, a yet-to-be-said not imported from the outside, in a metaphysical mode, but drawn from within, as a knowledge haunting the text unbeknownst to the text – an unconscious knowledge always-already there, intimately incorporated into Derrida's language, fluent in and fluid on Derrida's tongue, hollowing it out, dancing upon it and, as it were, signing in his place.

However, the *Portrait de Jacques Derrida en jeune saint juif* is not, of course, restricted to these nine surlined pages. These pages are surrounded by a critical text of 104 less unusually presented pages, to the extent that the annotated documents may well seem to the reader so many anecdotal illustrations of the main discussion. I, for my part, would suggest that these nine exercises in surlineage are not at all cut off from the critical discourse, but, further, that they consti-tute its heart, with their veins and arteries, their blue, venous and red, arterial blood. These operations of surlineage thus set off the critical discourse of the *Portrait*, just as any piece of machinery is set off, triggered or set in motion by an irrigating pump. What we have to understand here is that to sign 'Cixous' – and this is the only author's name inscribed on the cover of the work – that is to say to survive Derrida, whilst remaining one of his intimates, is the prerogative of she who manages to be leading the spectre to sign in Derrida's place, of the writer who in consequence has managed to bleed Derrida, to find his secret vein, which is also to say to ape Derrida.[15] In so saying I am, of course, referring to a form of monkey business that takes us a long way from imitation or animality, as defined by metaphysics: animality without spirituality, and also, as Derrida explained, animality without hand, without the creative work of the hand.[16] The ape in question here does not engage in an insensible, senseless repetition of the gesture of the other, for this monkey is also an organ-grinder; Cixous reproduces Derrida's gesture in such a way as to have him pour out his heart, in such a way as to have him give up his ghosts, so as to 'spiritualize' him. Cixous's surlineage, furthermore, only apes Derrida's hand (monkeys around with it) in order to fashion his text, his corpus, out of a line of thinking, a bloodline, whose production paradoxically guarantees the signatory of the portrait her authority-effect. For, when the second hand notes that which is spectrally expressed in the body of the text, in the text re(a)d to the letter, this trickle of blood, of meaning, of Derrida's text, she is not simply expressing a secretion: she *makes the text say* its spectral unknown. And it is through this 'making-say', this reinterpretation, that the signatory of the book is constituted as subject of her own utterance, as author of a lineage set off by reiteration, but also by excision, ob-literation, the author of a literature conceived as what I would like to call 'reiterature'. Cixous's hand redraws the path taken by Derrida's hand in a gesture that is also an erasure, an intimate and benevolent erasure, a positive erasure, inviting herself into 'Circonfession' in order to bring out its unbeknownst but also to graft herself onto it as author-subject.

There is no metaphysical dimension to this joint work of spiritualization and subjectivation: in order that the body should express all of its senses, all the senses circulating within it, it needs not an immaterial beyond, a privileged signified, but uniquely, and concretely, a feast for the senses. It is thus that the *Portrait* makes of itself not an anecdotal biography, but a literary work. The nine operations of surlining ask us, indeed, to allow the hand to become eyes, and the eyes ears, which can only take place within literature, by virtue of a poetic operation. To return once again to the first period of the *Portrait*, period 16, Cixous's hand invites us to hear the unheard of Derrida's text. The black ink issues a call in the name of Derrida's friend, Elie Carrive, in a subjunctivized verb form: 'qu'arrive Elie!', the condition of possibility of which is the aural. It is the 'subjunctivization' of language that grants us our Derrida, and at the same time irrigates Cixous's essay – Cixous, who only authorizes herself to become the signatory of her own text for having touched, seen and heard breathe the spirit of Derrida, or, to be more precise, the spirit of Derrida's language. In order to gain a still more precise sense of the subjectivation that is set into play in the work of surlining, we can refer to period 10.[17] For it is from this first work of surlineage that the signatory, Cixous, draws her first 'je': 'Reste que je suis'. Note that 'Reste que je suis' is given as a quotation ('Reste que je suis, citation'), without, however, being marked with the conventional signs for a quotation, namely quotation marks. To write 'citation' out in full is surely not the equivalent of a punctuation mark (that marks the borrowing of a secondary statement embedded within a principal statement, the subject of which may be clearly identified). The pronominal indecision by which the whole speech apparatus is taken over thus enables us to be there at the birth of an 'I' that is of course that of Derrida's text, but also that of the signatory, since the sentence continues, 'Reste que je suis reste d'Ester', down to the foot of the page, 'à la lettre reste d'Ester', in the mode of a creative reiteration, a 'recontextualized' quotation, which the signatory appropriates for herself and squeezes back out having, in a sense, grafted herself onto it.[18] Thus, it will have been necessary for the black ink of Cixous's handwriting to articulate the unknown of the text, namely that the verb 'reste' is an anagram of Derrida's mother's first name, Ester, 'nom des noms à partir duquel il fait tout descendre de tout des cendres', concludes Cixous, who clearly sets out this time, through the use of the third person pronoun 'il', that the first 'je' was already not fully that of Derrida. To that precise extent, if Derrida can be said, to the letter, 'reste d'Ester' (Esther's remains), the signatory of the essay produces herself in turn as remains of the remains, daughter of the son, replacement for the replacement, in his line, produced by the surlineage, as Derrida's survivor, Derrida's ghost.

All of the metaphors that this reading of the text have invited turn around the body, around the corpus as body and the body as corpus. To surline is to a certain extent to extract a fragment of tissue, of an organ, or some of the organism's fluid, with a view to subjecting it to analysis. My reading of the *Portrait* through the prism only of these few handwritten pages has, however, brought out the fact that we need here to imagine not so much a scalpel, which would cut away, or slice off – an instrument of circumcision – as a stylus, a tricoloured stylograph, which would tap into the vein of writing, leaving a puncture mark – much, then, like a syringe. But a syringe that could also write, like the ink cartridge of a fountain pen. We should therefore imagine Cixous's stylograph as she writes the *Portrait* as a hollow-stemmed stylus, like a needle, an impossible needle, a magic needle, capable at one and the same time of puncturing and injecting, via the same channel. Puncture and injection, at the same time: the putting into circulation of the meaning of a life, a lifeblood, constantly renewed, constantly re-oxygenated, with an ever-differing sense. Ghost writer and guest writer: at the same time as Cixous invites herself into the 'Circonfession' in order to conjure the ghosts of the text, the ghosts invite themselves into her own text of 'reiterature' so as to make her speak in Derrida's place. It could thus be said that there is no greater intimacy in deconstruction than the haunting of style, of style as the true blood tie between the texts.

Notes

1   This is a variant of a previous essay published under the title 'Derrida un-cut: Cixous's art of hearts', in *Paragraph: A Journal of Modern Critical Theory*, 30, 2 (July 2007), 1–16. We wish to thank *Paragraph*, and more particularly Nicholas Harrison and Keith Reader, for their permission to use this material.
2   Hélène Cixous, *Jours de l'an* (Paris: des femmes, 1990), p. 79.
3   Paris: Galilée, 2001.
4   Jacques Derrida, 'Circonfession', in Geoffrey Bennington (ed.), *Jacques Derrida* (Paris: Seuil, 1991).
5   'Si ce n'était pas Michel Delorme qui me l'avait expressément demandé je n'aurais simplement jamais proposé cette maquette', states Hélène Cixous in her published exchange with Frédéric-Yves Jeannet, *Rencontre terrestre* (Paris: Galilée, 2005), p. 86.
6   Translator's note: the neologism 'surlining' has here been chosen as a translation of the original French 'sur-lignement' in preference to

the more familiar 'highlighting'. The intention is to render, by the prefix 'sur-' (from the Latin meaning at once 'over', 'above' and 'beyond'), the polysemic materiality of Cixous's intervention in relation to Derrida's own writing. Whereas 'to highlight' is to introduce a change of colour in order to indicate privileged significance of a part of a corpus, Cixous's hand here takes up an ambiguously spatialized position with regards to the body of Derrida's text which resists the hierarchical implications suggested by the idea of 'highlighting'.

7　See Jacques Derrida, *Spectres de Marx: l'état de la dette, le travail du deuil, et la nouvelle Internationale* (Paris: Galilée, 1993), p. 18.

8　Hélène Cixous, 'Le Lieu de l'autre', interview with Frédéric Regard, March 1991, in Frédéric Regard (ed.), *Logique des traverses* (Saint-Étienne: PUSE, 1992), pp. 11–26.

9　Claude Lévi-Strauss, *La Pensée sauvage* [1962], 2nd edn (Paris: Plon/Pocket, Agora, 2002), pp. 31–6.

10　Cixous, *Portrait de Jacques Derrida en jeune saint juif* (Paris: Galilée, 2001), p. 31.

11　Ibid., p. 43.

12　The piece had originally been put together for the 'Jewishnesses' conference on Jacques Derrida. See Cixous and Jeannet, *Rencontre terrestre*.

13　The 'moment spectral', says Derrida, is never 'docile au temps' (*Spectres de Marx*, p. 17).

14　Cixous, *Portrait*, p. 15.

15　Translator's note: in the 'Prière d'insérer' to the French edition of the *Portrait*, Cixous insists that her eponymous 'Saint juif' should also be read according to the near homophony between the two terms in French as 'Singe juif'. The original French of the present article here plays on 'signer', 'saigner' and 'singer', which cannot be retained in an English translation.

16　Jacques Derrida, 'Geschlecht I' [1983], in *Heidegger et la question* (Paris: Flammarion, 'Champs', 1990), pp. 193–203.

17　Cixous, *Portrait*, p. 17.

18　See Derrida, 'Signature événement contexte', in *Marges de la philosophie* (Paris: Minuit, 1972), p. 381. Derrida here speaks of 'reiteration' as a 'citational graft'.

Chapter Ten
Shadowy Figures of Oneself: Robert Pinget's *Passacaille*

Sarah Tribout-Joseph

One critic has described Robert Pinget's *Passacaille* (1969) as *À la recherche du temps perdu* written by an amnesiac.[1] The comparison is highly telling, for it allows us to see a very different dynamic at work behind each of the texts. The Proustian narrator is imbued with a sense of nostalgia and perturbed by the passing of time and the transience of life. Far more frightening for Pinget's 'narrator' figure in *Passacaille* is the horror of losing one's memory and not knowing for certain what one's past life has been. Furthermore, whereas writing in Proust offers a possibility of recuperating the past, Pinget's fraught and unresolved narratives offer only chilling discomfort as the past seemingly returns to haunt the present.

The narrative in Pinget's works is unreliable to the extent that the reader is not able to tell what happens. What is *Passacaille* about? There is mention throughout of a dead body but at no point is it ever possible to establish any concrete facts such as time, place, identity of victim, identity of perpetrator, motive, weapon, cause of death, circumstances under which the body was found, or indeed whether there in fact is a dead body. In other words, it is the hard facts which are missing: that which can be pieced together by rational logic and which make detective novels such page-turners. Time, space and the material world are collapsed. A body that appears, disappears and reappears with no explanation would seem to take us beyond into another dimension: one which is haunted by the irrational.

At the outset of *Passacaille* the main 'character', identified only as 'the Master', appears to have found a body, or alternatively the body may in fact be his own. In later permutations of the story, the body may have been found by the neighbours' boy, or again perhaps the

body is that of the boy himself, or perhaps it is somebody else's, or
nobody's. There is no single or clearly identifiable narrative voice
but it often seems to emanate from the Master in an extension of
his conversations with his friend, the doctor, and likewise across an
emulation of an apparent extract from his memoirs. This equation
of narrative voice or concerns with the Master may indicate a reason
why the character is referred to as 'the Master', suggesting that he
somehow controls the narrative. The phantoms of the text would
therefore appear to come from inside the Master's mind. As Colin
Davis emphasizes in chapter one of the present volume, the
Enlightenment's triumph of rationalism does not banish ghosts;
instead, with the advent of psychoanalysis, the dark side is identified
as emanating from within ourselves: 'the ghosts are now inside our
heads rather than roaming the outside world'.[2]

In Pinget the reader finds himself in the disconcerting position of
never being able to get a grip on the story, of never being able to
account for the happenings. In the absence of any conventional
storyline or characters, the tale becomes a confusion of imaginings.
There are multiple layers of haunting in the text. The story comes
to us via disembodied voices. The past seems to coexist with the
present and the beyond-the-grave. Perhaps, as I will explore, the
manifestation of the conscience and the collective subconscious can
account for these parallel worlds and realities which merge.
Nevertheless, if we are dealing with the Master's imaginings, the
result is no less frightening and it is the unsettling nature of the
work that will be examined here. The last layer of the ghost story is
the element of the story itself.

John O'Brien explores a reading of *Passacaille* in the light of
Pinget's statement that the book is a talisman against death. He
argues that: 'The protagonists of Pinget's farce of consciousness
escape extinction only by the rehearsal of their obituary.'[3] This
imagining of the world at our death, or at the news of our death,
would explain why characters are treated in the text as alternatively
both dead and alive. Peter Broome looks at ghosts in the text. From
looking specifically at the passage in the text which presents 'a
surrealist description of a mass exodus of mental phantoms', he
concludes that all the characters are just shadows, verbal or optical
illusions.[4] Laurent Adert looks at how the ghostly presence is
conveyed through discourse: 'ce qui a lieu ici et maintenant se
produit simultanément ailleurs et dans un autre temps … un tel

dispositif a pour effet de spectraliser les discours et les voix, de les décoller de leur lieu et temps d'énonciation et de leur conférer un statut de fantômes: mortes ou vivantes, les voix sont ici des revenantes'.[5] Voices in the text have become disembodied as they are displaced and cannot be situated in time and place. Iwata, amongst others, looks at alchemy.[6] In *Passacaille* the theme is linked to the transformation of colours. Having completed the École des Beaux-Arts in Paris, Pinget's first artistic calling was painting and he explores the possibility of writing his text in different colours. From the grey opening passage we progress to blood-red passages. Alchemy, however, also suggests links with magic, witchcraft, devil worship – Faust being no doubt the most famous alchemist – and the underworld. Across all these studies there is a concern to locate the haunting presence in the text. The writer in *Passacaille* is haunted by himself. Having looked at how the ghostly presence in the text makes itself felt, this essay will suggest that the spectres in the text are shadowy figures of the fictional author himself; it will consider why he creates them and what it is that haunts him. The text is in fact a staging of conscience but whether there is any saving grace for the central character of the Master is highly debatable.

The haunting presence

The Master's fate is bound up with that of another character in *Passacaille*, the neighbours' boy. The latter is accused of having too much imagination: 'comment se fier au gamin, il a trop d'imagination'.[7] The boy elaborates on the truth and invents. The result is an unreliable narrative which the listener cannot place. Bordering on reality in its account of events, the tale has credibility and may well take in the listener. The fictional elements no doubt make the tale more appealing. The boy who suffers from an overdeveloped imagination is symptomatic of the nature of *Passacaille* as a whole. The position of the author as storyteller is likened to that of the boy who tells stories in a way which, rather than being belittling, has a grace-saving effect, as will be seen at the end.

The tale is built up like a rumour. Critics have suggested that the title of the book, *Passacaille*, is derived from Spanish and means something like 'passing through the streets'. The portmanteau word seems to be a running together of the two words 'pasar', 'to pass through', and 'calle', 'street', such as would happen were the

words whispered quickly. The word thus reproduces the spirit of
gossip and rumour prevalent in *Passacaille* as word passes from
mouth to mouth on the streets. Pinget's novels in fact all deal with
the subject of gossip. Furthermore, their narratives themselves are
woven out of gossip. Although Pinget has been criticized for getting
rid of plot, character and everything else that literature has traditionally been about, his stories, I would argue, constitute a
continued engagement with what lies at the heart of storytelling.
Information is presented in a way that reveals both the tale and the
reaction to the tale. Every snippet is a mini-saga which reproduces
both the position of the storyteller and the reader's interpretative
role in the form of the listener's reaction. Furthermore, the reader
is drawn into the tale and implicated as his mind naturally tends to
fill in the missing information to make sense of subjective titbits, the
'murmures, formules divinatoires, rabâchage' that he is given.[8] This
implication of the reader in the construction of meaning is deliberate and I will return to this towards the end. In Barthes's terms,
Pinget's works are 'scriptible' not 'lisible': it is the reader who is
responsible for making sense of the text.

People talk either about their daily lives or else they elaborate on
half-heard stories and generate further talk or indeed invent stories
of their own. The reliance on oral narrative positions the writing
ambiguously between the very ordinary and the fantastic. When
Pinget transposes such talk into the novel the result is that the texts
are shrouded in uncertainty and mystery. It is this space of oral
storytelling that ghosts are wont to haunt. Ghost stories are just that:
stories. They are tales that are told and that exist in the human
imagination and are passed on usually from mouth to mouth even
when recounted within a literary text. In the archetypal story
someone from foreign parts arriving at an old house is told the
house's secrets by the servants, those denied access to literacy but
whose receptive imagination brings storytelling to life along with
the dead, the ghostly and the monstrous. At one point in *Passacaille*
we see that the existence of the Master himself has shifted into
another dimension and that he has become a sort of bogeyman of
the imagination, invoked by mothers to scare their children: 'on
finissait par le montrer du doigt et les mères disaient à leurs
marmots qu'elles les feraient manger par le vieux s'ils n'étaient pas
sages'.[9] When people die, or are absent, they live on in the thoughts
and verbal articulations of others. This is their afterlife; their

continued presence conveyed to the living sometimes also through written testimony, photos, objects etc.

Passacaille borrows many elements from the genre of the ghost story that we have all heard before. Our familiarity with the signs casts an eerie sense of foreboding over the tale. The scene is set in a cold dark empty mansion one winter's night. The 'story' which is outlined revolves around the visions of a dead and mutilated body which mysteriously displaces itself. It is first 'ce cadavre sur le fumier' and then on the next page the body seems to have slumped from a sitting position at the kitchen table.[10] Black crows caw ominously. A scarecrow hangs on the cross. It is a restless narrative that displays a compulsion to repeat, haunted by recurring images. As we know from all the stories we have heard, ghosts are doomed endlessly to reappear in the same places, compelled to perform forever the same actions. Hamlet's father is the most well-known ghost in Western culture. Often these ghosts are the spirits of people that have been killed at an untimely hour and that now exist in a state of limbo not yet permitted to enter the next world, as is the case with Hamlet's father. Their presence shows that something is amiss. Thus the fact that something is amiss is signalled in *Passacaille*, but exactly what it is we are never sure.

Todorov in his study of 'le fantastique' distinguishes the concept from 'l'étrange' and 'le merveilleux'. Faced with supernatural elements in a story, the reader hesitates between two possible explanations: either it is an illusion or it is part of reality but the reality is different from that which we know: 'Le fantastique occupe le temps de cette incertitude; dès qu'on choisit l'une ou l'autre réponse on quitte le fantastique pour entrer dans un genre voisin, l'étrange ou le merveilleux.'[11] If the supernatural is accepted, it constitutes 'le merveilleux'; if it is explained it falls into the category of 'l'étrange'. Todorov's system perhaps seems rather overdetermined. Nevertheless, *Passacaille* could fit the category of the 'fantastique'. The system of suggestive reporting means that the reader of *Passacaille* is never quite able to account for the events. As stated in the text itself, the source of the information is missing: 'Source d'information défaillante.'[12] I will nevertheless propose an explanation for the supernatural elements as emanating from the Master's mind and thus no longer qualifying the tale for the category of the 'fantastique'.

Figures of oneself

At the outset of *Passacaille*, the Master stops the clock. The story at
various points seems to offer itself as the Master's account of his own
death, the stopping of the clock symbolizing the arresting of his
life.[13] Accordingly, no longer subject to time, the story and the characters are of another dimension. They have a spectral presence,
being but outlines, memories from an imaginary beyond-the-grave.

At various points we see an image of a man who lives off his past,
kept alive by a few fading memories: 'Dans le livre qu'il feuilletait
une image vieillotte qui faisait ses délices, drôle de bonhomme,
passions inexplicables, le murmure faiblissait, remâchant ses jours
sans gaieté, les conversations avec le docteur, les allées et venues
dans la cour pavée, la solitude.'[14] The Master is this 'image vieillotte'. He is obviously now an old man, shut up, like his cold, old
mansion, in his own thoughts. The Master is also now a shadow of
his former self. He spends his remaining days reminiscing and storytelling in the company of the doctor. We are told that he is also
writing his memoirs and it seems that he is perhaps reading or
going over passages from them with the doctor. The Master refers to
'la rédaction pour une feuille mensuelle de mes mémoires'.[15] This
makes it seem as if the Master has been asked to write his memoirs.
Or perhaps the monthly page is not for publication, and there is
certainly no indication as to why he would be commissioned for it.
As distinct from autobiography, memoirs usually detail only part of
a life, typically during a period of public office. They have not traditionally focused on intimate detail (although the focus is perhaps
now changing as stars from popular culture have developed an
interest in the genre). The apparent extract from the memoirs with
which we are presented and which will be discussed later deviates
from accepted practice in focusing on intimate and sordid detail.
Furthermore, in accordance with the norms of the genre, we would
expect a person's memoirs to be an effort to capture and hold an
image of the self. The Master, however, also defies the genre by
further destabilizing the image he gives of himself.

Memoirs are written for posterity. The Master seems to become so
obsessed with a posthumous image of himself that he fixates on the
moment of his death, constantly rehearsing it and fantasizing about
it. This may be how he hopes to ward off death; this is O'Brien's
talisman effect discussed earlier. It would be possible to offer a
Blanchotian reading of the text and see it as the Master's trying to

control his death by taking his own life. This latter reading might account for the endless repetition of the moment at which the body is found, of the moments immediately before and after his death. Blanchot himself shows how the suicide victim's thoughts are flawed since it is not possible to 'want' to die because the active 'wanting' always stops short of death. The 'Master' is not 'Master' of his own death and the more he fantasizes about it, the more it seems to escape him: the dead body, indeed, is often designated as 'l'autre'. Blanchot focuses in *L'Espace littéraire* on suicide uniquely from the perspective of cheating death: it is difficult for us to accept death and Blanchot interprets suicide as the deluded idea of not letting death claim us but rather deciding ourselves to embrace death.[16] He does not, however, consider that we may simply not want to live. He does not consider that attempted suicides are often pleas for attention. In fixating on the moment of the discovery of the body we may think that the Master is fantasizing about a similar desire to be the centre of attention. Yet his body, if it is his, is not discovered by loved ones and neither do there seem to be any loved ones to mourn his passing. Instead, the body is found either by the neighbours' boy, or by the *sentinelle*, or the goatherd. All of them are nameless and, despite the proximity to the Master, remain strangers to him.

More important, I believe, in this staging of his own death, is a concern for what will become of his memory after death. There is a fear of ending up forgotten on the rubbish heap. The text reproduces his fading away: '[Il] rédigeait ses souvenirs' becomes '[il] bafouillait des excuses ou des souvenirs, on entendait mal'.[17] The written memoirs become mutterings or excuses which border on the inaudible. Or perhaps it is not that this whisper, the retelling of his life, cannot make itself heard but, rather, that he only half wants it to be heard. With the day of judgement approaching, by the living and possibly a Higher Authority in the afterworld, these 'excuses' are perhaps his confessions.

The dead body appears not always to be that of the Master. Sometimes it is that of a young boy or the postman. Perhaps the Master is haunted by a dead body because he has killed or sacrificed someone. Another possible explanation is that the 'Master' is called the 'Master' because he controls the story and the other characters are mere adjuncts of himself. The doctor would thus represent the psychoanalytic aspect; the *sentinelle* the desire to view oneself both from the inside and the outside.[18] The Master's personality, indeed, begins to split up and disintegrate like the material decomposition of the body on the compost heap.

The spectre of conscience

Of all the stories that are told and of all the various versions of the Master that seem to coexist, there is one more insidious than any other. A twenty-page section towards the end of the book, pages 99– 118, which constitutes about a fifth of the total text, stands out for being written in the first person singular. It would appear to be an extract from the Master's memoirs.

The passage revolves around a boy of about fifteen whom the Master has adopted. The boy seems half-witted, the Master refers to him as 'le crétin' and 'l'idiot';[19] he is half-wild, sleeping, the Master thinks, in 'un fossé ou un fourré ou un fumier' – the alliteration serves to recall the fact that it is the 'fumier' where the body appears most.[20] The Master tells us that because the boy sometimes smells, the only house rule is that he must take a bath once a week. The tale is elaborated on each time it is retold:

> *Je n'exigeais qu'une chose, le savonner moi-même dans son tub tous les samedis ou à peu près, sans calendrier ni passion il m'arrivait de me tromper et je me sentais moins seul à ces moments, j'ai sa peau sous ma main, je le savonne partout sans exception de A à Z, peut-être plus le Z, à dire vrai c'est moins une corvée qu'un plaisir, ou si dans ma hâte à être moins seul je le savonne deux fois par semaine mettant mon erreur de calcul sur le compte de l'absence de calendrier.*[21]

If 'Z' is for 'zizi', 'A' must be for 'anus'. In any case the washing sessions focus on the boy's genitals. By chiasmic reversal in the following sentence, the boy's innocence certainly throws guilt on the Master: 'Il me tendait le savon et ma main tombait sur le Z, l'innocent se mettait à durcir.'[22] The interludes between the sessions become shorter: the Master half-hiding behind a pretence of duty and mutual agreement requires only that the boy submit to the Master's washing him when the boy smells bad. The latter, however, frequently smells bad. The innocent soap bubbles cannot conceal a paedophile.[23]

The exposed dead body, variously that of a man or a boy, has in later variations of the story been mutilated and at times it is specified that it has been castrated. Whether it is the boy or the Master himself who has been castrated, the spectre is undoubtedly a projection of the Master's guilt. One of the many phrases that reoccur in the text is 'Tourner, retourner, revenir'.[24] Much as the Master may try to turn the page on his past he cannot. 'Tourner, retourner, revenir' may also refer to his sleepless nights that are the result of a troubled conscience. There seems to be an inability to rewrite the past. His past returns, it shadows his conscience, it is the *revenant*. In the following passage, in dismissing the farce of conscience, there is nevertheless a remnant of guilt in the idea that one may be held to account:

> *Je soussigné dans la pièce froide, ciguë, pendule détraquée, je soussigné dans le marais, chèvre ou carcasse d'oiseau, je soussigné au tournant de la route, au jardin du maître, vieille femme à maléfices, sentinelle des morts, satyre, simulacre, en camionnette sur ce trajet dévié par le mauvais œil, jouet de cette farce qu'on nomme conscience, personne, je soussigné minuit en plein jour, chavirant d'ennui, vieille chouette, pie ou corbeau.*[25]

The undersigned here, and more clearly elsewhere, identifies himself with Oedipus at the crossroads where the latter kills the man that he will later discover was his father: 'je soussigné sentinelle des morts, aux croisements des routes'.[26] A fear of castration is accompanied by an Oedipean knowledge of having done something wrong.

The guilt seems to shift between his conscience, which takes account of what he may actually have done or thought, and his subconscious. It is difficult to lay accusation squarely upon him. There are no witnesses who can speak up. The boy himself has disappeared and seemed not to be able to speak anyway. The Master tells us how he invites another man along to their bathing sessions but nothing happens in the presence of a third party: 'pour tromper l'ennui de cette soirée, faire bander le crétin, peine perdue, la présence d'un tiers le dérangeait'.[27] For the reader, nevertheless, this sentence incriminates rather than exonerates the Master.

However, the whole of *Passacaille*, I would argue, is predicated on the story of the boy with too much imagination and the parallel with the Master as storyteller, as I outlined at the beginning. It is clear that the Master has nothing to do all day and spends his time reminiscing and fantasizing. Just as happens to those who believe in ghosts, his imagination seems at times to get the better of him: 'Dans cette maison froide hantée par des années d'insouciance, fantasmes de la nuit qui ne laissent rien intact des suggestions de la mémoire.'[28] Fact and fiction merge. The haunted house may be a metaphorical extension of the Master's mind. Another reason why the Master may be so called is because he owns what seems like a large manor house and the others are dependants on his land: they people the space of his mind. Having led a carefree life, inactivity now sets his mind racing. Perhaps never having thought twice about anything he has done, now, with time and imagination, the smallest misdemeanours and the subliminal flicker of wayward thoughts are inflated into potentially enormous sagas. Perhaps in old age, with mild memory loss or the onset of senility, he has become so detached from the person he was that he applies worst-case scenarios to his former self. Rumour, gossip, newspaper headlines, the collective unconscious: all no doubt play upon his mind, making him feel guilty for things he has not done. He merges into the 'personne', the everybody and the nobody of the above quotation: 'personne, je soussigné minuit en plein jour, chavirant d'ennui'.[29] The phantoms in *Passacaille* certainly seem to be figments of the writer figure's imagination. This would appear to be a case of the Freudian relocation of the dark side within the mind. What is more difficult to diagnose is the guilt complex producing this ghostly return of the repressed.

Critics have accused Pinget of doing away with the storyline and being difficult to follow. What ensues, I will call the 'reader's predicament'. It is what *Passacaille* is all about. The story is befuddled. The Master's memoirs are befuddled. Is the central character a paedophile or not? We are left in the uncomfortable position of not being sure. Throughout the book there runs an interest in alchemy and the desire to extract something pure. This could be interpreted as the reader's own quest for knowledge – the desire to extract the essence from the various stories he is being told. At times we are lured by the possibility of a colour-coded hermeneutics behind the narration. However, the opening and oft-repeated phrase 'Le calme, le gris' denies us any such certainty. The 'gris' seems to reproduce the hesitation between black and white pronouncements that makes the story so unsettling. The Master's story is watertight and what affronts our morality cannot be judged: 'À sa table dans la maison froide notait en marge d'une phrase murmurée, on entendait mal, l'histoire demeurera secrète, sans faille sur l'extérieur.'[30]

The story of *Passacaille* is the very multiplicity of its stories and the impossibility of being able to decide what happens. It is a befuddling of the story. One very disturbing story hides behind the others as being just another story. The haunting presence in the text is the spectre of possibility, imagination and uncertainty. The coexistence of these various planes of reality defies the conventional rules of narrative and might seem to lend the story the fantastic dimension that Todorov outlines. However, that the oscillation of these planes of reality arises out of the Master's state of mind, or our interpretation of his state of mind, excludes the story from the category of the 'fantastique' by offering an explanation. It therefore ceases to conform to Todorov's definition of the 'fantastique' as precisely the moment of hesitation between the two possible explanations: illusion (the irrational can be accounted for, as in the case of *Passacaille*); or a different order of reality (the supernatural). One explanation would be that something which lies heavily on the Master's conscience is enacted before him. Yet the possibilities raised in the text also haunt the collective subconscious of all of us. This spectre of possibility is glimpsed in rumour, storytelling, sensational reporting, all of which can create a 'faux mystère'.[31] It is perhaps the hint of something sinister in all of us which delights in a story and which the text solicits through scenarios which the reader has stored up in the back of his mind. It is perhaps the impossibility of refining our souls down to a state of purity. The clamour for a story is what is left over in *Passacaille*. There may be a confession that the writer is also implicated in the desire to tell stories. The slumped body of the Master which sometimes appears in a writing position at the kitchen table certainly suggests identification with the writer. Like the little boy who tells stories and like those who believe in ghosts, our imaginations like to run away with us.

Notes

1 Peter Broome, 'Pinget's *Passacaille*', *Nottingham French Studies*, 12 (1973), 86–99 (p. 90).
2 See p. 17 above.
3 John O'Brien, 'Pinget's *Passacaglia*: birds wings beating the solid air', *The Review of Contemporary Fiction*, 3 (1983), 147–51 (p. 149).

4 Peter Broome, 'Pinget's *Passacaille*', 96. The passage in *Passacaille* only takes up a few sentences but stands out as key in the text as seemingly belonging to another narrative: 'La mère dans le wagon de l'exil … ils se traînaient par masses ou se hissaient sur les poutrelles ou plongeaient dans les caves par les trappes' (Robert Pinget, *Passacaille*, (Paris: Minuit, 1969) p. 35).

5 Laurent Adert, *Les Mots des autres: Flaubert, Sarraute, Pinget* (Paris: Septentrion, 1996), p. 272.

6 Yoshinori Iwata, *Écriture et intériorité dans quatre romans de Robert Pinget* (Geneva: Slatkine, 2003).

7 *Passacaille*, p. 50.

8 Ibid., p. 47.

9 Ibid., p. 24.

10 Ibid., p. 14.

11 Tzvetan Todorov, *Introduction à la littérature fantastique* (Paris: Seuil, 1970), p. 47.

12 *Passacaille*, p. 35.

13 This is a reading which J. P. Szarka supports in 'The farce of consciousness: a study of Pinget's *Passacaille* and *Fable*', *Nottingham French Studies*, 26 (1987), 81–96 (p. 86).

14 *Passacaille*, p. 12.

15 Ibid., p. 23.

16 Maurice Blanchot, *L'Espace littéraire* (Paris: Gallimard, 1988).

17 *Passacaille*, pp. 22 and 34.

18 Fernand Meyer equates the sentinelle 'qui voit mal' with the position of the reader, in 'Robert Pinget: Le livre disséminé comme fiction, narration et objet' (*Nouveau roman: hier, aujourd'hui* (Paris: Union Générale d'Éditions, 1972), vol. 2, pp. 309–10).

19 *Passacaille*, pp. 116 and 119.

20 Ibid., p. 101.

21 Ibid., pp. 101–2.

22 Ibid., p. 116.

23 John O'Brien has also noted the possibility of sexual abuse and the fact that anything is possible in Pinget, with suggestions often thrown in as if in passing as in the following gloss on the text: 'Oh, I forgot to mention we were pederasts'. See 'Pinget's *Passacaglia*: birds wings beating the solid air', 149.

24 *Passacaille*, p. 49.

25 Ibid., p. 130.

26 Ibid., p. 131.

27 Ibid., p. 117.

28 Ibid., p. 69.

29 Ibid., p. 130.

30 Ibid., p. 74.

31 Ibid., p. 52.

Chapter Eleven
Haunting Canons: Ethics of Mourning in *Vie secrète* by Pascal Quignard

Henriette Korthals Altes

Ghosts are familiar company in the works of Pascal Quignard. Ever since Quignard started writing in the 1970s, loss, transformation and recuperation have formed leitmotivs in his works. As a translator, he has rescued classic authors from oblivion and given them a second life. As a critic, he has spun his own narratives from his erudite reading of both classic and obscure texts. In both capacities, he has let himself be haunted by voices of others in order better to resurrect them. As a novelist, he has made mourning a recurrent theme in his fiction, with both his novels and short stories recounting how characters and destinies are shaped by haunting presences of the past.

Vie secrète (1998), an essay on love and desire, may appear to be a surprising choice when the themes of haunting and mourning are so readily available in Quignard's fictions.[1] In *Vie secrète*, however, the author conjoins the themes of love and mourning, joy and melancholy, writing and reading in a radically novel way. Mourning and haunting become crucial metaphors that account for an ethical mode of connecting with others, be they present, absent or deceased. For Quignard, to love, to know, to read and to write are processes that entail engaging with the singularity of another. They suppose we acknowledge its irreducible otherness, which is experienced more acutely when we mourn a loved one. Quignard conceives of intimacy as a form of mourning in so far as it is an emotional and intellectual state in which one recognizes that the person loved, whether present or absent, remains radically other, with his emotions in part resisting empathy.

In this respect, *Vie secrète* occupies an original space within the larger body of literature and theory about mourning and phantoms, as it restores a positive value to the notions of haunting and mourning. For Freud, ghosts par excellence elicit an uncanny feeling because they embody the return of the repressed. For Otto Rank, the phantom and the double are imaginary figures that function like an insurance against death.[2] Colin Davis, however, has usefully brought to the fore how the notion of *hauntology*, which Derrida developed in *Spectres de Marx*, has marked an ethical turn in the story of the ghost: 'Attending to the ghost is an ethical injunction insofar as it occupies the place of the Levinasian Other: a wholly irrecuperable intrusion in our world, which is not comprehensible within our available intellectual frameworks, but whose otherness we are responsible for preserving.'[3] Derrida's spectres signal that present and past, absence and presence are categories that are not as reassuringly impermeable as we would like them to be. Colin Davis also reminds us how Abraham and Torok, in their essay *L'Écorce et le noyau*, have made the phantom the metaphor of foreclosed secrets that keep returning from one generation to the next.[4] In Quignard's works, ghosts are not so much the bearers of unspoken and unspeakable secrets; neither are they experienced as uncanny. Instead, they give body and shape to the present. Aphorisms about knowledge and love, desire and mourning, music and resonance cross-fertilize so as to challenge current perceptions of melancholy and loss. Melancholy, it emerges, is not so much a pathological form of mourning, as Freudian theory has it. For Quignard, it represents instead a psychological engagement with the irreducible singularity of another. It is a form of radical identification inherent in the processes of reading and writing, as well as in loving and mourning. The spectre, in *Vie secrète*, becomes the signifier of what is past, yet survives into the present. It is also the signifier of what our curiosity, intellectual or emotional, seeks to grasp whilst recognizing it cannot be fully grasped.

By exploring the canonical texts that haunt *Vie secrète* and the ways in which they are transmuted and subverted, this essay shows how the book composes an ethics of reading and knowledge that is also an ethics of love and mourning. In the first section, it reveals the way in which the figure of the ghost and the principle of ghostliness or 'spectrality', to keep up Derrida's metaphor, break several oppositions between past and present, self and other, passive and active roles. In a second section, I argue that the dismantling of such binary categories translates into both an aesthetic and an ethical stance. Self-effacement emerges as an ideal ethical relation with others. For Quignard, writing is foremost an act of reading and *Vie secrète* abundantly rewrites and subverts the classics. Writing is a practice that consists in hosting the texts of literary forebears and paradoxically Quignard is most idiosyncratic when he 'ghost-writes' his own readings. Self-effacement also defines the act of mourning: it allows the mourner to resonate with voices of the past.

The haunted text: knowledge, recognition and the familiarity of the unknown

In 'Mourning and melancholia', Freud argued that successful mourning is a psychological process consisting in the progressive transformation of the attachment to a lost love object into another attachment.[5] By contrast, the melancholic who is incapable of such transformation internalizes the lost object. Freud's analysis of closure rests on the principle of transformation. In his view, no psychic energy ever dies, it only mutates. The expression 'work of mourning' refers precisely to that transformation of affect, when one attachment grows into another.

Interestingly, *Vie secrète* rests on multiple transformations. Cast in a hybrid form where the traditional boundaries between autobiography, fiction and theory break down and blur, *Vie secrète* provides an arresting example of the ways in which affect and emotions feed into theory, as a way of mourning. The book indeed opens with a fictionalized autobiographical account of the narrator's relationship with his now deceased violin teacher, Némie Satler. He remembers this relationship as a formative experience marked by learning, secrecy, music and silence, all themes that find further theoretical developments in the subsequent aphorisms. While the text alternates between its philosophical and fictional guises, its very subject is the transformation of love. In *Vie secrète*, love is linked to loss, as the tale of the narrator's past relationship with Némie is echoed by a relationship with a younger woman who is referred to by the initial M. and which takes place in the present of narration. Even though the text never explicitly establishes connections between Némie and M., the relationship with the latter is implicitly presented as a continuation and rebirth of the former.

Mourning, in *Vie secrète*, is not only construed as the capacity to transform affect into creativity and an old attachment into a new one. The narrator is aware of the continuities between past and present. From the start, Quignard warns: 'Ce que je cherche à penser ne se discerne en rien de ce que j'ai vécu et surtout de ce que je vis et ce que je veux poursuivre de vivre.'[6] This statement of intent points to the metamorphic nature of experience and thought, but also to an unusual temporality in which past, present and future are blurred. The past is haunting the present, which in turn is haunting the future. With such multiple transformations, *Vie secrète* offers fertile ground to explore the relation between love and knowledge as well as desire and mourning. I will show how haunting rather than transformation provides a metaphor for the relationship between knowledge and learner, between text and reader. This seems all the more relevant since the text revisits the Platonic tradition of *Symposium* insofar as it makes love a subset of knowledge, just as physical love is an avatar of curiosity and erudition. If the narrative of love functions as an allegory of knowledge and the aphorisms on knowledge as small vignettes emblematizing passion, love lost transmutes into creativity. That it is one and the same energy that drives knowledge, passion and poetry has been well established by Freud's theory of libido and affect and Lacan's more radical dismantling of the opposition between affect and intellect, both thinkers having amply drawn on the Platonic and neo-Platonic tradition in their essays.

Further parallels with *Symposium* are more obvious. The narrator's bond with Némie is mediated through the teaching of music. Quignard implicitly imitates and extrapolates from Plato's text in which the pedagogical relation was conceived of as erotic.[7] More importantly, Némie teaches him to learn, that is to love to learn, as both good teaching and good learning exceed their scope and intention. Quignard writes: 'Il y a trente ans de cela, j'avais bien conscience que Némie m'enseignait quelque chose, mais j'estimais qu'il s'agissait de musique. J'ai le soupçon maintenant qu'elle enseignait peut-être alors tout simplement ce que je recherche, avec un tel entêtement, à chercher.'[8] The platonic heritage indeed considered love as a subset of knowledge, or, more exactly, of the love for knowledge. Yet Quignard does more than reformulate such a legacy. The construction of the above sentence, based on repetitions and variations of a same word and its cognates ('elle m'enseignait',

'Némie m'enseignait', 'recherche', 'chercher') imitates the motion of curiosity and desire, its very plasticity and mutability, until it settles into its paradoxical metamorphic nature ('ce que je recherche à chercher'). Quignard does more than rewrite one of the main lessons bestowed by *Symposium,* namely that love sublimates into intellectual curiosity. He highlights how knowledge has a haunting effect. It has a temporality of its own: meaning comes with a delay, however open ended, in unexpected forms that we do not always recognize. Recognizing meaning triggers new associations of its own; the ingestion and working-through of knowledge remains therefore a dynamic process par excellence.

Quignard, however, goes further in his aphorisms. He also re-defines the process of gaining knowledge as, paradoxically, a passive activity: 'Qui n'éprouve pas de joie quand il apprend ne doit pas être enseigné. Se passionner pour ce qui est autre, aimer, apprendre c'est le même.'[9] The prohibition of the first line makes joy a moral imperative and seems to echo and bring together two philosophical traditions. First, this negative imperative reformulates the Epicurean adage that joy comes not as a reward of learning but is concomitant with the dynamic process itself.[10] Secondly, in keeping with the Spinozan tradition, it makes joy an ultimate virtue, a state of self-reflexive intelligibility when man recognizes that he is just a fragment or a manifestation of an infinite world with which he is continuous.[11] Quignard would run the risk of repeating the Masters, were it not for the wilful grammatical mistake that brings about an additional ethical corollary. Indeed, this mistaken passive construction makes the indirect object of *enseigner* an agent, which is possible in English of course but not in French, thus insisting on the passivity of the learning process. The deliberate mistake implicitly has *enseigner* behave as if it were a transitive instead of an intransitive verb, thereby suggesting an unmediated link between pupil and teacher, pupil and knowledge. This finds corroboration in the second set of equivalences established between learning, love and passion for differences and otherness. This declaration reads like a pastiche of a Pre-Socratic saying, in particular Parmenides' equation between thinking and being, which has often been trans-lated into French as 'Le même, en vérité, c'est à la fois penser et être'. Whether wilful or unconscious pastiche, whether active or passive copying, such phrasing shows how Quignard lets himself be captive of his own readings. He allows himself to be haunted by texts that have a phantom-like status, that is to say, at once present and absent, at once extraneous and part of oneself. In that respect, such an imitative formulation also illustrates its content, namely that love and knowledge are paradoxically passive activities, during which new material is ingested, and the boundaries between self and other, passive and active roles vacillate. Quignard virulently rejects the notion that learning and knowledge are the domination of new material. In order to preserve its freshness and irreducible difference, discovery needs to be experienced in full passivity.

I am not suggesting that Quignard is short-circuiting the main pitfalls and questionings of Western metaphysics with a grammatically mistaken passive construction. Yet, repeatedly, his works invite the reader to reflect on moments of self-effacement when one no longer assimilates the unknown into known categories. Like reading, these are processes of passive intake of knowledge, eliciting both awe and wonder. Quignard exemplifies his position most strikingly in *Le Sexe et l'effroi*, where he analyses how such awe is domesticated through the social distribution of passive versus active sexual roles in Ancient Rome:

> *Il y a un mot de Septumius énigmatique et terrible.* Amat qui scribet, paed-
> icator qui leget. *(Celui qui écrit sodomise. Celui qui lit est sodomisé.)*
> *L'auctor demeure un* paedicator. *C'est le vieux* status *de l'homme libre*
> *romain. Mais le* lector *est* servus. *La lecture rejoint la passivité. Le lecteur*
> *devient l'esclave d'une autre* Domus. *Ecrire désire. Lire jouit ... Tout*
> *homme, toute femme sont passifs quand arrive la jouissance ... La volupté*
> *surprend toujours le corps qui désire. Platon faisait de l'effroi le premier*
> *présent de la beauté. C'est la familiarité de quelque chose d'inconnu.*[12]

Quignard actually over-translates the violence of Septumius' image, and in so doing, he forcefully reminds his reader of a simple but easily forgotten paradox, namely that the most frantic and active pursuit of knowledge or love is only rewarded with success in passivity. 'Eureka!' is a cry of victory but also of surrender – surrender, that is, to the unknown. This may be viewed as a sophism, a mere rhetorical figure. Yet, as the text elaborates on the social and sexual role distribution between 'domus', the free citizen and master, and 'servus', the slave, a series of oppositions emerge: freedom, active sexuality, writing and desire versus slavery, passive sexuality, reading and pleasure. This paradigmatic opposition reverses through a strange dialectic when in the next paragraph sexual pleasure and awe are conjoined in the experience of beauty, with beauty being redefined as the familiarity of the unknown. This new set of associations between beauty, awe and the familiarity of the unknown is rather unexpected. Reading, like sexual pleasure, is a passive activity; they both have a paradoxical temporality of their own. The freshness of the present is imbued with an unconscious memory of the past. Reading, like aesthetic and sexual pleasure, is a process that mobilizes the memory of something unknown. Such ambiguity forms a ghostlike experience insofar as its emotional impact stems from the recognition that the past still permeates the present experience. In that respect, ghosts and spectres hover and are ubiquitous in aesthetic, learning and reading experiences. They always manifest something known of old, which cannot consciously and fully be brought up in a mental representation. Rather than eliciting an uncanny feeling, the 'spectrality' of such experiences is associated with pleasure.

In effect, Quignard demands that his readers break down the polarity between active and passive roles and make them permutable categories, reading being par excellence a moment when passivity turns into activity. Quignard summarizes this in an enigmatic formula, which intimates that reading and writing are concomitant, indeed, even inextricably bound: 'Je cherche à écrire un livre où je songe en lisant.'[13] Tellingly, the narrator and his companion M. are often seen reading, either alone or together, like Dante's lovers. In the text, reading scenes epitomize privileged moments of being, moments of silent symbiosis and harmony, when the self is regenerated in a dynamic process of receptivity. And, in *Vie secrète*, the feeling of familiarity with the unknown is extended to the activity of reading which in turn functions like a metaphor or paradigm for Quignard's ethics of knowledge and love: 'Les anciens Grecs usaient du verbe *anagignôskô* pour dire lire. Lire pour les anciens Grecs, c'est mot à mot, reconnaître ce qu'on attend.'[14] Reading is a recognition scene in so far as what has been experienced in confusion becomes joyfully intelligible. Quignard highlights here the paradox of reading: discovery of the new is the identification of something known of old. He plays with several loci classici of Ancient Greek philosophy and poetics. His statement finds resonances with Plato's paradox of knowledge exposed in Meno's dialogue, namely that we can be in search neither of the unknown nor of the known because the former we ignore and the latter we know.[15] Quignard's statement perhaps also echoes the germane notion of knowledge as recollection (anamnesis). Plato's metaphysics propose that knowledge is the remembrance and recognition of forms, the archetypes of all phenomena in the physical world.[16] More importantly, Quignard's etymological glossing refers to Aristotle's *Poetics* where recognition is considered to be one of the components of plot that holds greatest emotional impact on the reader, that is, it literally seduces him, leads him astray, outside himself.[17] Quignard elaborates on the notion in a short essay 'Anagnosis', where he defines reading as the recognition and the displacement of the boundaries of the self. He therefore makes Oedipus' recognizing himself as the murderer of his father an Ur-recognition scene because self and other so powerfully and tragically coincide. Recognition does indeed correspond to a hermeneutic resolution when emotion, passion and knowledge are concomitants in a single experience. It implies a new adequate rereading of reality that results from isolating similarities and differences between past and present, self and other. Thus in such moments, selfhood is challenged, identity changed and its boundaries displaced.[18]

Such poetics and ethics of reading are transmuted in *Vie secrète* on several levels. First, on the narrative level, the narrator's love for M. repeats the affair he had with Némie. It is construed as the survival of affect transferred to a new attachment. Love survives even after separations and therefore feeds on the recognitions of previous loves, Quignard intimates. Because affect perpetuates and mutates, recognition represents modes of knowledge or love that have a more violent emotional impact than discovery or love at first sight: 'Reconnaître est un régime aussi bouleversant mais encore plus fasciné que peut l'être la fulguration du coup de foudre.'[19] Secondly, on an aesthetic level, such ethics of reading transmute into the remembrance and resurgence of past texts in recycled forms. In a text replete with pastiche and references to the classics, Quignard obviously plays with recognition patterns. Thirdly, on a philosophical level, the notion that the past survives in the present finds expression in different aphorisms which variously assert that we are determined by an original imprint we occasionally glimpse and that we abide by linguistic, social and biological structures to which we are oblivious. More importantly, according to Quignard, we are haunted by a scene forever lost upon us: the moment of our conception. Throughout *Vie secrète*, Quignard elaborates upon the idea that we are defined by what we do and cannot know. This inscrutable yet haunting event is what he calls 'l'angle mort du langage': it renews and regenerates curiosity and fascination, be it intellectual, artistic, erotic or amorous. Quignard writes that: 'L'homme est celui à qui une image manque.'[20] Absent from the scene of his conception, he tracks down in artistic creation the mystery of his own individuation, all the more disquieting for being the result of the contingencies of sexual reproduction and death. For Quignard, dreams and desires are echoes of moments that predate our life stories. And all images are the avatars of this lost image.

The haunted subject: mourning, self-effacement and the language of affect

In *Vie secrète*, haunting and recollection constitute common principles that pervade language, literature, knowledge and desire. This principle of haunting defines both the aesthetics and ethics at work in Quignard's text. First, Quignard proposes a literary ideal resting on a language haunted by what he calls 'l'angle mort', that is a language haunted by its own inscrutable origins. Such a literary ideal of what I call a 'language of affect' has ethical consequences. For one of Quignard's prime concerns is the direct emotional communication with those absent or present. *Vie secrète* is indeed underpinned by a recurring question: what forms of empathy allow for relating to others. In this second section, I shall first define Quignard's language of affect and show how it promotes an aesthetic and ethical ideal of self-effacement that allows for an enhanced connection with others. Yet, language, because it is inherently wrought by mediation, is a lesser means to convey emotion. In this text, silence, paradoxically, and touch are upheld as higher means of communication. As Quignard construes and constructs music as a form of touch, it forms a language of empathy. Musical pleasure has a haunting quality. It lies in the recognition of harmonic and rhythmic patterns; it implies both anticipation and memory. Its aesthetic and emotional impact has therefore a double temporality. I shall argue that, by manipulating images of resonance, vibration and interpretation, Quignard makes music an ideal mode of connection, and that, in doing so, the author also redefines melancholy and haunting as an ethical mode of relating to others.

'Je cherche une pensée aussi impliquée dans son penseur qu'un rêve peut l'être dans le dormeur.'[21] This statement of intent provides a good illustration of what I called Quignard's language of affect. With this comparison between thinker and dreamer, he creates an aesthetic ideal where thought is an expression of the unconscious and a manifestation of affect; it is therefore, at once an active and passive process. Such an aesthetic ideal is assigned the momentous onus of expressing the secrecy of emotions that predate our affective and intellectual life. On several occasions, Quignard has professed his affinities with and admiration for Longinus and, with his suggestive and fragmented aphoristic writing, he intends, like his Greek forebear, 'not to persuade but to entrance'.[22] In *Le Dictionnaire du Littéraire*, Alain Viala explains how for both Longinus and Boileau, who translated and commented upon the first-century treatise, the Sublime is an aesthetic ideal that hopes to elicit in the reader a sense of the Beyond and a refracted feeling of the Infinite.[23] Quignard's writing endeavours to echo not so much a Beyond, but rather a Before, that is to say, the pure affectivity and originary unity that predates language and birth. In her essay *Soleil noir: dépression et mélancolie*, Kristeva examines whether mood is a language, in other words, whether affect can replace the symbolization operated by language.[24] In effect, Quignard reverses the question as his writing tends towards an aesthetic ideal where language is not the expression of affect, but is and coincides with affect. Sound and music have of course a special status. As Quignard remarks in *La Haine de la musique*, eyes have eyelids; ears do not. Audition is the only sense that links the adult to his prenatal life insofar as sound, rather than touch, is the sole link the foetus has with the outside world. More importantly, to fulfil his quest for a language able to capture the uncharted emotions of a prenatal life, Quignard summons Latin and Greek: 'Ce qui est avant notre langue renvoie à ce qui est avant notre naissance. La couche la plus ancienne (le latin) dira la scène la plus ancienne.'[25] Latin and Greek are the languages of the primitive scene and this performative statement composes Quignard's articles of faith in a fantasized parent language. *Vie secrète* is indeed studded with Latin and Greek words, whose foreign sound interrupts the familiarity of reading the French text. Quignard's etymological glosses, rather than being monolithic or explicative of semantic evolutions, are poetic and playful. They bring out the disparity between archaic meaning of a classic word and the contemporary meaning of its etymological descendant. They reactivate old and disused meanings that are still haunting words.

Quignard obviously delights in the paradox that the meaning of old words refreshes new ones. His fascination for the origins of words displays a wish to capture the dawn of meaning. His glosses play with the embryonic potentials of words and as the latter develop, they give the illusion of a cratylic, motivated language. Quignard prefers, for instance, to use the Latin noun *fascinus* for *phallus*, because its cognate *fascinatio*, meaning fascination, defines both the awe and joy in the lover's or the reader's relation to the unknown. *Fascinus* is also dynamically redefined by Quignard's glossing of fascination as the blind spot of language: it imposes silence. In other glosses, Quignard develops his ethical stance: '*Coire* est le verbe romain qui signifie l'amour. *Ire*, c'est aller ensemble.'[26] Love, then, is a state of togetherness and not a state of union or fusion; contrary to sexuality it maintains distances. Quignard's stance is never definitive. It constantly readjusts, with different glosses cross-fertilizing. 'Lire, c'est le plaisir de penser avec l'autre sexe', he writes in the same chapter.[27] Read against each other, both aphorisms create a third meaning: ultimately reading and love overcome the scandal of sexual division. It enables the reader to think as, if not almost be, the other gender.

A paradox emerges, then, from this activity of etymological glossing. Quignard's writing is all the more idiosyncratic and subjectively invested when he takes dictation from ancient words. For his etymological glosses are indeed poetic creations. They function like archaic metaphors, composing brisk sets of equivalences that privilege identity over likeness. Quignard surrenders to language when he writes the lessons of classical etymology, thereby enacting his own self-effacement as a writer, his own 'disparition élocutoire'.[28] In this respect, his poetics do mimic his ethics. Authorship is a moment of dispossession, so is self-accomplishment through love.

Self-effacement is not an experience of dispossession but, rather, of plenitude. This is the logical consequence of Quignard's ethics of reading and writing. Reading finds its ultimate accomplishment in self-effacement, when the reader identifies with the text and suspends his own interpretation. Quignard writes: 'Aimer: lire à

livre ouvert.'[29] Self-effacement, being haunted, are prerequisite
states of mind that allow for both an ethical mode of relating to
others and an enhanced form of intimacy. Quignard asks obsessively
what form of communication exists between people and what forms
of empathy are possible. In a chapter entitled 'Sur le sentiment de
l'adieu', he strips melancholy of its negative valence. Freudian
psychoanalysis has brought to the fore that melancholy is a pathological form of mourning insofar as the subject refuses to let go of
his loss, instead internalizing it. Such internalizing implies that the
mourner fails to recognize his loss as other, considering it instead as
part of himself. Freud therefore argued that the melancholic suffers
from a form of narcissism. Interestingly, Quignard challenges the
specific issue of narcissism, reversing melancholia into a form of
connection with another, present or absent:

> *Celui qu'on aime est à mi-chemin du fantôme.*
>
> *Dans les bras l'un de l'autre, rêvant l'un de l'autre, il arrive que nous
> rêvions à l'intérieur de notre crâne de celle qui respire à nos côtés, et dort, et
> rêve à celui qui la rêve. On peut croire aux fantômes des amants quand on a
> vécu leur amour et alors que le destin les sépare. L'amour vit l'autre comme
> l'endeuillé vit le mort qui ne le quitte pas.[30]*

That a loved one has a phantom-like quality may come as a paradox.
And, yet, the image forcefully reminds us that the loved one is
always present and absent at once. He/she hovers between two
states, that of being an emanation of personal projections and
desire and that of being a radical stranger, because intimacy and
communication are inherently intermittent and imperfect. Yet this
aphorism, as it rests upon a series of semantic repetitions, oppositions and echoes between the inside and the outside of the body,
between closeness and separation, experience and dreaming, reinforces the image it describes: that of intimacy and reciprocity having
a dreamlike if not phantom-like quality, despite the very palpable
presence of the lover. Being in love, like being in mourning, is a
state that does not suffer that intimacy can only be intermittent.
Paradoxically, the imaginative internalizing and keeping alive
described vividly in the above quotation is a form of receptivity to
another. Quignard writes that 'La mélancolie veille sur l'altérité
dans l'amour.'[31] It is the phantom-like quality of the lover that
ensures such vigilance: he haunts, he is being dreamt of and yet
remains at once intimate and a radical stranger.

This receptivity to another may also be seen as a kind of spiritual exercise, a form of connection with those absent or bygone. Mystical images are regularly called up and voided of their religious context. In a sense, one may argue that Quignard is a secular mystic insofar that he seeks to invent a language that transforms absence into presence in order to relate to, not so much an absent God, but those who are no more.[32] One understands why the metaphors of music, resonance and vibration take on special importance in *Vie secrète*. They compose images of ideal communication, of ideal propagation and transmission of affect, ensuring that an initial emotion persists and survives in its very corporeality, dies out until it is interpreted again. It elevates interpretation to an act of revival. Music may be seen as a language, at once the expression of emotion and the locus of its taming. According to Adorno, the figures of Apollo and Orpheus both convey that music has the power at once to elicit passions but also to pacify their violence.[33] The latter, after he has lost Eurydice, both expresses his love and overcomes his grief by playing the lyre. Significantly, rather than invoking Orpheus, Quignard appropriates instead the story of the flaying of Marsyas, another mythological figure associated with music. He does so in order to suggest that music is primarily an instrument of empathy and compassion, and sometimes violently so: 'Pourquoi dans le mythe grec écorche-t-on le musicien? Pour aller derrière le visage. Parce que la musique s'introduit inexplicablement, invisiblement, aussitôt derrière la surface.'[34] Quignard plays with the literal meaning of Marsyas' defining quality, his being flayed. He is 'un écorché vif': literally meaning flayed alive, and metaphorically referring to a sensibility on edge. His emotions are neither contaminated by language nor any longer refracted by his epidermis. Music, the author intimates, is about empathy pushed to an unbearable limit. Quignard's image forcefully conveys that musical experience induces a state of intense receptivity, because music is an unmediated language. It is the propagation of affect made almost palpable, however evanescently, in the form of vibrations; it also has haunting effect, because musical phrases emerge as patterns retrospectively and in silence.

Music, as it transmutes touch into vibration, undoes the limits of the self and provides, therefore, an experience of continuity. With its haunting effect, the lingering and fading of vibration also undoes the linearity of time. In one of his aphorisms, Quignard expresses his wonder that the sound post is designated by the word 'âme' in French: it is the piece of wood that holds the violin together and which transforms the vibrations of the strings into sound and music. If the narrator of *Vie secrète* so readily divests himself of his own subjectivity, he perhaps does so in order to find finer resonance with voices of the past. In return, he is rewarded with a soul. Telling the past story of his violin teacher, Némie, he makes the act of recollecting haunting memories a very physical experience:

> *Cette femme que j'ai aimée il y a des années, il y a même des dizaines d'années ne vit plus dans ce monde – ni dans aucun autre – mais quelque chose qui est son corps circule encore dans le mien. Cette trace vivante ... est domiciliée dans le corps qui répond à l'appel de mon nom. Plus encore que l'âme qui s'en détache peut-être comme un echo, tout corps aimé est à demeure dans le corps où il n'a fait, dès le premier instant où sa forme s'est consentie dans l'emprise, que retrouver la place qui le guettait.*[35]

The lingering of echoing voices of the past gives the narrator's body a remarkable new topography, granting it both enhanced interiority and multiple extensions. Némie is no more and yet, the text insists, something of her body still dwells in the narrator's and animates it. With this image, the processes of incorporation and internalization of the absent and the dead are not just a convenient psychological metaphor; they constitute a very corporeal and dynamic experience. With the metaphors of resonance, vibration, reverberation and echoing, the body and the name and soul it houses are like a musical instrument. In keeping with the image of the sound post, the narrator echoes the existence of those who are no more. He acquires a heightened sense of self by refracting the legacies of bygone voices. Here Quignard would seem to be in tune with Derrida's reflection on mourning, when apropos Louis Althusser's death, he writes: 'Il ne m'entend qu'en moi, en nous (mais nous ne sommes jamais nous-mêmes que depuis ce lieu de résonance en nous même de l'autre, et de l'autre mortel).'[36] For both the philosopher and writer, identity is a point of resonance, where voices of others merge with and enrich the self. One understands why the notion of psychological closure would find little currency in *Vie secrète*. Mourning is a dynamic, ubiquitous and silent process, taking place in excess of any conscious intention. The self-effacement that characterizes Quignard's narrator whilst in love, in mourning or in the process of writing is not so much a feeling of uncanny dispossession; rather, self-effacement enables the sounding of voices of the past. One may understand better why Quignard puts writing and mourning on a par. As forms of experiential knowledge, they require a state of self-effacement in order to resonate with the Other. This brings not only a heightened sense of self, but also what Julia Kristeva calls 'une jubilation résurrectionnelle': the pleasure of casting characters and voices of the past into an imaginative afterlife and seeing them remain the same yet different.[37]

Notes

1   Pascal Quignard, *Vie secrète* (Paris: Gallimard, 1998).
2   Otto Rank, *The Double: A Psychoanalytic Study*, trans. Harry Tucker (New York/London: Meridian Books, 1971).
3   Jacques Derrida, *Spectres de Marx: l'état de la dette, le travail du deuil, et la nouvelle Internationale* (Paris: Galilée, 1993); see Colin Davis, *État présent*: hauntology, spectres and phantoms', *French Studies*, 59, 3 (July 2005), 373–9.
4   Nicolas Abraham and Maria Torok, *L'Écorce et le noyau* (Paris: Flammarion, 1987; first published 1978).
5   Sigmund Freud, 'Mourning and melancholia' (1917), in *The Standard Edition of the Complete Psychological Works of Sigmund Freud*, vol. 14, trans. James Strachey (London: Hogarth Press, 1953–74), pp. 237–58.
6   Quignard, *Vie secrète*, p. 14.
7   Plato, *Symposium* (Cambridge, MA, vol. 3, first published 1917; Loeb Classical Library, 1999). See in particular Pausanias' speech (183d–5c).
8   *Vie secrète*, p. 17.
9   Ibid., p. 28.
10   'Ce n'est pas, en effet, après la recherche que nous éprouvons de la joie, mais pendant la recherche même.' (Epicure, *Sentences Vaticanes*, 27, in *Lettres* (Paris: Éditions Bordas, 1982), p. 86).
11   Baruch de Spinoza, 'On the origin and nature of the affects', in *Ethics* (London: Penguin, 1994), pp. 76–7. Quignard pays tribute to Spinoza's philosophy in his essays, in particular in 'Dieu', *Petits Traités* (Paris: Gallimard, 1990), pp. 35–41 and 'Ut Sol', in *Abîmes* (Paris: Grasset, 2002), pp.18–19.
12   Pascal Quignard, *Le Sexe et l'effroi* (Paris: Gallimard, 1994), p. 260.
13   *Vie secrète*, p. 286.
14   Ibid., p. 146.
15   Plato, *Meno* (Cambridge, MA, vol. 2, first published 1917; Loeb Classical Library, 1999). See paragraph 80e.

16 Plato, *Phaedo* (Cambridge, MA, vol. 1, first published 1917; Loeb Classical Library, 1999). Knowledge is linked to metempsychosis in Plato's myth. For him, the intellect occasionally has access to archetypal forms when a person remembers the visions his soul had when it travelled through the ideal realm of forms during metempsychosis.

17 Terence Cave, *Recognitions* (Oxford: Clarendon, 1988). For further details on the meaning of such impact, see the interpretation of Aristotle's *Poetics*, in the introduction, 'Beginning with the poetics'. For further details on the common etymological root between anagnostes (reader) and anagnorisis (recognition), see the chapter 'Recognition and the reader'.

18 See Quignard's essay 'Anagnosis': 'Effet de retour de la parole sur cette sorte de 'soi' au sein de nous-mêmes – le 'soi' et le 'non-soi' que la lecture révèle qu'elle met à nu et qu'elle déplace, qu'elle exalte et brime, qu'elle humilie et qu'elle illumine, qu'elle cultive et bouleverse' (Pascal Quignard, *Petits Traités II* (Paris: Gallimard, 1997), pp. 67–90).

19 *Vie secrète*, p. 12.

20 *Le Sexe et l'effroi*, p. 12.

21 *Vie secrète*, p. 404.

22 Longinus, *On Sublimity* (Oxford: Clarendon Press, 1965): 'For the effect of elevated language is not to persuade but to entrance' (p. 45).

23 See Alain Viala's article on the Sublime in Paul Aron, Denis Saint-Jacques et Alain Viala (eds), *Le Dictionnaire du Littéraire* (Paris: Presses Universitaires de France, 2002).

24 Julia Kristeva, *Soleil noir: dépression et mélancolie* (Paris: Gallimard, 1987).

25 *Le Sexe et l'effroi*, p. 260.

26 *Vie secrète*, p. 422.

27 Ibid., p. 429.

28 See Stéphane Mallarmé, 'Crise de Vers', in *Œuvres* (Paris: Classique-Garnier, 1985), pp. 275–6.

29 *Vie secrète*, p. 217.

30 Ibid., p. 469.

31 Ibid., p. 453.

32 On the secular mystic, see Michel de Certeau's *La Fable mystique* (Paris: Gallimard, 1982). Interestingly, in his introduction, he defines mystical discourses as 'une théologie du fantôme' insofar as they seek to render present an absent God (p. 10).

33 See Theodor W. Adorno, 'On the fetish-character in music and the regression of listening', in *Essays on Music*, selected, with introduction, commentary and notes by Richard Leppert (Berkeley: University of California Press, 2002), pp. 289–90.

34 *Vie secrète*, p. 321.

35 Ibid., p. 14.

36 Jacques Derrida, *Chaque fois unique la fin du monde* (Paris: Galilée, 2003), pp. 149–50.

37 Julia Kristeva, *Soleil noir*, p. 114.

Bibliography

Abraham, Nicolas and Torok, Maria, *L'Écorce et le noyau* (Paris: Flammarion, 1987; first published 1978).

Adert, Laurent, *Les Mots des autres: Flaubert, Sarraute, Pinget* (Paris: Septentrion, 1996).

Adorno, Theodor W., 'On the fetish-character in music and the regression of listening', in *Essays on Music*, selected, with introduction, commentary and notes by Richard Leppert (Berkeley: University of California Press, 2002).

Alizart, Mark and Kihm, Christophe (eds), *Fresh Théorie II* (Paris: Éditions Léo Scheer, 2006).

Aristotle, *Poetics*, ed. and trans. S. Halliwell (Cambridge, MA: Harvard University Press, 1995).

Aron, Paul, Saint-Jacques, Denis and Viala, Alain (eds), *Le Dictionnaire du Littéraire* (Paris: Presses Universitaires de France, 2002).

Asibong, Andrew, 'Meat, murder, metamorphosis: the transformational ethics of François Ozon', *French Studies*, 59, 3 (July 2005), 203–15.

Aston, Margaret, 'Death', in Rosemary Horrox (ed.), *Fifteenth-Century Attitudes: Perceptions of Society in Late Medieval England* (Cambridge: Cambridge University Press, 1994), pp. 202–28.

Barthes, Roland, *La Chambre claire: Note sur la photographie* (Paris: Cahiers du Cinéma/Gallimard/Seuil, 1980).

Barthes, Roland, *Œuvres complètes* (Paris: Seuil, 1993).

Blanchot, Maurice, *L'Espace littéraire* (Paris: Gallimard, 1988).

Bloom, Harold, *The Anxiety of Influence: A Theory of Poetry*, 2nd edn (New York/Oxford: Oxford University Press, 1997).

Boccaccio, Giovanni, *Famous Women*, ed. and trans. Virginia Brown (Cambridge, MA./London: Harvard University Press, 2001).

Boccace 'Des cleres et nobles femmes' , ed. Jeanne Baroin and Josiane Haffen, 2 vols (Paris: Les Belles Lettres, 1993).

Borie, Monique, *Le Fantôme, ou le théâtre qui doute* (Arles: Actes Sud, 1997).

Bouvet, Honoré, *Medieval Muslims, Christians, and Jews in Dialogue: The 'Apparicion Maistre Jehan de Meun' of Honorat Bovet*, ed. Michael Hanly (Tempe: Arizona Center for Medieval and Renaissance Studies, 2005).

Bowie, Malcolm, *Proust Among the Stars* (New York: Columbia University Press, 1998).

Braden, Gordon, *Renaissance Tragedy and the Senecan Tradition: Anger's Privilege* (New Haven: Yale University Press, 1985).

Brantôme, Pierre de Bourdeille, seigneur de, *Recueil des dames, poésies et tombeaux*, ed. Étienne Vaucherat (Paris: Gallimard, 1991).

Brombert, Victor, *Victor Hugo and the Visionary Novel* (Cambridge, MA: Harvard University Press, 1984).

Broome, Peter, 'Pinget's *Passacaille*', *Nottingham French Studies*, 12 (1973), 86–99.

Buse, Peter and Stott, Andrew (eds), *Ghosts: Deconstruction, Psychoanalysis, History* (Basingstoke: Macmillan, 1999).

Butor, Michel, 'Victor Hugo romancier', *Répertoire II* (Paris: Minuit, 1964).

Castle, Terry, *The Female Thermometer: Eighteenth-Century Culture and the Invention of the Uncanny* (New York/Oxford: Oxford University Press, 1995).

Cave, Terence, *Recognitions* (Oxford: Clarendon Press, 1988).

Cerquiglini-Toulet, Jacqueline, *L'Écriture testamentaire à la fin du moyen âge: identité, dispersion, trace* (Oxford: EHRC, 1999).

Certeau, Michel de, *La Fable mystique* (Paris: Gallimard, 1982).

Cixous, Hélène, *Jours de l'an* (Paris: des femmes, 1990).

——, 'Le Lieu de l'autre', interview with Frédéric Regard, March 1991, in Frédéric Regard (ed.), *Logique des traverses* (Saint-Étienne: PUSE, 1992), pp. 11–26.

——, *Portrait de Jacques Derrida en jeune saint juif* (Paris: Galilée, 2001).

——, *Rencontre terrestre* (Paris: Galilée, 2005).

Clark, J. M., *The Dance of Death in the Middle Ages and the Renaissance* (Glasgow: Glasgow University Press, 1950).

Cox, Fiona, 'The dawn of a hope so horrible: Javert and the absurd', in James Hiddleston (ed.), *Victor Hugo – Romancier de l'abîme* (Oxford: Legenda, 2002).

——, 'Money and identity in *Les Misérables*', in Sarah Capitanio, Lisa Downing, Paul Rowe and Nick White (eds), *Currencies – Fiscal Fortunes and Cultural Capital in Nineteenth Century France* (Bern: Peter Lang, 2005), pp. 121–32.

Crétin, Guillaume, *Apparition du Mareschal sans reproche*, in *Œuvres poétiques de Guillaume Crétin*, ed. Kathleen Chesney (Paris: Firmin-Didot, 1932), pp. 143–81.

D'Aubignac, *La Pratique du théâtre*, ed. Hélène Baby (Paris: Champion, 2001).

Davis, Colin, '*État présent*: hauntology, spectres and phantoms', *French Studies*, 59, 3 (July 2005), 373–9.

——, *Haunted Subjects: Deconstruction, Psychoanalysis and the Return of the Dead* (Basingstoke: Palgrave Macmillan, 2007).

Delcourt, M., 'Jodelle et Plutarque', *Bulletin de l'Association Guillaume Budé*, 42 (Janvier 1934), 36–52.

Deleuze, Gilles, *Cinéma*, vol. 1, *L'Image-Mouvement* (Paris: Minuit, 1983) and vol. 2, *L'Image-Temps* (Paris: Minuit, 1985).

Derrida, Jacques, 'Signature événement contexte', in *Marges de la philosophie* (Paris: Minuit, 1972).

——, 'Fors: Les mots anglés de Nicolas Abraham et Maria Torok', preface to Nicolas Abraham and Maria Torok, *Le Verbier de l'homme aux loups* (Paris: Flammarion, 1999, first published 1976), pp. 7–73.

——, 'Geschlecht I', in *Heidegger et la question* (Paris: Flammarion, 'Champs', 1990).

——, 'Circonfession', in Geoffrey Bennington (ed.), *Jacques Derrida* (Paris: Seuil, 1991).

——, *Spectres de Marx: l'état de la dette, le travail du deuil, et la nouvelle Internationale* (Paris: Galilée, 1993).

——, *Chaque fois unique la fin du monde* (Paris: Galilée, 2003).

Detambel, Régine, *Album* (Paris: Calman-Lévy, 1995).

Dosmond, Simone, 'Folie d'Eraste, folie d'Oreste', in Jean-Louis Cabanès (ed.), *Littérature et médecine*, vol. II (Bordeaux: Université Michel de Montaigne Bordeaux III, 2000).

Dubos, Jean-Baptiste, *Réflexions critiques sur la poésie et sur la peinture* (Paris: Jean Mariette, 1719).

DuBruck, Edelgard E., 'Death: poetic perception and imagination (Continental Europe)', in Edelgard E. DuBruck and Barbara I. Gusick (eds), *Death and Dying in the Middle Ages* (New York: Peter Lang, 1999), pp. 295–313.

Ducoudray, Gustave, *Les Origines du parlement de Paris et la justice aux XIIIe et XIVe siècles* (Paris, 1902).

Duffy, Jean, *Reading Between the Lines – Claude Simon and the Visual Arts* (Liverpool: Liverpool University Press, 1998).

Duras, Marguerite, *L'Amant* (Paris: Minuit, 1984).

Du Verdier, Antoine, *Bibliotheque d'Antoine du Verdier, seigneur de Vauprivas* (Lyons: Barthélémy Honorat, 1585).

Eden, K., *Poetic and Legal Fiction in the Aristotelian Tradition* (Princeton: Princeton University Press, 1986).

Elliot, Revel, *Mythe et légende dans le théâtre de Racine* (Paris: Lettres Modernes, 1969).

Epicure, *Lettres* (Paris: Éditions Bordas, 1982).

Ernaux, Annie, *La Place* (Paris: Gallimard, 1984).

——, *Une Femme* (Paris: Gallimard, 1988).

——, *Je ne suis pas sortie de ma nuit* (Paris: Gallimard, 1997).

——, *La Honte* (Paris: Gallimard, 1997).

——, *L'Occupation* (Paris: Gallimard, 2002).

—— and Marie, Marc, *L'Usage de la photo* (Paris: Gallimard, 2005).

Evans, David, *'Le Tombeau de la Poésie*: strategies of textual resurrection in Mallarmé and Banville', in Lisa Downing, Nigel Harkness, Sonya Stephens and Tim Unwin (eds), *Birth and Death in Nineteenth-Century French Culture* (Amsterdam: Rodopi, 2007), pp. 63–79.

ffrench, Patrick, 'The memory of the image in Chris Marker's *La Jetée*', *French Studies*, 59, 1 (January 2005), 31–7.

Finucane, R. C., *Appearances of the Dead: A Cultural History of Ghosts* (London: Junction, 1982).

Freud, Sigmund, 'Mourning and melancholia' (1917), in *The Standard Edition of the Complete Psychological Works of Sigmund Freud*, vol. 14, trans. James Strachey (London: Hogarth Press, 1953–74), pp. 237–58.

Frost, Thomas, *The Wicked Lord Lyttelton* (Stroud: Nonsuch Publishing Ltd, 2006; first published 1876).

Garat, Anne-Marie, *Photos de familles* (Paris: Seuil, 1994).

Garnier, Robert, *Two Tragedies. Hippolyte and Marc Antoine*, ed. Cathleen M. Hill and Mary G. Morrisson (London: Athlone, 1975).

Gaudon, Jean, *Le temps de la contemplation: l'œuvre poétique de Victor Hugo des Misères au Seuil du gouffre (1845–1856)* (Paris: Flammarion, 1969).

Gordon, Avery F., *Ghostly Matters: Haunting and the Sociological Imagination* (Minneapolis and London: University of Minnesota Press, 1997).

Gossip, C. J., 'Oreste, *amant imaginaire*', *Papers on French Seventeenth-Century Literature*, 20, 39 (1993), 353–67.

Greenleaf, J. H., 'L'unité de lieu dans la Cléopâtre de Jodelle', *Wisconsin Studies in Language and Literature*, 20 (1924), 62–73.

Griffiths, Kate, 'Scribbling ghosts. The textual spectres and spectral texts of Émile Zola', in J. Horn and L. Russell-Watts (eds), *Possessions: Essays in French Literature, Cinema and Theory* (Oxford: Peter Lang, 2003), pp. 51–65.

——, 'Descartes and Lacan. Print and the subject of citation', *New Zealand Journal of French Studies*, 27, 2 (2006), 16–28.

Grossman, Kathryn, *Figuring Transcendence in Les Misérables – Hugo's Romantic Sublime* (Carbondale and Edwardsville: Southern Illinois University Press, 1994).

Guibert, Hervé, *L'Image fantôme* (Paris: Minuit, 1981).

Helmreich-Marsilien, Armand, 'Un inspirateur paradoxal du tragique racinien: Corneille comique', *Australian Journal of French Studies*, 2 (1965), 291–312.

Hénin, Emmanuelle, 'Fantôme et *mimèsis* à l'âge classique: la théorie hantée', in Françoise Lavocat and François Lecercle (eds), *Dramaturgies de l'ombre* (Rennes: Presses universitaires de Rennes, 2005), pp. 229–45.

Hicks, Eric (ed.), *Le Débat sur 'le Roman de la rose'* (Paris: Champion, 1977).

Horowitz, Louise K., 'The second time around', *Esprit Créateur*, 38, 2 (summer 1998), 23–33.

Hugo, Victor, *Les Contemplations* (Paris: Gallimard, 1973).

——, *Romans 2 – Les Misérables* (Paris: Robert Laffont, collection Bouquins, 1985).

——, *Œuvres critiques* (Paris: Robert Laffont, collection Bouquins, 1985).

——, *Chantiers* (Paris: Robert Laffont, collection Bouquins, 1990).

Iwata, Yoshinori, *Écriture et intériorité dans quatre romans de Robert Pinget* (Geneva: Slatkine, 2003).

Janin, Jules, 'Une histoire de revenant', at *http://www.bmlisieux.com/litterature/janin/histoire.htm*

Jodelle, Étienne, *Cléopâtre captive*, ed. Kathleen M. Hall (Exeter: University of Exeter Press, 1979).

Jondorf, G., *Robert Garnier and the Themes of Political Tragedy in the Sixteenth Century* (Cambridge: Cambridge University Press, 1969).

Kristeva, Julia, *Soleil noir: dépression et mélancolie* (Paris: Gallimard, 1987).

Lacan, Jacques, *Écrits* (Paris: Seuil, 1966).

——, *Le Séminaire de Jacques Lacan. Livre XI* (Paris: Seuil, 1973).

——, *Le Séminaire de Jacques Lacan. Livre I* (Paris: Seuil, 1975).

——, *Le Séminaire de Jacques Lacan. Livre XX* (Paris: Seuil, 1975).

——, *Le Séminaire de Jacques Lacan. Livre II* (Paris: Seuil, 1978).

———, *Le Séminaire de Jacques Lacan. Livre III* (Paris: Seuil, 1981).

———, *Le Séminaire de Jacques Lacan. Livre XVII* (Paris: Seuil, 1991).

Lang, Andrew, *The Valet's Tragedy, and Other Stories* (1903), at *http://www.gutenberg.org/dirs/etext00/vlttr10.txt*

La Farce nouvelle ... de la resurrection de Jenin Landore, in *Ancien théâtre français*, ed. by M. Viollet le Duc, 10 vols (Paris: Jannet, 1854–7), II (1854), pp. 21–34.

Lecouteux, Claude, *Au-delà du merveilleux: essai sur les mentalités du moyen âge*, 2nd edn (Paris: Presses de l'Université de Paris-Sorbonne, 1998).

Le Fèvre, Jean, *Les Lamentations de Matheolus* and *Le Livre de leesce*, in *'Les Lamentations de Matheolus' et 'Le Livre de leesce' de Jehan le Fèvre, de Resson: poèmes français du XIVᵉ siècle*, ed. A.-G. van Hamel, 2 vols (Paris: Bouillon, 1892–1905).

Le Franc, Martin, *Le Champion des dames*, ed. Robert Deschaux (Paris: Champion, 1999).

Lemaire de Belges, Jean, *Épitaphe en maniere de dialogue*, in *Œuvres*, ed. J. Stecher, 4 vols (Geneva: Droz, 1969), IV, pp. 318–38.

Lemaitre, Barbara, 'Sans soleil, le travail de l'imaginaire', in Philippe Dubois (ed.), *Théorème 6, Recherches sur Chris Marker* (Paris: Presse Sorbonne Nouvelle, 2002).

Lévi-Strauss, Claude, *La Pensée sauvage*, 2nd edn (Paris: Plon/Pocket, Agora, 2002, first published 1962).

Longinus, *On Sublimity* (Oxford: Clarendon Press, 1965).

Lupton, Catherine, *Chris Marker: Memories of the Future* (London: Reaktion Books, 2005).

Madius, Vincent and Lombardius, Bartholomew, *Vincentii Madii et Bartholomaei Lombardi in Aristotelis librum Poetices communis explanationes, Madii vero in eundem librum propriae explanationes. Ejusdem de ridiculis et in Horatii librum de Arte poetica interpretatio* (Venice: V. Valgrigio, 1550).

Mallarmé, Stéphane, *Œuvres* (Paris: Classique-Garnier, 1985).

Mannoni, Octave, *Clefs pour l'imaginaire* (Paris: Seuil, 1968).

Marker, Chris, *Le Dépays* (Paris, Herscher, 1982).

Marks, Laura U., *The Skin of the Film: Intercultural Cinema, Embodiment, and the Senses* (Durham/London: Duke University Press, 2000).

Martineau-Génieys, Christine, *Le Thème de la mort dans la poésie française de 1450 à 1550* (Paris: Champion, 1978).

Mary, Georges, 'La Folie d'Oreste ou l'écart minime à l'équilibre', *Poétique*, 98 (1994), 171–80.

Maskell, David, *Racine: A Theatrical Reading* (Oxford: Clarendon Press, 1991).

Maupassant, Guy de, *Contes et nouvelles*, ed. Louis Forestier, 2 vols (Paris: Gallimard, Bibliothèque de la Pléiade, 1974–9).

Meyer, Fernand, 'Robert Pinget: Le livre disséminé comme fiction, narration et objet', in *Nouveau roman: hier, aujourd'hui* (Paris: Union Générale d'Éditions, 1972).

Michault, Pierre, *Le Procès d'Honneur Féminin, La Complainte sur la mort d'Ysabeau de Bourbon*, and *La Danse des aveugles*, in *Pierre Michault: œuvres poétiques*, ed. Barbara Folkart (Paris: Union Générale d'Éditions, 1980).

Milet, Jacques, *La Forest de tristesse*, in *Le Jardin de plaisance et fleur de rethorique: reproduction en fac-similé de l'édition publiée par Antoine Vérard vers 1501*, ed. Eugénie Droz and Arthur Piaget, 2 vols (Paris: Firmin-Didot, 1910–25), I (1910), fols 204r–24v.

Milton, John, *Paradise Lost* (New York: Norton, 1993).

Modiano, Patrick, *Dora Bruder* (Paris: Gallimard, 1997).

Molière, *Œuvres complètes*, ed. Georges Couton, vol. II (Paris: Gallimard, Bibliothèque de la Pléiade, 1971).

Monteleone, J., 'Spectante te potetur (Thy. 66), un simbolo senechiano', *Latomus*, 68 (1989), 604–26.

Muratore, M. J., 'The pleasures of re-enactment in *Andromaque*', *Dalhousie French Studies*, 24 (spring–summer 1993), 57–70.

Nimier, Marie, *La Reine du silence* (Paris: Gallimard, 2004).

O'Brien, John, 'Pinget's *Passacaglia*: birds wings beating the solid air', *The Review of Contemporary Fiction*, 3 (1983), 147–51.

Pinget, Robert, *Passacaille* (Paris: Minuit, 1969).

Piroué, Georges, *Victor Hugo ou les dessus de l'inconnu* (Paris: Denoel, 1964).

Plantinga, C. and Smith, G. M. (eds), *Films, Cognition and Emotion* (Baltimore/London: Johns Hopkins University Press, 1999).

Plato, *Phaedo* (Cambridge, MA: Loeb Classical Library, 1999, vol. 1, first published 1917).

——, *Meno* (Cambridge, MA: Loeb Classical Library, 1999, vol. 2; first published 1917).

——, *Symposium* (Cambridge, MA: Loeb Classical Library, 1999, vol. 3; first published 1917).

Pontalis, Jean-Bertrand, *Traversée des ombres* (Paris: Gallimard, 2003).

Proust, Marcel, *À la recherche du temps perdu*, ed. Jean-Yves Tadié, 4 vols (Paris: Gallimard, Bibliothèque de la Pléiade, 1987–9).

Quignard, Pascal, *Petits Traités* (Paris: Gallimard, 1990).

——, *Le Sexe et l'effroi* (Paris: Gallimard, 1994).

——, *Petits Traités II* (Paris: Gallimard, 1997).

——, *Vie secrète* (Paris: Gallimard, 1998).

——, *Abîmes* (Paris: Grasset, 2002).

Racevskis, Roland, 'Generational transition in *Andromaque*', *Dalhousie French Studies*, 49 (winter 1999), 63–72.

Rank, Otto, *The Double: A Psychoanalytic Study*, trans. Harry Tucker (New York/London: Meridian Books, 1971).

Ransom, Amy J., *The Feminine as Fantastic in the Conte fantastique* (New York: Peter Lang, 1995).

Raser, Timothy, *The Simplest of Signs: Victor Hugo and the Language of Images in France 1850–1950* (Newark: University of Delaware Press, 2004).

Saint-Gelais, Octovien de, *Séjour d'honneur*, ed. Frédéric Duval (Geneva: Droz, 2002).

Seneca, *Tragedies*, ed. and trans. F. J. Miller (Cambridge, MA: Harvard University Press, 1987).

Siebers, Tobin, *The Romantic Fantastic* (Ithaca/London: Cornell University Press, 1984).

Shaviro, Steven, *The Cinematic Body* (Minneapolis/London: University of Minnesota Press, 1993).

Simon, Claude, *Les Géorgiques* (Paris: Minuit, 1981).

Sontag, Susan, *On Photography* (London: Penguin, 1973).

Spinoza, Baruch de, 'On the origin and nature of the affects', *Ethics* (London: Penguin, 1994), pp. 76–7.

Sprinker, Michael (ed.), *Ghostly Demarcations: A Symposium on Jacques Derrida's 'Specters of Marx'* (London/New York: Verso, 1999).

Swift, Helen J., *Gender, Writing and Performance: Men Defending Women in Late Medieval France (1440–1538)* (Oxford: Oxford University Press, 2008).

Szarka, J. P., 'The farce of consciousness: a study of Pinget's *Passacaille* and *Fable*', *Nottingham French Studies*, 26 (1987), 81–96.

Taillepied, Noël de, *Traicté de l'apparition des esprits. A sçavoir, des Ames separées, Fantosmes, Prodiges, et autres accidens merveilleux, qui precedent quelquefois la mort des grands personnages, ou signifient changement de la chose publique* (Paris: Jean Corrozet, 1627).

Taylor, Jane H. M., 'Un miroer salutaire', in Jane H. M. Taylor (ed.), *Dies Illa: Death in the Middle Ages* (Liverpool: Cairns, 1984), pp. 29–43.

——, 'The dialogues of the Dance of Death and the limits of late-medieval theatre', *Fifteenth-Century Studies*, 16 (1990), 215–32.

Thomas, Lyn, *Annie Ernaux: An Introduction to the Writer and Her Audience* (Oxford/New York: Berg, 1999).

Todorov, Tzvetan, *Introduction à la littérature fantastique* (Paris: Seuil, 1970).

Trafic, 6 (spring 1993), (Paris: POL).

Voltaire, *Œuvres de 1746–1748 (I)* (Oxford: Voltaire Foundation, 2003).

Wilson, Emily R., *Mocked with Death: Tragic Overliving from Sophocles to Milton* (Baltimore/London: Johns Hopkins University Press, 2004).

Žižek, Slavoj, *For They Know Not What They Do: Enjoyment as a Political Factor* (London/New York: Verso, 1991).

——, *Looking Awry: An Introduction to Jacques Lacan Through Popular Culture*, (Cambridge, MA/London: The MIT Press, 1991).

——, *The Indivisible Remainder: An Essay on Schelling and Related Matters* (London/New York: Verso, 1996).

——, *Welcome to the Desert of the Real: Five Essays on September 11 and Related Dates* (London/New York: Verso, 2002).

Zola, Émile, *Le Rêve*, in *Les Rougon-Macquart. Histoire naturelle et sociale d'une famille sous le Second Empire*, ed. Henri Mitterand, 5 vols (Paris: Gallimard, Bibliothèque de la Pléiade, 1960–7), IV (1966), pp. 813–994.

——, *La Débâcle*, in *Les Rougon-Macquart. Histoire naturelle et sociale d'une famille sous le Second Empire*, ed. Henri Mitterand, 5 vols (Paris: Gallimard, Bibliothèque de la Pléiade, 1960–7), V (1966), pp. 399–912.

Index